SUPPLEMENT TO THE HANDBOOK OF MIDDLE AMERICAN INDIANS

Volume 5 Epigraphy

SUPPLEMENT TO THE HANDBOOK OF MIDDLE AMERICAN INDIANS

 VICTORIA REIFLER BRICKER, General Editor

VOLUME FIVE

EPIGRAPHY

VICTORIA REIFLER BRICKER, Volume Editor

With the Assistance of Patricia A. Andrews

UNIVERSITY OF TEXAS PRESS, AUSTIN

First edition, 1992

Requests for permission to reproduce material from this
work should be sent to Permissions, University of Texas
Press, Box 7819, Austin, TX 78713-7819.

∞ The paper used in this publication meets the
minimum requirements of American National Standard
for Information Sciences—Permanence of Paper for
Printed Library Materials, ANSI Z39.48-1984.

LIBRARY OF CONGRESS CATALOGING-IN-
PUBLICATION DATA

Epigraphy / Victoria Reifler Bricker, volume editor,
    with the assistance of Patricia A. Andrews.
      p.   cm. — (Supplement to the handbook of
    Middle American Indians : v. 5)
    Includes bibliographical references and index.
    ISBN 0-292-77650-0
    1. Indians of Mexico—Writing. 2. Indians of Central
    America—Writing. 3. Mayas—Writing. I. Bricker,
    Victoria Reifler, (date). II. Andrews, Patricia A. III.
    Series.
F1219.3.W94E65   1992
497'.6—dc20   91-14769
                                          CIP

CONTENTS

SUPPLEMENT TO THE HANDBOOK OF MIDDLE AMERICAN INDIANS
Volume 5 Epigraphy

1. Introduction

VICTORIA R. BRICKER

E PIGRAPHY DID NOT occupy a prominent position in the *Handbook of Middle American Indians*. No one volume
of that series was dedicated to this topic, and
articles on Mixtec, Zapotec, Maya, and Aztec
writing were buried in two volumes concerned with the archaeology of Middle America (Wauchope and Willey 1965; Wauchope,
Ekholm, and Bernal 1971). The purpose of
this volume of the *Supplement* is to recognize
the important role that epigraphy has come
to play in Middle American scholarship and
to document significant achievements in three
areas: dynastic history, phonetic decipherment, and calendrics.

In Chapter 2, Gordon Whittaker tells us
that the earliest clear evidence of writing in
Middle America appeared during the first millennium B.C., in a region of southern Mexico
encompassing the Valley of Oaxaca and the
Isthmus of Tehuantepec, where it was associated with two Preclassic cultures, those of the
Zapotecs and the Olmecs. Zapotec writing,
like Middle American scripts in general, was
highly pictorial, and it had a close relationship with iconography. At first, writing was
less important than iconography and was used
only for recording names and numbers. By
Late Preclassic times, writing had become
dominant and was monopolizing the space on
large stelae. It began to decline in importance during the Early Classic period, and,
by the Middle Classic, iconography had re-
gained the prominence it had enjoyed during
the Middle Preclassic.

At its height, Zapotec writing had begun to
resemble the Maya script, with glyphs for
verbs ("death," "capture," and "conquest") as
well as for numbers, the days in the twenty-
day "week," personal names, and places ("emblems"). However, the Zapotec system seems
to have been less developed phonetically and
grammatically. It was apparently based entirely on logograms, with phoneticism restricted to rebus usage. And no grammatical
affixes have yet been identified in the Zapotec
script.

In Chapter 3, Maarten Jansen describes
another Oaxacan script, which was used by
the Mixtec people. In Mixtec codices, pictures are paramount. The glyphs that refer to
places are usually embedded in pictures, and
personal name glyphs are sometimes incorporated into the costumes of the men and

1

women to whom they refer. The pictorial manuscripts that are the major sources of Mixtec hieroglyphs cover the Late Postclassic and Early Colonial periods and are of much more recent date than the Zapotec inscriptions. It has therefore been possible to enlist the help of Colonial ethnohistorical sources in unraveling the dynastic histories that are the principal subject of those codices. For this reason, epigraphers such as Alfonso Caso, Maarten Jansen, Mary Elizabeth Smith, and Emily Rabin have been more successful in explaining the content of the Mixtec codices than scholars studying the Preclassic and Early and Middle Classic Zapotec inscriptions have been.

Another group of pictorial manuscripts was produced by the Tlapanec people, who lived west of the Mixteca Alta in what is today the state of Guerrero. In Chapter 4, Constanza Vega Sosa discusses their calendar and analyzes the toponymic glyphs and pictures that appear in their codices. She also provides a semantic reading for each of the folios that make up the *Codex Azoyú 1,* in which she documents the history of the Kingdom of Tlachinollan and its relationships with neighboring Mixtec and Nahua peoples and its later domination by the Mexica, or Aztecs.

Although the layout of folios in the Codex Azoyú 1 is very different from the format of Mixtec codices described by Jansen in Chapter 3, the Mixtec and Tlapanec scribal traditions share a reliance on pictures for describing events. In neither case is the scope of the hieroglyphs associated with the pictures broad enough to communicate the full message intended by the scribe. The hieroglyphs anchor the pictures in time and space, but they lack the grammatical "glue" that would permit them to stand alone as a text.

In Chapter 5, Hanns Prem offers a formal definition of the relationship between picture writing (what he calls "narrative pictography") and hieroglyphic writing among the Aztecs of Central Mexico; his definition applies equally well to Mixtec and Tlapanec writing. Of particular interest to him are the different functions of the two types of writing. Narrative pictography has the advantages of being independent of language and of giving the reader the freedom to vary the length of the narration. Its disadvantages are that it bears no direct relationship to speech and it communicates the intended message less exactly than hieroglyphic writing can. On the other hand, because hieroglyphic writing is language-specific, it can be more difficult to interpret. Furthermore, because Aztec writing is very pictorial, and because many pictures are subject to different interpretations, even native readers who were familiar with the tradition sometimes had trouble assigning the correct phonetic value to a particular sign.

Prem explains that this problem was a result of the fact that Aztec writing was predominantly ideographic. Phonetic complements were employed only rarely to resolve the ambiguity between two or more possible readings, and even full syllabic spellings were difficult to process because of a lack of consistency in the ordering of signs. Thus, the phonetic component in Aztec writing was incompletely developed and was seldom useful for decoding messages.

The coverage of Maya writing in the original *Handbook* is now largely out of date. Since 1965, when J. Eric S. Thompson's "Maya Hieroglyphic Writing" was published, there has been an explosion of knowledge in two major areas: dynastic history and phoneticism. Thompson (1965: 635–636) mentioned the pathbreaking articles by Heinrich Berlin (1958) on emblem glyphs and Tatiana Proskouriakoff (1960) on Piedras Negras, which revealed, for the first time, the historical content of the Maya monumental inscriptions. Research on the dynastic sequences at Maya sites was still in its infancy, however, and most of what we know today about the lives of the rulers of Maya cities has been discovered in the past twenty years.

One of the sites whose inscriptions have received a great deal of attention since 1965 is Palenque, which is situated at the western edge of the Maya Lowlands. Floyd Lounsbury, Linda Schele, and Peter Mathews have together worked out the intricate dynastic sequence at this site, and the results of their research are summarized by Linda Schele in Chapter 7. Their task was complicated by the fact that there are no stelae as such at Palenque, and the monuments are not arranged as neatly into groups as at Piedras Negras, so much more effort was required to determine the correct sequence of events at this site. The key to their success has been a method of breaking texts down into clauses and paraphrasing their contents.

During the same period, Berthold Riese was analyzing the inscriptions of Copan, a city on the eastern periphery of the Maya area, and his article in this volume covers the long dynastic sequence at this site. Among Riese's previous contributions to decipherment is his determination of the meaning of the "hel" hieroglyph, whose coefficients refer to the positions of rulers in such sequences (1984b). At Copan, this information on two key monuments and on a third monument containing a gallery of sixteen rulers permitted him to reconstruct the dynastic history of the site.

The work of Schele and others at Palenque and Riese at Copan rests on Proskouriakoff's (1960) method of seriating monuments in terms of their references to historical personages, events, and dates. When that information is combined with references to emblem glyphs (Berlin 1958), it is possible to infer intersite relations for a region. That approach was first developed by Joyce Marcus (1976a) and is now refined by Stephen Houston in his article on Dos Pilas (Chapter 8), in which he describes the complex mesh of political and kinship relations among the rulers of several cities in the Pasion drainage of Central Peten. In the process, he clarifies the meaning of emblem glyphs and contrasts them with other glyphs ("toponyms") that refer to specific localities.

The other major area of development in Maya epigraphy has been the demonstration that the Precolumbian Maya had a full-fledged writing system, composed of both logographic and syllabic signs and incorporating the basic grammatical structures of the Classical and Modern Cholan and Yucatecan languages. In his *Handbook* chapter, Thompson (1965:653) said that, "although there is at present, in my opinion, no adequate reason for supposing that the Maya possessed a syllabic writing in pre-Spanish times, yet there is good evidence that grammatical particles were expressed as affixes." In fact, as I show in Chapter 6, grammatical particles were not only expressed by affixes, but were also formed by concatenations of syllabic signs. Today, in 1990, there is ample evidence of the logosyllabic nature of the Maya script, and my chapter gives examples not only of the use of grammatical affixes, but also of syllabic spellings of both words and affixes.

With the phonetic characteristics of the Maya script no longer in doubt, it is instructive to compare it with Aztec writing, which, as Prem shows in Chapter 5, also contains some evidence of phonetic usage. The Aztec sources contain a few examples of syllabic writing, but there is no consistent reading order: in some cases, the signs are read from top to bottom, in others, from bottom to top; in a few cases, there is no real pattern at all. In this respect, the Aztec script constrasts markedly with the Maya one, which has a fixed reading order, from left to right and from top to bottom.

The Aztec script also has a few examples of the use of phonetic complements with logograms, whereas Maya writing has numerous examples of this spelling pattern. Both scripts abbreviate words, but this convention is much more common in Aztecs than in Maya writing. On balance, phoneticism in Maya writing is much more deeply rooted and has a much longer history.

One characteristic that Aztec writing shares with Maya writing is the use of noun roots, instead of stems, for logographic signs. In both cases, nouns are stripped of stem suffixes (*-tl, -tli, -itl,* and *-li* in Nahuatl; *-il* in Maya) before being used in rebuses. This explains why only the roots *coyo* in *coyotl* 'coyote' and *cac* in *cactli* 'shoe' appear in the syllabic spelling of the place name Coyocac

3

(as *coyo-cac*). The absolute suffixes *-tl* and *-tli* were not regarded as part of the intrinsic meaning of the words (see Karttunen 1983:20, 43, for an analysis of these stems).

In all Middle American scripts described in this volume, there is a close relationship between iconography and writing. Hieroglyphic signs are highly pictorial, and they follow the same formal conventions as pictures. At one extreme, Mixtec hieroglyphs are usually embedded in pictures; there is no hieroglyphic text as such. At the other, Maya hieroglyphs are normally segregated from pictures, occupying clearly defined zones that sometimes frame the accompanying pictures, although, in rare instances, a picture of an object may substitute for its hieroglyph in the textual part of a composition, or a hieroglyph may be embedded in a picture.

Not all texts are accompanied by pictures in Maya writing, although most are. Whittaker includes illustrations of several Zapotec texts that are not associated with pictorial scenes. The other writing systems considered in this volume are more closely identified with pictures.

Thus the relationship between writing and pictures is one that characterizes all Middle American scripts, from the earliest to the most recent. There are differences in the degree of spatial overlap between the two systems of communication, but in all cases the formal properties of writing have been heavily influenced by iconography throughout Middle American history. This is one of the unifying traits of the culture area.

Another widely shared trait in Middle America was, of course, the calendar, and especially the fifty-two-year cycle known among scholars as the Calendar Round, which was analogous to our century. The Calendar Round was a permutation of two smaller cycles, a ritual calendar of 260 days and a solar calendar of 365 days. Munro Edmonson has found evidence of the use of these cycles among approximately sixty different linguistic groups in Middle America. All known writing systems had glyphs for the numerals from 1 to 13 and for the 20 days in the ritual calendar, and some of them had glyphs for the divisions of the 365-day year as well. There was considerable variation in the glyphs for the days in the versions of the ritual calendar used by different ethnic groups in the region, as well as in the choice of days that could serve as "bearers" of the year (New Year's Day). Edmonson summarizes these variations in Chapter 10 and argues that the differences in the reckoning of New Year's dates can be treated as part of a single historical system, which had as its goal the adjustment of the Middle American year calendar to the stations of the tropical year.

It is clear that Middle American epigraphy has come a long way since the original *Handbook* was published. We now have dynastic histories for regions that were formerly terrae incognitae (especially for the Maya and the Tlapanecs, but also for the Mixtecs). The nature of the Zapotec, Aztec, and Maya scripts is now much better understood than it was in the 1960's, when the chapters for the *Handbook* were written. In addition, the different versions of the Calendar Round have been placed in a regional and historical perspective. The advances in epigraphy during the past two decades have moved it from the margins of archaeological and ethnohistorical scholarship into the mainstream of research on the culture history of Middle America.

2. The Zapotec Writing System

GORDON WHITTAKER

INTRODUCTION

O N PRESENT KNOWLEDGE, writing in the Americas first began to develop at some point in the early first millennium B.C. From the middle of this millennium onward, sequences of two or more signs begin to appear on stone monuments in southern Mexico, providing us with the first indisputable evidence of writing. Since early monuments of this kind can be found in both the Valley of Oaxaca and the Isthmus of Tehuantepec regions, there has been some debate as to whether the ultimate invention of writing in Mesoamerica should be attributed to Zapotec-speaking Oaxacans or to Mixe-Zoque-speaking Olmecs (see the recent discussions in Whittaker 1983:101–105; 1990: 147–249; Justeson et al. 1985:31–37; Justeson 1986). No sufficiently cogent evidence has been advanced to date which would resolve the issue decisively, and it may well be that the development of writing came about less as the result of internal factors in a Oaxacan or Olmec polity than as the outcome of the dynamic interaction of the graphic and symbolic systems of both cultures in response to the growing demands of incipient and competing statehood.

Writing, the use of graphic elements to represent words in language, may occur in the absence of a full-fledged system of writing. Signs, graphic units that may take the form of simple or composite graphic elements, often occur in cultures in which a system of writing is lacking, such as those of the tribes on the North American plains. In such cultures, signs are used to render, for example, names and ritual terms, but have not been further developed for the purpose of recording the varied constituents of actual sentences. Graphic information in such societies is predominantly iconographic in nature, with writing serving as a mere adjunct to names and numbers.

Southern Mesoamerica began to turn from reliance on a single graphic system, in which writing played a subordinate role, to the adoption of dual systems, in which iconography and writing might occur independent of each other or in varying proportions of combination, at the latest by the end of the Middle

5

Preclassic period (that is, by the sixth century B.C. in round terms). By way of contrast, Mesoamerica north and west of Central Oaxaca probably did not begin to pursue a line of development toward separate iconographic and writing systems until the eve of the Spanish Conquest.

With Period I (c. 500–200 B.C.) at the Valley of Oaxaca site of Monte Alban—the beginning of the Late Preclassic—comes the first compelling evidence that a system of writing had come into being in Mesoamerica. During this period, which coincides with Monte Alban's rise to power in the valley, a number of massive stelae were erected in the center's main plaza, all boasting orderly columns of gracefully executed signs and all free of accompanying iconography (Caso 1946). Beside the repeated occurrence of signs followed by bar-and-dot or finger numerals, suggesting the notation of calendrical data, there appear other signs, both compound and simple, which can be suspected on formal and comparative grounds of having a nominal or verbal function (Whittaker 1980; 1981).

Short sequences of writing were also added to a number of prominently placed iconographic monuments belonging to the extensive series of *danzantes* (Scott 1978), so named because of their sculpted reliefs of sprawling individuals. The majority of monuments bearing inscriptions, whether stelae or *danzantes*, appear to have made up groups sharing related texts, a pattern that continues into the Classic (Marcus 1976b; 1983c; Whittaker 1977; 1983).

Period II (c. 200 B.C.–A.D. 250), marking the close of the Late Preclassic, saw a vigorous expansion of the might and influence of Monte Alban both within and beyond the Valley of Oaxaca. This is reflected not only in the archaeology of the region but also in an impressive series of stone tablets adorning the walls of Mound J in the main plaza at Monte Alban itself. These tablets have been interpreted on formal grounds as records of Monte Alban's conquest of Oaxacan towns (Caso 1946:137). With few exceptions, the glyphic sequences are limited to a three-glyph column with signs of varying size, all of which appear to be toponymic in nature. Nevertheless, a handful of tablets, perhaps the earliest, include dates and, rarely, additional calendrical or ritual data.

The writing system of Monte Alban, which had shown great vitality in Period I, flourished still and may even have increased its repertory of hieroglyphs, but by the end of Period II it had leveled off and, it seems, already entered on a decline in its usage. The elite medium that had documented the growth and military prowess of the Zapotec state now gave way increasingly to iconography in importance and versatility, gradually resuming its prior role as an adjunct to the latter. Monte Alban was now at the height of its power, yet, with rare but notable exceptions, the writing of Period IIIA (c. A.D. 250–450), the Early Classic, had become limited to calendrical sequences and probable names of people and places, all other functions having been taken over again by iconography.

By the Middle Classic, the Zapotec writing system had come full circle. The former flexibility and artistic elegance of this graphic medium was now replaced by an increasingly crudely executed iconographic system. Monte Alban was on the decline. The late monuments of Period IIIB (c. A.D. 450–700) exhibit a devastating collapse of the stylistic conventions and structural organization so evident in the works of earlier periods. As in the following, politically post–Monte Alban, Period IV (c. A.D. 700–950), calendrically oriented information alone, including names of individuals, is as abundant and important in Central Oaxaca as at any point in the development of Zapotec writing, though now lacking the ordered and complementary date sequences of the Preclassic.

We are confronted with the unparalleled instance of a writing system that began to decline even as the state that developed it was reaching its height of power and prestige (Whittaker 1977). This devolution, as it were, is perhaps to be attributed to the growing internationalism of the Zapotec elite at a time when the iconography of Teotihuacan, which lacked a writing system, was gaining currency in Mesoamerica. The perception of iconography as a universally interpretable medium may well have led to a negative assessment of the propaganda value of a language-specific system of writing, one whose message was accessible only to a local Oaxacan elite.

THE LANGUAGE OF THE INSCRIPTIONS

It has been widely assumed since the time of the first scientific excavations early in this century that the material culture brought to light at Monte Alban was the product of a Zapotec population. Alfonso Caso, whose excavations and hieroglyphic studies laid the basis for our understanding of early Oaxaca, noted the cultural continuity that flows from Monte Alban to Postconquest Zapotec society and consequently identified the writing system he found at the site as Zapotec (Caso 1928:9–13). In later years, however, Caso drew a distinction between what he regarded as the full-blown Zapotec culture of the Classic and the, for him essentially non-Zapotec, developments leading up to it. He tended to view the matter of Preclassic Monte Alban's ethnic affiliation as an unsolved problem. Although little has been done to test the validity of the assumption, students of early Oaxacan writing today accept the likelihood that, given the geographical distribution of the Zapotec language (or languages) at the time of the Conquest, the language behind the inscriptions of Monte Alban, located near the center of the Zapotec linguistic area, was Zapotec from the very beginning.

The very limited number of hieroglyphs, often three or fewer, occurring between identifiable calendrical sequences on the Period I stelae and Period II tablets, or without calendrical data on the *danzantes* of both periods, suggests that the script was not syllabic. This is in accord with what one would expect at such an early point of development. The noncalendrical glyphs frequently take the form of (1) heads—*pars pro toto* representations of humans, supernaturals, and animals; (2) hands—fingers as numeral digits; thumbs;

open hands compounded with other elements; or (3) feet—singly, in pairs, or as footprints pointed up, down, or to the side. Most other glyphs appear to depict physical objects, some of which are clearly recognizable, such as rattles, arrows, and axes.

It is probable that Zapotec signs are logographic. In other words, they represent lexemes, or word-bases minus affixes. Except in the area of verbal morphology, Zapotec has many of the characteristics of an isolating language, in which affixation plays no major role. Because of the low frequency with which graphic elements repeat from compound to compound, elements in such compounds are probably also lexemic, the affixes occasionally required to complete words being supplied by the reader rather than by the script itself. This is a typical feature in the early development of a predominantly logographic writing system, such as the Sumerian, the Japanese, or the Maya. The telegraphic, and often phonetically opaque, nature of this kind of incipient script makes decipherment an extremely difficult task. Since a syllabic system or subsystem did not grow out of Preclassic Oaxacan writing, retrieving exact details of grammar and precise readings will be slow, limited, and dependent on the discovery of phonetically employed logographs.

To date, few instances of rebus phonetics (the use of logographs for their sound value only) have been thought to be discernible in Zapotec inscriptions, and these remain highly tentative at best (Whittaker 1980:42–55; cf. Justeson et al. 1985:46–48). A reasonable case can, nonetheless, be made for a flower-and-stem element (Fig. 2-1) assuming what is probably a phonetic role from Period II on. In its more elaborate form, the latter is part of a three-stem plant glyph classified as W446. The reduced element, a variant of W291, turns up in (1) the hill sign used with place names, (2) an elaborate version of the sign for the numeral 1 when it is a coefficient of day names, (3) an iconographic symbol for rain, often downturned, that adorns representations of the numen of rain and thunder, Cocijo, and (4) the glyph (W291, W297) for the

7

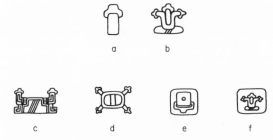

FIGURE 2-1. The flower-and-stem phonetic element: *a*, the base form, a single-stem element; *b*, W446, a three-stem variant element. The base form is probably phonetic in: *c*, W593, the so-called hill sign; *d*, WIb variant, the calendrical prefix for the numeral 1; *e*, W291, the day name Rain; *f*, W297, the three-stem variant for the day Rain.

day name that is equivalent to Rain or Lightning in most Mesoamerican calendars.

The word for 'flower' in the sixteenth-century Valley (of Oaxaca) Zapotec recorded by Fray Juan de Córdova (1942) is *qui(j)e*, related to modern Isthmus Zapotec *guie'* (Pickett 1971). 'Rock' and 'rain' are Córdova's *quie* and *qui(j)e*, respectively (Isthmus *quie* in both cases). *Quie* and *qui(j)e* are homophones in Valley and Isthmus Zapotec, even with regard to tone, the sole distinction being that the term for 'rain' occurs always in conjunction with an additional noun or adjective. Similarly, the day-name prefix associated with the number 1 in the Zapotec calendar is recorded in sixteenth-century orthography as *quie* or *quia* (see, e.g., Córdova 1886:204–212). The only published reconstruction of Proto-Zapotec forms for these words are Morris Swadesh's (1947:223) **kkĕ'ya* 'flower' and **kkéya* 'stone', which, although in need of revision, clearly demonstrate the antiquity of the resemblances.

In addition to Córdova's grammar and dictionary, reliable linguistic data describing the modern dialects of Zapotec and their lexicon and a thorough reconstructive analysis of

Proto-Zapotec based on information derived from the latter are indispensable for studying the language of the inscriptions and for recognizing phoneticism. Although some important vocabularies have been produced in recent years by the Summer Institute of Linguistics, extremely little work in Zapotec historical and comparative linguistics, so vital to hieroglyphic studies, has reached print. Beside Swadesh (1947), only one other short contribution (Suárez 1973) has appeared on the subject of Proto-Zapotec, and this is based largely on a still-unpublished, extensive dialect survey prepared in 1961 by the late María T. Fernández de Miranda, whose manuscript and data are not generally accessible to scholars. The only published study both touching on Proto-Zapotec and including a partial reconstruction of its ancestors, Proto-Zapotecan and Proto-Otomanguean, is the pathbreaking but problematical monograph by Calvin R. Rensch (1976). For valuable introductions to the Valley Zapotec reflected in Colonial manuscripts and in the works of Juan de Córdova, see Joseph W. Whitecotton (1982) and Roger Reeck (1982).

THE CORPUS OF TEXTS AND PRIMARY REFERENCE TOOLS

Progress in deciphering, or at least interpreting, the Zapotec script is also largely dependent on the size of the corpus available to us. At the present time, this corpus consists of only a few dozen, for the most part very short, texts in stone from Preclassic and Early Classic Monte Alban, plus several hundred usually very brief sequences of dates and calendrical names, with the occasional noncalendrical glyph, incised in stone and ceramics hailing from Monte Alban and sites scattered throughout the Valley of Oaxaca and beyond. Many sites in Central Oaxaca have yet to be excavated, and so it is as yet unknown whether the writing system of Monte Alban, in its full form, took hold elsewhere or even whether monuments were set up in outlying regions by the central power. Those sites that have been partially excavated, such as Dainzu, Yagul, and Lambityeco in the Tlacolula, or eastern arm of the Valley of Oaxaca, have so far yielded very few monuments with hieroglyphic information; what we have is almost entirely calendrical in nature (e.g., Bernal and Seuffert 1973; 1979). Even the Postclassic Zapotec capital of Zaachila, a few kilometers to the south of Monte Alban, has not been extensively excavated, although a small number of well-worn monuments from the Late Classic, some of them lying underfoot in the town's square and streets, have been reproduced by Caso (1928), partly in the form of photographs and partly as line drawings. Unfortunately, the quality of these illustrations is inadequate for exact hieroglyphic analysis.

North of the Valley of Oaxaca, the Zapotec sierra is virtually terra incognita with regard to Prehispanic monuments. A large and skillfully carved stela lying in the town of Yaguila has been published in part (Caso 1965a: 858–860), but beyond that, little more has reached print concerning this region. Far to the northwest, however, Zapotec writing appears on a tomb stela found in the Zapotec quarter of Teotihuacan, although the sequence is limited to a single date or calendrical name. The influence of Monte Alban is, moreover, traceable in the Mixtec graphic system and its Aztec descendant (Whittaker 1977).

Zapotec writing is, therefore, at the present time a field of study largely concerned with the analysis of hieroglyphic evidence from Monte Alban itself, complemented by a scattering of calendrical data from other Central Oaxacan sites. Perhaps because of the extreme paucity of the available material and the high degree of glyphic variability, relatively few works have appeared that are devoted exclusively to the script of Monte Alban: these include monographs and papers by Alfonso Caso (1928; 1946; 1965b), Gordon Whittaker (1976; 1980; 1981; 1982), and Joyce Marcus (1980; 1983a). In addition to these, a small number of publications by these authors and other scholars discuss Zapotec writing incidentally or in relation to a variety of special themes. These contributions will be referred to in the course of this chapter.

The Preclassic hieroglyphs of Monte Alban have been classified and catalogued in Whittaker 1980:198–227, which supplies the context of every sign, details on compounding, and preliminary interpretations. For the corpus of monuments at Monte Alban with hieroglyphs, a two-volume work by John Scott (1978) on the *danzantes* and an inventory of virtually all sculpted monuments from the site (García Moll et al. 1986), containing photographs and drawings of most pieces listed, are essential reference tools. With regard to drawings and technical descriptions of monuments, the publications of Caso (1928; 1946) and Scott (1978) are preferred because of their markedly greater accuracy. The early stipple and line drawings executed by Agustín Villagra for Caso, and reproduced by Caso (1946) and Scott (1978), remain unsurpassed in quality and exactness, and an even earlier study by Leopoldo Batres (1902) provides photographs and illustrations of sculpted monuments that reveal details not found in later works. Further sources of data are the calendrical glyphs that turn up frequently in Zapotec ceramic sculpture, often as ornaments or insignia on urn figurines. Many such vessels and sculptures are documented by Caso and Ignacio Bernal (1952) and Frank H. Boos (1966).

PERSONAL AND PLACE NAMES IN THE INSCRIPTIONS

The two most frequent identifiable components of Zapotec inscriptions are names and calendrical data. Names of individuals may be descriptive or calendrical. Calendrical names are often indistinguishable from dates but may be recognized as names if they occur alone beside an individual at chest or, more often, head level. Descriptive personal names are common on *danzantes*, where they are usually located beside the head. Frequently,

9

the final glyph in a name clause is a quincunx staff (or rattle) sign or a glyph that Caso (1928: 65) identified as a tied bag (Fig. 2-2). These are almost certainly verbal or adjectival elements with the approximate meanings 'killed, died' and 'captured', respectively (Whittaker 1980:41–45). Sacrificial clauses, probably indicative of heart sacrifice, are found on the chests of *danzantes* (Fig. 2-3).

Place names are recognizable by virtue of their association with the so-called hill glyph identified by Batres (1902:Pl.II). On Stelae 2–8 of Period IIIA, variable elements infixed to the hill glyph serve to name, as Caso (1928:82) first theorized, towns subjugated by Monte Alban in the Early Classic. This is indicated not only by the bound human and animal figures, probably vanquished supernatural patrons or defeated rulers dressed as such, standing on top of the place glyphs, but also by the freestanding individual, presumably a Zapotec ruler, spearing the place sign on Stela 4. For this the Aztec Stones of Tizoc and Motecuhzoma I provide a good analogy.

In the Preclassic, place glyphs, many of them glyphic compounds, were composed in essentially the same manner as in the Classic, but the pattern is somewhat obscured by a format convention of Period II which dictates that, if two place signs occur in succession, the first dispenses with its hill sign for aesthetic reasons. In later texts and iconography a glyph that recurs is always altered to avoid unsightly repetition.

Let us now examine the incised tablets set in the walls at Monte Alban's central Mound J. Of all the inscriptions associated with this building, only two bear no more than a single hieroglyph, consisting of a hill glyph with varying infixed element. The first, Tablet 44, is located at the top of the stairway on the northeast side of Mound J (Fig. 2-4a). Its distinctive feature is a trilobate element similar to that breathed out by canines and felines in Teotihuacan iconography (see Miller 1973: Figs. 18, 289, 339), and is interpretable as 'vital essence, air, wind' (Whittaker 1980:116, 127; cf. von Winning 1987:II:8).

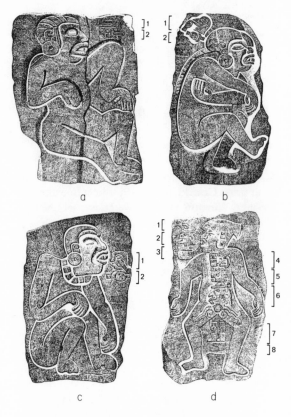

FIGURE 2-2. Death and capture clauses. *a*, Danzante 2 (from Caso 1946:Fig. 1): (1) Atlatl Wielder? (2) was slain. *b*, Danzante 6 (from Caso 1946:Fig. 3): (1) Kingfisher (2) was slain. *c*, Danzante 8 (from Caso 1946:Fig. 4): (1) Face Striker (2) was slain. *d*, Danzante 55 (from Caso 1946: Fig. 16): (1) Were- (2) Jaguar (3) was captured (and) (4) sacrificed (5) to (6) the Wind (or Cocijo?). (7) Leg vessels (8) were set down as offerings.

The place glyph, which may name Mound J as 'Place of the Wind', is also recorded in a side panel on Stela 8 of the nearby South Platform (Fig. 2-5). In the relief, the place glyph is being struck by a downward-snaking band on which the glyph for day name 17 is superimposed. The latter position corresponds to the name Xoo 'turbulent, raging' and, taken together, the depiction suggests Zapotec *quije pèexoò* 'storm wind, whirlwind'. The trilobate element occurs twice more on Stela 8:

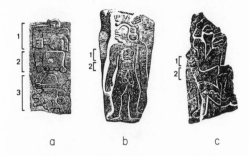

a   b   c

FIGURE 2-3. Sacrifice clauses. *a*, Stela 17, detail (from Caso 1946: Fig. 15): (1) Sacrificed (2) to (3) the Wind (or Cocijo?). *b*, Danzante 59 (from Scott 1978: Fig. D-59): (1) Sacrificed (2) (to) the Waters. *c*, Danzante 63 (from Scott 1978: Fig. D-63): (1) Sacrificed (2) (to) the Sun.

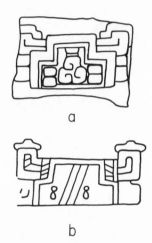

a

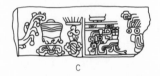

b

FIGURE 2-4. Monte Alban place names: *a*, Tablet 44 (drawing: G. Whittaker), glyph for Mound J; *b*, Tablet 42 (drawing: G. Whittaker), glyph for Monte Alban.

a

b

c

FIGURE 2-5. Stela 8. *a*, Front (drawing: G. Whittaker), with depiction of bound ruler atop place name of vanquished town and facing text: (1) (On?) Rain 3 (2) captured. *b*, Lower side (after Caso 1928: Fig. 47a), with personage in final panel atop place name of Mound J and facing whirlwind (or lightning?). *c*, Upper side (after Caso 1928: Fig. 47b), with rain wind at right in initial panel.

iconographically in the panel on its upper side, where it occurs between converging downward streaks from which the glyph for rain descends, and glyphically on its lower side, apparently as the day name that is equivalent to general Mesoamerican Wind, recorded beside a skull and a sacrificial brazier from which a heart rises.

There is a second inscription at Mound J, the sole glyph of which is a place name. This is found on a stone block, now split in two as Monuments 20 and 51, lying near the foot of the structure. The glyph it bears (Fig. 2-4b) is distinguished by an infix consisting of two or three diagonal bands and a neutral filler element, flanked by what has been described as jade ornaments or pendant jewels (Caso 1946: 134; Whittaker 1980: 53, 148) in the form of double circlets or a circlet with pendent trapezium or oval element. A more ex-

11

FIGURE 2-6. Inscribed monuments depicting Monte Alban rulers. *a*, J-45 (drawing: G. Whittaker); *b*, Stela 4 (drawing: G. Whittaker), depicting ruler named Deer 8 driving lance into place name of vanquished town.

plicit version of the place name can be seen on a much-eroded Protoclassic slab set into the upper level of Mound J, J-45 (Fig. 2-6), where a staff-bearing personage in elaborate dress (by analogy with Stelae 1 and 4, probably a ruler) faces a glyphic sequence to his left that consists of what was probably a day name (now eroded) with a coefficient of 4. Here, as on Stela 4, this is presumably the calendrical name of the ruler, and floats above a squat hill sign that is embellished only by internal filler lines. A numeral 1 with necklace element is attached to the base of the hill sign. Given the lack of militaristic iconography or additional hieroglyphs, and weighing the overall context, it is likely that this Terminal Period II carving names and depicts the personage as ruler of Monte Alban itself.

The traditional names for the Zapotec capital speak for this. The Mapa de Xoxocotlan (Smith 1973a:202–210), which gives the Mixtec and Nahuatl names for the hills of Monte Alban that make up part of the Mixtec town's territorial boundaries, corroborates evidence from the later Zapotec capital, Zaachila, that the ancient city was originally known as the 'Hill of Precious Stones' (Whittaker 1980: 150–151). In Córdova's "classical" orthography, the Zaachila form would be Tàniquie-càche. It is this name that we find recorded on all the Mount J inscriptions proclaiming Monte Alban's conquests or victories. On J-45 the full rendition of the center's name is aided by rebus phoneticism. The glyphic numeral 1, the calendrical prefix for which is *quie*, functions here as a phonetic indicator for *quie* 'stone'.

GLYPHIC FORMAT IN THE PERIOD II CONQUEST TABLETS

The place sign for Monte Alban occupies a central position on all the conquest tablets (Fig. 2-7). Its importance is highlighted by its size—it is twice as wide as its column—as well as by its position relative to the glyphs above and below it. Together they form a distinctive iconographic cross. Within the cross, three, sometimes four, signs appear, each belonging to a separate category:

(1) place sign of the subjugated town;
(2) verb;

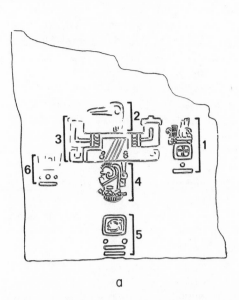

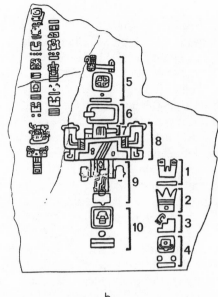

a

b

FIGURE 2-7. Conquest tablets. *a*, Table 10 (from Caso 1946: Fig. 42): (1) In the year Rabbit 6 (2) at Town X (3) Monte Alban (4) (struck down) District A (5) on the day House (feline variant) 12 (6) of Trecena 8. *b*, Tablet 14 (from Whittaker 1980: Fig. 9): (1) Trecena 5, (2) named Reed, (3) descended/elapsed to (4) Rain 4. (5) In the year Rabbit 6 (6) at the town of Yanhuitlan (8) Monte Alban (7) struck down (9) District H (10) on the day House 11 (7 days after Rain 4).

(3) glyph for Monte Alban;

(4) downturned head.

Category 2, which is often unfilled (glyphic ellipsis), consists of only two signs: arrows (usually clutched by a hand), and a quincunx staff that may be a rattle. On the basis of the analogy of Mixtec iconography, in which an arrow penetrating a place sign indicates the conquest of the town in question, the Zapotec arrow verb can be interpreted as a verb of conquest. The quincunx staff, found in tomb inscriptions and on *danzante* slabs, is apparently a verb of death or, in this case, destruction.

Zapotec word order is generally verb-subject-object (see, e.g., Marlett 1985). In the Period II inscriptions, this rule appears to hold. The verb is followed by the place sign for Monte Alban, its subject, from which its object, a downturned glyph usually in the form of an anthropomorphic head, is suspended. Caso (1946:137) has suggested that the heads depict the kings of the places con-

quered, perhaps dressed in the guise of the local patron deities. Since some downturned glyphs are not heads but, rather, abstract symbols, it is unlikely that rulers are intended. An alternative theory (Whittaker 1980:54, 110–144; 1982) proposes that Category 4 names the political and geographical units to which the subjugated towns named in Category 1 belong. This theory is based on the observation that the heads (probably supernatural patrons) and symbols fall into only ten discrete groups, each having diagnostic features that distinguish it from the next. The groups have been termed "emblem groups" by analogy with the Maya category of the same name.

Under verbs translating the Spanish *vencer*, Córdova (1942) differentiates in the military sense between verbs signifying 'to defeat causing (someone) to flee' and those meaning 'to defeat by casting (someone) down'. The latter sense is implied strongly by the downturned emblem glyphs. The ancestor of Cór-

13

dova's *tocàayòo(a)*, literally '(I) strike (*càa*) to the ground (*yòo*)', is the verb that would best fit the arrow glyph. For the second verb on the conquest tablets a reading such as *to-xiñe(a)* 'to destroy' or the related *tiquíñeyòo(a)* 'to thrash to the ground' is suggested. It should be noted that the first of the two (without the first-person suffix) is attested in Colonial-period Zapotec references to conquest (e.g., Whitecotton 1983:71n.17). Moreover, in Nahuatl enumerations of conquests, two verbs, as here, are usually employed: a verb 'to defeat, conquer' and a verb 'to destroy'.

If Categories 2–4 match typical Zapotec sentence structure, then what about Category 1? From the point of view of Zapotec linguistics, there is an obvious explanation for its initial position: one of the elements in the standard Zapotec sequence, verb-subject-object (-oblique reference), has been shifted into the so-called focus position at the beginning of the sentence. In the context of the inscriptions of Monte Alban, this would mean that either the direct object or the locative reference has been brought forward for reasons of emphasis. The whole sequence can be read: "At Town X Monte Alban struck down Polity Y" or "As for Town X, Monte Alban struck it down in Polity Y." It should be noted that, in Zapotec, as in Otomanguean languages in general, there is rarely a formal distinction between place names as objects and place names in a proper locative context.

The identification of the towns in Category 1 has been a primary concern of epigraphers. Caso (1946:136–137), followed by Marcus (1976b:128–131; 1980:52, 55), compared a small number of these glyphs with Aztec place signs for towns located, for the most part, in Oaxaca. A problem with this approach is that isolated place-sign comparisons are untestable and not automatically substantiated by the discovery of a Monte Alban presence at the sites in question, since a faulty comparison might still involve sites within Monte Alban's known or conjectured orbit (see the detailed discussions in Whittaker 1982; in press).

Of the comparisons just mentioned, one

does seem convincing: a Zapotec place sign consisting of a human head with ornate speech scroll on Tablet 47 clearly resembles the Aztec sign for Cuicatlan 'Place of Song', a site to the northwest of Monte Alban. Names for this town match in several languages, and the area has been shown to have come under Monte Alban's control as a border region in Period II. Unfortunately, the emblem glyph for Tablet 47 is found on no other stone, and the new García Moll catalogue (see Monument 18) fails even to confirm the details of the distinctive place sign. John S. Justeson et al. (1985: 47), like Marcus, take the quincunx staff (or rattle) glyph that follows it to be part of the place sign.

Set in two rows along the western and southern faces of Mound J's so-called arrowhead section, a sequence of conquest tablets, dubbed the Arrowhead Series, provides contextual evidence for the identification of places in relation to their polities or "districts" (Figs. 2-8 and 2-9). The sequence is especially valuable because the lower row is in situ and the upper row is restored on the basis of the position of the fallen stones. If Mount J parallels the chronological pattern of the Danzante Wall (Scott 1978:68–71), then the lower the row, the earlier the record. This would mean that the earlier towns subjugated occur in districts closer than the latest recorded on the upper row. Six of the tablets on the lower row share a single emblem glyph, and these are all located along the western face of the building, where they are interrupted by only one tablet with a differing emblem. The lower row's southern face, by way of contrast, displays six different emblem glyphs, each face of the upper row having four. The lower western face is probably the beginning of the sequence, which continues to the right and then in reverse direction on the upper row. Marcus (1980:51–52) has postulated that the places named in the inscriptions on Mound J are only those towns situated along Monte Alban's Period II borders. The alternative hypothesis (Whittaker 1982) sees the Arrowhead Series as a pro-

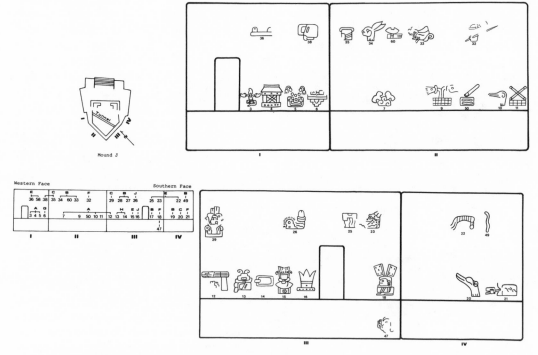

FIGURE 2-8. The Arrowhead Series (from Whittaker 1980: Fig. 66): *a*, orientation of the tablet series at Mound J; *b*, classification of tablets according to emblem glyph; *c*, western, and *d*, southern, faces of series, with schematic arrangement of place names alone.

pagandized record of Monte Alban's military victories in Periods I and II. Very tentative identifications of vanquished districts and towns are ventured in Table 2-1.

DATE FORMULAE AND READING ORDER

In view of the fact that the corpus of inscriptions known from Period I is very limited, few exact statements can be made about the extent of elaboration of its calendrical system. Clearly present, however, from this period onward are the following:

(1) a 260-day divinatory calendar composed of 20 day names and 13 numerals in constant rotation;

(2) a division of the divinatory calendar into 13-day *trecenas;*

(3) a 365-day solar calendar, each sequence of which is named after its 360th day; and

(4) a division of the solar calendar into 18 months of 20 days plus a final set of 5 days (Whittaker 1983; 1990).

Day names and derivative calendrical names of individuals are recognizable by virtue of the fact that they are almost always enclosed in a rounded frame, or cartouche, and are followed by a numeral below 14.

Date formulae usually occur at the beginning of an inscription. When they are found both at the beginning and the end of a text, or text passage, the year date is almost always given first, while secondary data, such as the day and the *trecena*, are normally placed at the end. In the inscriptions of the Period II Arrowhead Series, such date formulae are often balanced iconographically at two or more opposing points of the central textual cross.

Numeral coefficients consist of small circles

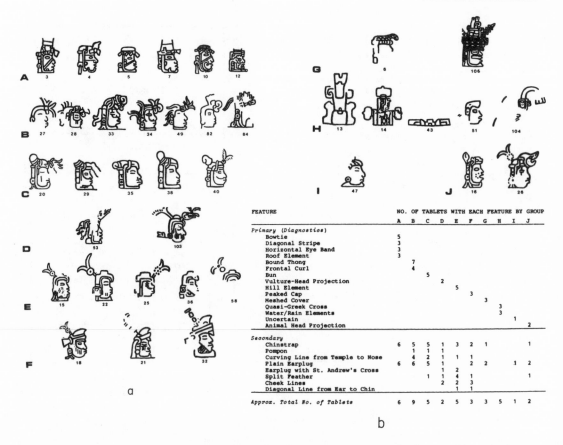

FEATURE	NO. OF TABLETS WITH EACH FEATURE BY GROUP									
	A	B	C	D	E	F	G	H	I	J
Primary (Diagnostic)										
Bowtie	5									
Diagonal Stripe	3									
Horizontal Eye Band	3									
Roof Element	3									
Bound Thong		7								
Frontal Curl		4								
Bun			5							
Vulture-Head Projection					2					
Hill Element						5				
Peaked Cap							3			
Meshed Cover								3		
Quasi-Greek Cross									3	
Water/Rain Elements									3	
Uncertain									1	
Animal Head Projection										2
Secondary										
Chinstrap	6	5	5	1	3	2	1			1
Pompon	1	1	1							
Curving Line from Temple to Nose	4	2	1	1	1					
Plain Earplug	6	6	5	1		2	2		1	2
Earplug with St. Andrew's Cross					1	2				
Split Feather		1		1	4	1				1
Cheek Lines					2	2	3			
Diagonal Line from Ear to Chin						1	1			
Approx. Total No. of Tablets	6	9	5	2	5	3	3	5	1	2

FIGURE 2-9. Zapotec emblem glyphs (from Whittaker 1982: Figs. 63 and 64): *a*, emblem glyphs according to district; *b*, distinguishing features of the emblem glyphs.

or rounded squares for up to four single digits, with the rare substitution of fingers for the numerals 1 and 2, and of bars for units of five. Recorded numbers of twenty or above are not known, the only proposed instance (Justeson et al. 1985:49) being a misidentified day name.

Numerals follow day names in accordance with the order of Zapotec calendrical naming known from the Conquest period. In the Preclassic the digits rest above the five-bars, but by the beginning of the Classic the pattern reverses to more closely match spoken Zapotec, in which the compound numerals 11 to 13 break down as "10-1," "10-2," "10-3."

Some of the day names can be identified either on the basis of a close tie-in between the glyphic representation and the known Conquest-period Zapotec name, or by analogy with other Mesoamerican calendars. Because a number of the sixteenth-century day names are semantically opaque, such equations require corroboration. Fortunately, the Preclassic writing system provides us with a means of confirming the identity of some day names and of ascertaining the calendrical position of others. The use of a numbered *trecena* glyph in a small number of inscriptions anchors the day name plus coefficient in a context that can be checked against a chart of the divinatory calendar. Year formulae also serve to anchor the four day names on which they are founded, since year names stand five

TABLE 2-1. Tentative Identification of Districts and Towns

	District	Town	Tablet
A	Central Section & N. Tlacolula Arm of Valley of Oaxaca	Chilateca	3
		Mitla	4
		Yatareni	7
		Zaachila	9*
		Caballito Blanco	11*
		Ixtlahuaca	12
		Tlacolula	50*
		Teotitlan	57
B	?		
C	Southern Arm of Valley of Oaxaca	Coyotepec	20
D	?		
E	Tehuantepec Valley	Taniquexopa (opposite Huilotepec)	15
		Tehuantepec	23*
F	S. Tlacolula Arm of Valley of Oaxaca	Lachigolo	18
		Teitipac	21
G	Etla Valley?		
H	Mixteca Alta (Ñudzavui)	Yanhuitlan	14
		Teita	43
I	Cuicatlan Cañada	Cuicatlan	46
J	Mixteca Baja	Acatepec	16
		Tequixtepec	26

Note: A detailed presentation of the reasoning behind each identification is to be found in Whittaker (1982).

*An asterisk following a number indicates that the emblem glyph is absent on the tablet in question. This occurs only when the flanking tablets bear emblem glyphs referring to one and the same district.

positions apart in the day-name sequence.

Six identifiable day signs appear on the stelae of Period I (Fig. 2-10), all but one of them in anchored positions. On Stela 13, a day, Face 1, is anchored in Trecena 4. In the general Mesoamerican calendar, the first day in the fourth *trecena* is 1 Flower, which in the sixteenth-century Zapotec calendar (Córdova 1886:204–212) is Quialao 1 'Face 1'. Similarly, on Stela 15 we find a day, Monkey 2, in Trecena 14. This too correlates exactly with the expected position for this day.

Three of the anchored signs on the Period I stelae represent year names. They are crowned by a graphic element identified by Caso (1928) as the year sign—a headband, usually with a cartouched cross at the front. This sign anchors the days naming the year at positions 3, 8, 13, and 18 of the day-name series (Fig. 2-11), and not 2, 7, 12, and 17, as Caso had thought. The day names that double as year names have glyphic forms in the latter capacity that are derived from symbols associated with the names rather than from direct representations of the names themselves. The day names for positions 3 and 13, equivalent to Zapotec and general Mesoamerican Night/House and Reed, respectively, are

17

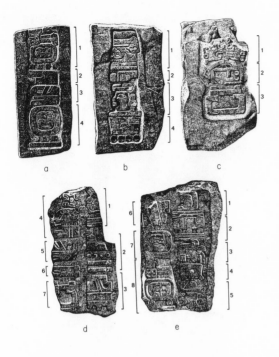

FIGURE 2-10. Period I stelae. *a,* Stela 12 (from Caso 1946: Fig. 10): (1) In the year Reed 4 (2) acceded? (3) Lord X (4) on the day Water 8. *b,* Stela 13 (from Caso 1946: Fig. 11): (1) In the year House 10 (2) he (Lord X) died/fell (3) on the day Face 1 (4) of Trecena 4. *c,* Stela 14 (from Caso 1946: Fig. 20): (1) Bat (2) Trapper? (3) was captured. *d,* Stela 15 (from Caso 1946: Fig. 14): (1) On the day Monkey 2 (2) of Trecena 14 (3) Monte Alban struck down (a town in?) District H, (4) Lord Bone? Jaguar (5) cast libations, and (6) its ruler? (7) was captured. *e,* Stela 17 (from Caso 1946: Fig. 15): (1) On the day Monkey 2 (2) of Solar Trecena 18 (3) human sacrifices were offered (4) to (5) the Wind (or Cocijo?). (6) The victims were dispatched? (7) on the day . . . 10 (or 2?) (8) of the year Flint 12.

represented both by the patron-related symbols (jaguar and dragon heads) and by forms corresponding directly to the names. With the exception of the dragon head for Reed, the symbolic glyphs are replaced in the Early Classic by the more familiar flint, house, and rabbit forms.

Month names are apparently not present in the date formulae. There is, however, a single attestation of an alternative system. On Stela 17, which begins with the same day as Stela 15, the anchoring is set not in a divinatory *trecena* but in Solar Trecena 18, that is, in the eighteenth *trecena* calculated from the beginning of the year named, which is Flint 12 (Whittaker 1983: 108–112). The sign in question is the depiction of the left half of the glyph for the divinatory *trecena*, which has been laid on its side.

Since the year name is usually located at the top of the rightmost column or, following a calendrical sequence in that column, at the top of the next column to the left, it appears probable that reading order was from top to bottom and in single columns from right to left. An alternative left-oriented, double-column hypothesis (Marcus 1976c), based on the view that Stelae 12 and 13 were intended to be read together Maya-style, that is, from Glyph 1 of Stela 12 to Glyph 1 of Stela 13 and so forth, is rendered unlikely by the facts that (1) the initial glyphs on the stelae in question are both year dates rather than calendrical units of descending order, (2) the glyphs in the two columns are not horizontally aligned but askew, and (3) the glyphs of Stela 12 are stylistically at variance with those of Stela 13, suggesting different sculptors or dates of carving.

In conclusion, there are still many gaps in our understanding of Zapotec inscriptions. Although the basic structure of the calendrical system is now clear, the hieroglyphs for much of the day-name series remain either unattested or insecurely identified, a problem that increases with the passage of the Classic. There is far more uncertainty with regard to inscriptional evidence for higher units of time below the year. As for toponyms, place-name signs and the higher-level emblem glyphs are readily identifiable as such, but precision in reading them and pinpointing their geographical location is exceedingly difficult to achieve. Attempts at distinguishing calendrical names of individuals from dates in the divinatory calendar are largely a matter of enlightened conjecture at this stage. Finally, very little headway has been made in the area of verbs, owing to a scarcity of contextually identifiable event glyphs. A small number of these, however, occur frequently enough to be recognizable as verbs, but only two or three can actually be assigned a probable meaning. Examples of preliminary interpretations of whole inscriptions can be found in Figs. 2-2, 2-3, 2-7, and 2-10.

Progress in these areas is very much dependent on an expanded corpus with longer inscriptions, more rigorous internal analysis of texts, a better understanding of Zapotec languages, particularly Proto-Zapotec, and a thorough comparison of Zapotec writing with the early Isthmian and Maya scripts.

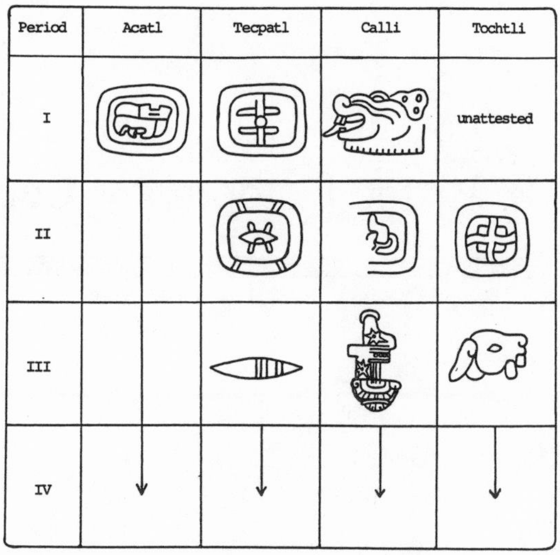

FIGURE 2-11. Year-naming signs (from Whittaker 1980: Fig. 2). Positions 3 (House), 8 (Rabbit), 13 (Reed), and 18 (Flint) correspond to Mexican Calli, Tochtli, Acatl, and Tecpatl. Sixteenth-century Zapotec terms are not employed here, since they are not recorded in a consistent manner and cannot occur without prefixes (see Whittaker 1983: 127–129).

3. Mixtec Pictography: Conventions and Contents

MAARTEN JANSEN

AN ANCIENT MEXICAN pictorial manuscript represents a special and unique form of writing. It does not record a number of sentences phonetically, but conveys information more directly through images, with only incidental interference of the language. Nevertheless, the result is a book, made up of a series of figurative paintings which can be read as a text. The possible readings may differ in their phonetic and idiomatic realizations, but, given effective communication, their contents will agree. The high degree of conventionalization of the images and signs certainly contributed to a conventional reading.

A specific group of codices was painted in the Mixtec region, in the southwestern part of Mexico, during Late Postclassic and Early Colonial times. These manuscripts contain unique historical data about the elite lineages that ruled the different kingdoms, or *cacicazgos*, of that region, especially those of Tilantongo and Teozacualco in the Mixteca Alta. The Mixtec provenance and historical character of these codices were firmly established by the works of Alfonso Caso, who laid

the foundation for modern Mixtec studies.[1]

The challenge of interpreting the Mixtec codices today is to "read" them, both by relating the pictographic images to the spoken language and its concepts and by relating the contents of the scenes to Mixtec culture. Historical and archaeological studies have to be combined with an understanding of the language and the heritage that is still alive today (Anders and Jansen 1988).

Colonial sources are few, and they are often incomplete and distorted. Mixtec religion is documented by an early Inquisition trial (1544) against nobles from Yanhuitlan (Jiménez Moreno and Mateos Higuera 1940). General descriptions of the region, its customs, and its history can be found in the *Relaciones geográficas* of circa 1580 (Acuña 1984). A first synthesis of this material was written by the chronicler Antonio de Herrera. The Dominican friars Antonio de los Reyes (1976) and Francisco de Alvarado (1962) published a very valuable grammar and dictionary of the Mixtec language in 1593, in which several important traditions and concepts were also recorded. A crucial sacred text about the origins of the world and humankind was published in an abbreviated translation by Fray Gregorio García (1981 [1607]). Later in the seventeenth century, Fray Francisco de Burgoa discussed several aspects of Mixtec culture and history in his history of the Dominican missions in Oaxaca.

Today the Mixtec region is poverty-stricken and suffering from social injustice and violence, while the environment is threatened with an alarming desertification. In many ways, however, Mixtec culture and Mixtec language show a great continuity, which makes it possible to interpret the data of the past through an understanding of the present, and vice versa. The participation of modern Mixtecs on an equal footing in this study is an essential element and also an ethical imperative: it is *their* history and *their* culture.

On the basis of these various sources—both ancient and modern—one may venture to "read" the scenes, identifying the objects represented and the genre of representation, interpreting the themes and motifs as well as their social and historical context, and evaluating the whole in terms of more general scientific, social, and human principles.

The basic elements of pictography are (often highly) stylized iconic images, in combination with a limited number of arbitrary signs. They may merely represent the objects they depict, indicate an action or something else directly related to the objects depicted, or have either a symbolic or metaphorical significance or a purely phonetic value ("hieroglyphs"). These elements are ordered in scenes and, in most codices, are distributed along horizontal or vertical guidelines, following a reading order of "as the ox ploughs" (*boustrophedon*). *Lienzos*, which do not have the screenfold form but are large pieces of cloth, have a different reading order. Codices are well suited for conveying narrative sequences. *Lienzos*, however, may be better suited for representing a spatial ordering and, in fact, are sometimes real maps, locating toponymic hieroglyphs according to geographical reality and associating historical

personages and events with these places.

Generally speaking, the protagonists of the historical narrative are human beings, the ancient Mixtec lords and ladies. The individuals are identified by their names, which are painted beside them: calendrical names, consisting of the day in the 260-day Mesoamerican calendar on which they were born, and more poetic so-called personal names, which are given in a special ceremony at the age of seven (Herrera y Tordesillas 1947: Decade III, Book 3, Ch. 12). The personal names may also be represented in the clothing. For the men these names often refer to brave animals (eagles, jaguars), fire, blood, or divine beings (e.g., sun, rain, fire-serpent) and other indications of strength, nobility, and courage. For the women they are used to represent beauty and value: quetzal birds, butterflies, cobwebs, jade, flowers, fans, etc. (see Smith 1937b).

The lords usually have short hair and wear loincloths, sometimes in combination with long ceremonial shirts or attire in the form of animals—referring to their names and perhaps also their *nahuales* or *tonales* (animal alter egos). They often wear sandals. The ladies normally wear their hair long and braided and are dressed in *quechquemitls* (shawls) and long wrap-around skirts. Both men and women may appear adorned with gold and turquoise or jade jewelry (earplugs, necklaces, bracelets, etc.) and with feather ornaments.

Priests often appear painted black with soot or a hallucinogenic ointment. Sometimes they are represented as elderly persons with beards. Certain long skirts, known as *xicolli* in Nahuatl, are ceremonial garments. They are offered at special occasions (such as marriages) and may also represent the different ranks of the priestly career. Priests may carry on their backs precious gourds, in which the tobacco powder for the offerings is kept. A specific priestly function is indicated by the fire-serpent and the eagle; according to Antonio de los Reyes (1976:79), *yaha yahui* 'eagle, fire-serpent' is a title, meaning 'nigromántico señor' in Spanish, from which a reference to a shamanic *nahual* can be inferred. The existence of such a title explains why historical personages occasionally may appear in this outfit (e.g., Lord 8 Deer "Jaguar Claw" in *Codex Nuttall*, pp. 44, 50).

A man and a woman facing each other usually represent a marriage. The couple may be shown seated on a mat (*petate*) or just on a band, on top of the toponymic hieroglyph of the place they rule, or in a palace. Sometimes a vessel containing chocolate sits between them and enhances the festive character of the event. The marriage had been preceded by the proposals of a "marriage ambassador," after whose successful mediation the bride was carried off to the house of the groom, as is still the case in traditional Mixtec communities (see the biography of Lady 6 Monkey of Jaltepec in *Codex Selden* 3135 (A.2), pp. 6–8, and the story of Lady 3 Flint in *Codex Nuttall*, p. 19).

A year bearer and a day sign often accompany the couple, giving the date of the marriage. Deer and Eagle, both associated with the West in the mantic system, were considered favorable days. The children are represented as isolated persons, following the couple and looking away from them.

Sometimes the couple is first followed by a provenance statement of the bride or groom moving in, mentioning the names of his or her parents and the toponymic hieroglyph of their *cacicazgo*. The children are sometimes explicitly shown as having been born, by means of umbilical cords attached to them, or by means of footsteps leading from the parents to the children (Fig. 3-1). Their years of birth may be given, the days, of course, being the same as their calendar names.

In a detailed genealogical pattern, a couple is followed by its children. Then one of the children is shown again, on the occasion of his or her own marriage, forming a new couple. In a more condensed pattern, however, one couple just follows another, making it difficult sometimes to determine the relationship between the two, e.g., to ascertain which member of the second couple was the child of the first, and whether he or she was actually their

child and not a brother or sister.

The Mixtec elite, as depicted in the codices, married within their own group. Frequently, the descendants of a couple tried to reunite the divided inheritance by intermarriage, e.g., between cousins, or between uncle and niece (Spores 1974). This practice resulted in an extremely complex web of family relationships, which are portrayed in the codices. To interpret these relationships one should keep to the Mixtec kinship terminology.

In a few instances, the death of the individual is explicitly shown by means of a mummy-bundle accompanied by his or her name and the date of death.

Several people were so important that many more details of their biographies were recorded. The most famous of them is Lord 8 Deer "Jaguar Claw," born in a Year 12 Reed and killed fifty-two years later, also in a Year 12 Reed. His life story is told in the *Codices Colombino-Becker, Nuttall* (p. 42-end), and *Bodley 2858* (pp. 7–14). In such biographies, we read about meetings, rituals, pilgrimages, battles, conquests, etc. They often reveal a dramatic composition: tragedies, ambitions, and intrigues may be reconstructed from the images, as well as the love of beauty and the devout, ritualized respect for the divine powers (see Troike 1974; Jansen and Pérez 1986).

Meetings are represented by two or more people facing each other, often of the same sex (if not, the scene may possibly be confused with a marriage scene, but is generally clarified by the context).

A special gathering is one in which people pay their ceremonial respects and present an offering to one or two individuals. The offering may consist of a decapitated quail, tobacco, a burning torch, and some palm leaves or other plants. Sacrifices to divine beings (such as Bundles in temples) may include *copal* incense with a smoking ladle and tobacco powder, as well as a blood sacrifice involving ear-piercing with a bone perforator and performed by priests and heirs to the throne.

Human sacrifice is rarely depicted. Gener-

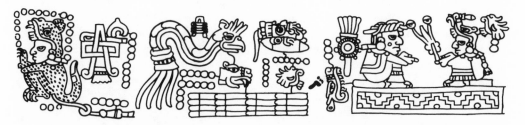

FIGURE 3-1. *Codex Bodley 2858*, p. 17–IV: Lord 2 Water "Fire Serpent of the Mexicans" is married to Lady 3 Alligator "Precious Fan," who has come from the Valley and is the daughter of Lord 11 Water "Rain Flint" and Lady 13 Serpent "Plumed Serpent of Cuilapan." In the Year 8 House, Lord 5 Reed "Twenty Jaguars" is born [the son of Lord 2 Water and Lady 3 Alligator].

Reconstructed Mixtec reading: *Iya Catuta "Yahui Sami Nuu" ninduvui sihi Iyadzehe Coquihui "Huichi nisaa Yusi," nindesi Yodzo, nicuvui dzayadzehe Iya Situta "Dzavui Yuchi" sihi Iyadzehe Siyo "Coo Ndodzo Saha Yucu." Nuu cuiya Nacuau nicacu Iya Q huiyo "Ocoñaña."*

ally speaking, it is a form of execution of enemies taken as prisoners in battle. Those to be sacrificed carry a white banner in one hand, have a black stripe painted across their eyes, and have their hair covered with white paper or white down.

Even though the character of the Mixtec codices under discussion is historical or, rather, descriptive and narrative, there are many references to religious beliefs and concise parallels with the religious, mantic, and prescriptive *Codex Borgia* group. The codices show the major Mesoamerican gods in their well-known iconography. A central religious concept is *ñuhu* 'God', which is painted in the screenfolds as a stony being, often colored red, with large teeth and round eyes (Smith 1973b:65ff; Jansen 1982a:Ch. V:4). The *ñuhu* is associated with the Holy Bundle. This Bundle, which is often related to the ancestors of mythological origin who founded the dynasty, is a central element in the dynastic cult: it is carried by priests (cf. the Aztec *teomama*) and adored in temples. The Bundle also appears in combination with the equipment for drilling the New Fire. The New Fire ceremony occurs in detail in the *Codex Vindobonensis Mexicanus 1* and is related to the foundation of the *cacicazgos*.

Christian churches have since taken the place of the ancient temples as *huahi ñuhu* 'Houses of God', and the *fiestas* of the Christian calendar have replaced most ancient public cults, but many elements and structures of the ancient worldview and rituals have survived in private life and intimate experience, enriched rather than destroyed by Christian beliefs. This is especially true of humanity's close relationship with nature, as well as of the awe surrounding the *temazcal* (steam bath), traditional curing, and the whole complex of *nahual* experiences.

Mixtec religion today has preserved many ancient concepts and essentially the same divine powers, combined with or translated into Christian saints. The *ñuhu*, which is often impersonated by a special rock or stone, is the spirit of the land: San Cristóbal and Santa Cristina, who provide for the harvest and may be responsible for cases of shock (soul loss, Spanish *susto*). Lord Rain continues to live in "his house" (a cave) and speaks in thunder. Lord Sun is the Eternal Father, who supervises our way and deeds. Lord Maize (Jesus Christ) is our brother and sustenance. Our Grandmother provides strength in the *temazcal* and watches over births, purity, and health. Obviously, these indigenous views and feelings are the background to any sound interpretation of the codices.

Music—an important element in ritual—is seldom represented in the codices; however, we occasionally find someone blowing a conch, shaking a rattle, or playing a drum or a

23

flute.

Battles are represented by two or more people standing opposite each other and wielding arms (spears, shields, axes, dart throwers). Victory is expressed by someone taking the enemy by the hair, making him a captive to be sacrificed. Conquest is expressed by a dart in the hieroglyph of the conquered place (see also Smith 1973a:33; Troike 1982).

In these scenes, as well as in the marriage scenes, toponymic hieroglyphs (place signs) play a crucial part: they indicate the extension of the power of the lord and the legitimization of the dynasty. These hieroglyphs follow the Mixtec practice of giving names to the diverse features of the landscape and generally consist of two elements (Smith 1973a): (1) a natural or cultural feature—a mountain or river (both conventionally drawn in cross section), a plain (a feather carpet), an altar, a ceremonial precinct (with its characteristic "battlements"), a city (a frieze with a geometrical pattern), a house, a ball court, or a *temazcal;* (2) a specifying element, such as a color, an animal or plant, a structure, or any other object that specifies the name of the geographical feature.

Not only the human beings but also the *cacicazgos* had their "calendar names": place-name hieroglyphs may form separate units with dates that are outside of durational time; i.e., they do not have a chronological function but belong to the place as a ceremonial or founding date, comparable to today's *fiesta del pueblo.* These place-date combinations occur where the beginning of a new dynasty is mentioned and are consequently quite frequent in the initial segments of Mixtec historiography (Jansen 1988b).

In some cases, the toponymic hieroglyphs may be identified through the glosses that accompany them. Other places have to be located in a more indirect way: The correspondence between the hieroglyph and the meaning of the Mixtec name has to be established, but, because individual place names are repetitive, such a procedure should com-

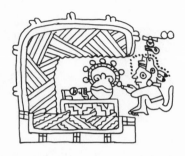

FIGURE 3-2. *Codex Selden 3135* p. 6–II: Lord 2 Rain "Twenty Jaguars" consulting the Jade Heart of the Mixtec People in the cave above the river. After an armed conflict in Jaltepec, Lord 2 Rain "Twenty Jaguars" (Ocoñaña), a prince of Tilantongo, sits in front of a cave, facing a complex sign composed of the *ñuu*-frieze surmounted by a head of the Rain God, a heart, and above the heart a jewel or jade·stone, i.e., 'the jade heart of the people of the Rain God', 'the jewel which is the heart of the Mixtec people'.

Fray Francisco de Burgoa (1934:1:319–333) describes the cult of the 'Heart of the People' (Corazón del Pueblo), which was an emerald wrapped in a Holy Bundle and adored in a cave in Achiutla, where the Mixtec lords came to hear oracles.

prise a significant *cluster* of place-name hieroglyphs or associated historical personages in order to be convincing. The work was initiated by Alfonso Caso and continued by other investigators, especially Mary Elizabeth Smith (1973a). Obviously, a study of the Mixtec language and topography is a prerequisite for this work. Tonal and dialectic differences sometimes make it difficult to determine the etymology of a place name. It is, furthermore, important to know whether a certain modern town was already in existence in precolonial times or, vice versa, whether certain precolonial towns were eventually abandoned and are now known locally only as archaeological sites. The toponyms associated with rulers and dynasties, one may assume, refer to the main towns of the *cacicazgos.* Others might refer, as well, to

FIGURE 3-3. *Codex Nuttall*, p. 36: the landscape around River with the Hand Holding Feathers. Seated as rulers are Lord 1 Flower, Lady 13 Flower, and their daughter Lady 9 Alligator, married to Lord 5 Wind. Above them are four priestly figures making an offering in front of a cave.

places that were important to the Mixtecs in some other way, e.g., holy places, each with a small temple, but not necessarily settlements (Fig. 3-2).

The Mixtec terms for *cacicazgo*, or "nation," are *ñuu teyu*, literally, 'place of a throne', and *yuvui teyu* 'mat and throne', which do occur in pictography. Rulers may sit on thrones and mats (e.g., *Selden 3135*, p. 5-II); place signs may include the *ñuu* frieze and a throne (e.g., *Bodley 2858*, p. 35-III).

Following are some of the more important toponymic hieroglyphs that have been deciphered:

River with the Hand Holding Feathers (= river that plucks or pulls out) (*Nuttall*, p. 36; *Vindobonensis Mexicanus 1*, p. 35): *Yuta tnoho*, Apoala, the place of origin of the

Mixtec dynasties (Caso 1957:45; Smith 1973a: 75; Jansen 1982a: Ch. 2; Figs. 3-3, 3-4).

Heaven, Place of the Rising Sun (Fonds mexicain 20; *Vindobonensis Mexicanus 1*, p. 13): *Andevui* or *Nuu nicana ndicandii*, East. In some cases, this may be identical with the "Place where Heaven was" near Apoala, which is mentioned in the sacred text recorded by Gregorio García, i.e., *Cahua caandihui*, the 'Rock on which Heaven rests' or 'Rock that rises into Heaven' (Jansen 1982a: Ch. 4; Fig. 3–5).

Dark Mountain ("Checkerboard Mountain") (Fonds mexicain 20; *Vindobonensis Mexicanus 1*, p. 21): *Yucu naa*, North (Jansen 1982a: Ch. 4).

River of Ashes (Fonds mexicain 20; *Vindobonensis Mexicanus 1*, pp. 17–16: *Yaa yuta*,

FIGURE 3-4. Apoala as seen from the Mountain of Heaven *Cahua candihui*. To the left is one of the sources of the *Yuta tnoho* (locally pronounced as *Yutza tohon*), the cave called *Yahui coo maa*. In the middle of the valley, this river is joined by another small stream coming from the opposite side of the valley. To the right the river drops into a valley below (*yodo maa*), forming an impressive waterfall not seen in the photograph.

West, probably Rio Nejapa (Jansen 1982a: Ch. 4).

Temple of Death (Fonds mexicain 20; *Vindobonensis Mexicanus 1*, pp. 15–14: *Andaya*, South, probably the cave near Chalcatongo where, according to Burgoa (1934:1:337–341), the Precolonial Mixtec elite were buried (Jansen 1982a: Ch. 4).

Altar of Flowers (*Selden 3135*, p. 5-III; *Nuttall*, p. 5): *Chiyo yuhu*, Santa Maria Suchixtlan (Smith 1973a:79).

Mountain of the Rain (*Nuttall*, p. 2): *Yucuñudahui* (Jansen 1982a: Ch. 4).

Black Town—Heaven Temple (*Mapa de Teozacualco; Nuttall*, p. 42): *Ñuu tnuu—huahi andevui*, Tilantongo (Caso 1949).

Broken Frieze (*Mapa de Teozacualco; Bodley 2858*, p. 16-III): *Chiyo cahnu*, Teozacualco. The Mixtec name means 'Big Altar'. The word for 'big' (*cahnu*) is represented by the homonym for 'breaking' (*cahnu*), with a different tone (Caso 1949).

Sand Mountain (*Vindobonensis Mexicanus 1*, p. 42-IV) or Mountain of Mouth with Sand ("Belching Mountain") (*Selden 3135*, passim): *Añute*, Magdalena Jaltepec (Smith 1983).

Fractured Mountain (*Nuttall*, p. 23): *Ñuu ñañuu*, San Juan Tamazola (Jansen 1982a: Ch. 4:13).

Temple of Beans (*Selden 3135*, p. 13-IV): *Yucun nduchi*, Etlatongo (Smith 1988).

Place of Beans (*Bodley 2858*, p. 18-I): *Ñuu*

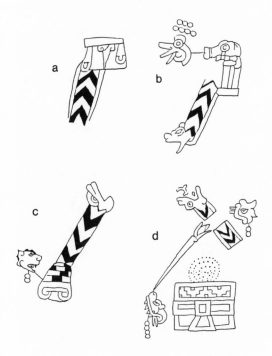

FIGURE 3-5. The hieroglyphs of the four cardinal points in the *Lienzo of Tlapiltepec,* combined with the *yecu* 'war band' (drawing by Ross Parmenter): *a,* Heaven = East; *b,* Temple of Death = South; *c,* Checkerboard Hill = North; *d,* Altar (elsewhere, River) of Ashes = West.

nduchi, Etla (Smith 1988).

Burning Town (*Bodley 2858* reverse, passim; *Selden 3135,* p. 2): *Ñuu ndecu,* San Miguel Achiutla (Jiménez Moreno in Jansen and Gaxiola 1978:12).

Place of Flints (*Vindobonensis Mexicanus 1,* p. 42-III; *Bodley 2858* reverse, passim): *Ñuu yuchi,* Mogote del Cacique (Jansen 1982a: 276; Byland and Pohl 1987).

Place of the Eye with Crossed Sticks or Crossed Legs (*Bodley 2858* reverse, passim): *Ndisi nuu,* Tlaxiaco (Smith 1973a:58–59; Jansen and Pérez 1983).

Plain of the Year (*Becker II,* p. 3): *Yodzo cuiya,* Juxtlahuaca (Smith 1979).

Plain of the Eagle (*Becker II,* p. 3): *Yodzo*

yaha, Tecomaxtlahuaca (Smith 1979).

Place of the Axes (*Lienzo de Zacatepec*): *Ñuu caa,* Putla (Smith 1973a:97).

Mountain of 7 Water (*Lienzo de Zacatepec*): *Yucu satuta,* Zacatepec (Smith 1973a:96).

Stone of the Bird (with a human chin) (*Bodley 2858,* p. 9-III; *Nuttall,* p. 45): *Yucu dzaa,* Tututepec (Smith 1973a:67).

Plumed Serpent (*Lienzo de Coixtlahuaca, Lienzo de Tlapiltepec*): *Yodzo coo,* Coixtlahuaca (Smith 1973a:65–66; Parmenter 1982).

Mountain of the Jewel (*Sierra,* pp. 4, 15): *Ñuu ndaa,* Tejupam (Smith 1973a:60–62) or *Yucu yusi* (*Egerton 2895,* pp. 20, 23, 24), Acatlan (Smith 1973a:60–62).

Mountain of the *Temazcal* (*Egerton 2895,* p. 15): *Ñuu niñe,* Tonala (König 1979).

The Mixtecs refer to themselves as 'the People of the Rain', *Ñuu Dzavui,* a concept which is also present in the codices (Fig. 3-2). Other ethnic groups may be indicated by specific attributes. The Nahuatl speakers (Toltecs, Aztecs) were called *sami nuu* 'those with the burned or burning eyes or faces' and consequently were characterized by dark circles around their eyes, flames emanating from their foreheads, or holding a torch with eyes in one of their hands (Smith 1973a:209). Their capital was Cattail Frieze. The ruler of this town entered into an alliance with the Mixtec prince Lord 8 Deer "Jaguar Claw," on whom the ruler bestowed royal honors in a nose-piercing ceremony (*Colombino,* p. XIII; *Nuttall,* p. 52; *Bodley 2858,* p. 9-II). Caso identified Cattail Frieze as Tula, the Toltec capital.[2] The Mixtec name for Tula was probably *Ñuu cohyo* 'Place of the Tule Reeds', which was later also used for Mexico City. A later interplay between Mixtecs and Nahuatl speakers is documented by the *Lienzo of Tlapiltepec* (formerly called "Antonio de León"; see Caso 1961). Ross Parmenter (1982) proved that part of the *Lienzo de Tlapiltepec* was actually a map locating the hieroglyphs of the major towns of the Coixtlahuaca Valley on the *lienzo* (upper right section) according to their actual geographical distribution. A study of this geographical arrangement of the *Lienzo de Tlapil-*

FIGURE 3-6. Lower right section of the *Lienzo de Tlapiltepec* (turned upside down).

Face, which can be identified as Cuauhtinchan and Tepeaca, respectively (Fig. 3-6).[3] Near Tepeyaca we find Altar of the Hut with Plant, which in *Lienzo Seler II* is glossed *chiyo tnuyaca* 'Altar of the *yaca* tree', the Mixtec name for Tecamachalco.

The last two towns occur together with a dynasty of rulers, which is also mentioned on the *Lienzo de Tecamachalco*. The parallel allows this whole story of an expedition from the Coixtlahuaca Valley toward the Cuauhtinchan region to be related to other historical sources, especially to the *Historia Tolteca-Chichimeca* (Kirchhoff, Odena, and Reyes 1976:205–206), the *Mapas de Cuauhtinchan* (Reyes 1977:59ff), and the *Anales de Tlatelolco* (Berlin and Barlow 1948:23).

The first couple in this dynasty shown on the *Lienzo of Tlapiltepec* is Lord 8 Movement (in other sources, 1 Movement) and Lady 6 Alligator. Their son, Lord 12 Lizard (Cuetzpaltzin), married Lady 5 Reed. They ruled over Tecamachalco, and one of their sons, Lord 8 House (in other sources, 10 House), became ruler of Quecholac, here represented as Mountain with River.

The comparison with the version on the *Lienzo de Tecamachalco* (Burland 1960) shows that this Lord 1 or 8 Movement was the son of Lord 13 Rain, the Mixtec lord who had led Mixtecs and Chocho-Popoloca from the Coixtlahuaca Valley to Cuauhtinchan and had established himself in that region, as the *Historia Tolteca-Chichimeca* tells us (Kirchhoff, Odena and Reyes 1976:205–206). According to the Nahuatl sources, the expedition took place in the fourteenth century A.D.

Probably related to this series of events is the story in the Codex Selden (pp. 11–12) about the military expedition of Lord 9 Lizard from Jaltepec and his ally, Lord 9 House from Tilantongo-Teozacualco (Fig. 3-7). After rituals in River of the Intertwined Plumed Serpents (Coixtlahuaca?) and Mountain of the Arrows (Miltepec?), they became involved in a battle near Valley or Split Mountain (Tepeji?) against the People with Burned Eye-Sockets, that is, *tay sami nuu*, or Nahuatl

tepec reveals a consistent orientation (east is in the upper left corner).

The map covers not only the Coixtlahuaca Valley, but also the area extending toward the northwest (lower right section). An expedition or conquest moves from Tlapiltepec (Hill of the Knot) in the direction of the Mixteca Baja and the Valley of Puebla. Given this general geographical framework (and also the interesting parallels in the *Lienzo Seler II* and the *Lienzo de Tecamachalco*), many places can be identified. The towns closest to Tlapiltepec—Stone of the Heron and Mountain of the Arrows, for example—have to be Aztatla and Miltepec (which are also present on the *Lienzo de Tecamachalco*). The expedition ends at House of the Eagle and Mountain with

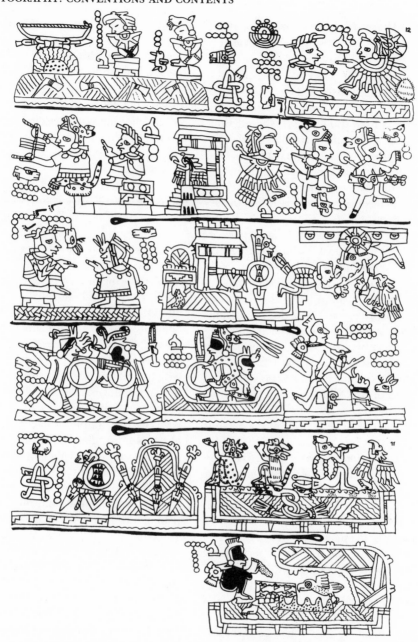

FIGURE 3-7. *Codex Selden 3135*, pp. 11–12: The Ritual of Eagle and Fire Serpent, of Coyote and Jaguar, performed in the River of the Intertwined Serpents (Coixtlahuaca?). The Ritual of the Holy Bundle and the *Ñuhu* of Arms, celebrated in the Mountain of Flowered Arrows (Miltepec?). In an attack on the Valley (Tepeji?), Lord 9 Lizard overcomes the Nahua Lord "Maize Hair," and Lord 9 House takes the Nahua Lord "Jaguar" prisoner and sacrifices him on the day 13 Deer, during a ceremony in which Eagle and Fire-Serpent (the *nahual* priests) offer human hearts to the Sun God in front of the Temple of the *Ñuhu* of Arms and the Holy Bundle in Jaltepec. Then Lord 9 Lizard marries Lady 12 Deer "War *Quechquemitl*," daughter of Lord 13 Serpent "Jaguar" and Lady 2 House from the Temple of the Eagle (Cuauhtinchan?).

speakers. Afterward, Lord 9 Lizard married a princess from Temple of the Eagle (probably Cuauhtinchan; see Caso 1964:39).

Contacts with the Zapotec area are also mentioned in the Mixtec codices. Caso (1966) observed that a whole dynasty, described in the Codex Nuttall (pp. 33–35), shared similar clothing types and attributes with personages represented in Tomb I of Zaachila. He therefore related this so-called "Xipe dynasty" to the Mixtec neighbor of Zaachila, Cuilapan, and consequently identified the associated town Quetzal River–Bent Rock–Tree as Cuilapan. A closely related place is "Cacaxtli Plain," which is also identified by Caso as Cuilapan (Smith 1973a:64; Caso 1977: I:111–114; Paddock 1983). Closer analysis, however, makes it more likely that the Xipe dynasty actually represented the ruling family of Zaachila itself, because the same genealogy seems to be represented on the *Lienzo of Guevea* (Jansen 1982a; Cruz 1983). Cacaxtli Plain, on the other hand, can be compared to the Cacaxtli Hill, which appears on a painting in Martínez Gracida's (1986) work. It can be glossed as the Coat of Arms of the ancient Coyolapan, that is, Cuilapan (Figs. 3-8, 3-9). In the *Codex Bodley 2858* (p. 24-III), the *cacaxtli* element is part of two place signs, the respective destinations of a sister and a brother, both belonging to the Tlaxiaco dynasty:

(1) Cacaxtli Plain, ruled over by Lord 6 Water, who belonged to the Xipe dynasty (see also *Nuttall*, p. 35 and *Selden 3135*, p. 13-I).

(2) Mountain of the Jaguar and the Flowers— Cacaxtli Hill. The second hieroglyph is similar to the Coat of Arms of Cuilapan in Martínez Gracida's (1986) work, which shows the Cacaxtli Hill together with a Hill of the Jaguar, a place of ancient walls and fortifications (Monte Alban?).[4]

The comparison leads us to the hypothesis that, in concurrence with Caso, the *cacaxtli* element refers to Cuilapan in both cases. According to the *Relaciones geográficas*, Cuilapan was given to the Mixtecs because of the bonds of marriage between the Zapotec and the Mixtec dynasties. The first of these interethnic elite marriages, according to the *Relaciones*, took place "more than 300 years ago," that is, shortly before A.D. 1280 (see also Rabin 1982).

These interethnic contacts have implications for the calculation and correlation of the dates in the chronological sequence of Mixtec historiography. This chronology was a theme of research and debate during the 1970's. It is a very complex problem and is basic to the understanding of the codices.

After telling the story of the dynastic origins, the Mixtec codices depict long and detailed genealogies that connect the rulers of the Late Postclassic *cacicazgos* (Tilantongo, Teozacualco, Jaltepec, Tlaxiaco, and so on) with their divine ancestors. Within this genealogical framework, Alfonso Caso analyzed the sequence of dates (years and days) associated with the lives of the protagonists. The dates, of course, are given in terms of the ancient Mexican calendar, which means that they are repeated in cycles of fifty-two years. The dates are given irregularly in the different codices, which raises the question of establishing how many fifty-two-year cycles are involved in all that has been recorded of Mixtec history. At the end of the sequence of cycles, it is possible to connect them with the Christian chronology.

The basis of such a synchronization is the fact that a Mixtec year 1 Reed roughly corresponded to an Aztec year 2 Reed, as different sources (the Cuilapan Stone, *Codex Sierra*, and others) make clear. These sources contain the equivalents of Mixtec dates for Aztec or Christian years (Jiménez Moreno and Mateos Higuera 1940).

FIGURE 3-8. Drawing of the coat of arms of ancient Coyolapan, showing the *cacaxtli* element, in the work of Manuel Martínez Gracida (1986).

FIGURE 3-9. *Codex Bodley 2858*, p. 24-III: Lady 1 Reed "Jade Sun" married Lord 6 Water "Coloured Stripes" from Cacaxtli Plain, and her brother Lord 3 Reed "Smoking Eye" went to the Mountain of the Jaguar and the Flowers—Cacaxtli Hill.

Some of the last generations of the Mixtec Precolonial dynasties depicted in the codices are also mentioned in Early Colonial Spanish sources. Starting from these dates one can calculate back into the past and establish a complete synchronization, as Caso (1960) did. A number of problems remain, however. Caso himself, stating explicitly that the correlation he proposed was by no means indisputable, was the first to criticize his own work. For the dates in the two centuries preceding the Conquest, he thought a change of one or two fifty-two-year cycles would be possible. For more remote periods, he emphasized, his correlation was merely tentative (1977:I:39).

Following Caso, we may distinguish two main periods in Mixtec historiography for the sake of this discussion: (1) the period between the lifetime of Lord 8 Deer "Jaguar Claw" and the Spanish Conquest; (2) the period before Lord 8 Deer "Jaguar Claw," i.e., the period in which the *cacicazgos* were founded and the first generations of Lords and Ladies ruled.

For the period between Lord 8 Deer and the Spanish Conquest, the dates are relatively clear. Caso's analysis follows the dates given in the codices and as such is impeccable. There are, however, some problems regarding the dates themselves. Emily Rabin (1981), who has made a careful and detailed analysis of the chronology problem, has suggested that in the latter part of this sequence of dates an error must have crept in somewhere and one fifty-two-year cycle too many was calculated. Rabin's hypothesis is supported by the possible connections with the above-mentioned Central Mexican and Zapotec data. If we follow Rabin's reasoning, the dates corresponding to the life of Lord 8 Deer "Jaguar Claw" would change from A.D. 1011–1063 (as calculated by Caso) to one cycle later, A.D. 1063–1115.

The period preceding Lord 8 Deer "Jaguar Claw" is that of the origins of the Mixtec dynasties. Here we also find among the chronological dates a number of dates in nondurational time, i.e., ceremonial founding dates

associated with the place signs of the *cacicazgos* (see Furst 1978; Jansen 1982a; 1988b). Caso, however, calculated those dates as chronological markers in the sequence of fifty-two-year cycles. Consequently, his correlation sequence became much too long here and contained a number of inconsistencies and biological impossibilities. Therefore, in this part of the chronology, Emily Rabin's revision of Caso's correlations is much more extensive and completely changes the picture.

One of the implications is that Lord 8 Deer's father, Lord 5 Alligator "Rain-Sun," cannot have been the successor of Lord 2 Rain "Ocoñaña," the grandson of Lord 12 Lizard "Arrow Legs" and the last descendant of the "first Tilantongo dynasty," as Caso thought. Nor was Lord 5 Alligator the founder of a "second Tilantongo dynasty." In fact, he was a high priest in Tilantongo who must have died fourteen years before this Lord 2 Rain did. It was Lord 5 Alligator's son, Lord 8 Deer "Jaguar Claw" himself, who, shortly after Lord 2 Rain "Ocoñaña" died, seized power in Tilantongo (Rabin 1981; Jansen 1982a: Ch. 6).

According to the revised chronology, Mixtec historiography starts with the marriage of Lady 1 Death and Lord 4 Alligator in the Year 6 Flint, Day 7 Eagle, i.e., A.D. 940. This date coincides with the beginning of the Postclassic period.

The interpretation of Mixtec chronology and its correlation with dates in the Christian calendar still raises many problems, as does the overall reading of the codices. Noticeable progress has been made, however. In the fields of history and geography, as well as in those of material and spiritual culture, the study of the codices is moving closer to an understanding of Mixtec reality and, we hope, closer to the Mixtecs themselves.

NOTES

1. A synopsis is Caso's (1965c) chapter in the *Handbook of Middle American Indians*. Many data can also be found in chapters by Glass (1975) and Glass and Robertson (1975).

Later reviews of progress in the field have been published by Troike (1978) and Gutié-rrez Solana (1987). For a general consideration of the interpretive practice within this paradigm, see Jansen (1988a). In another *Handbook* chapter, Robert Chadwick (1971) tried to relate the Mixtec codices to Central Mexican sources, but his work contains many unfounded speculations and is therefore of dubious validity.

2. Smith (1973a:71ff) expressed doubts about this identification and instead suggested Tulixtlahuaca, a subject town of Jica-yan in the Mixtec coastal area. The importance of the town and its consistent associa-tion with people wearing the facial painting characteristics of Nahuatl speakers, however, seem to support Caso's original hypothesis.

3. *Lienzo Seler II* (König 1984) contains the same hieroglyphs with Mixtec glosses: *Cahua dzoco yaa* 'Rock of the Eagle Temple'. This gloss must be the equivalent of *Huahi yaha* 'Temple or House of the Eagle', which is the Mixtec name for Cuauhtinchan in the list of place names given by Antonio de los Reyes (see also Codex Mendoza, p. 42).

4. A Hill of the Jaguar, Ocelotepeque in Nahuatl, is part of the configuration of Monte Alban on the 1771 Map of Xoxocotlan. See the discussion by Smith (1973a:205).

4. The Annals of the Tlapanecs

CONSTANZA VEGA SOSA

EVEN TODAY, Tlapanec, Mixtec, and Nahua groups coexist in that part of the Sierra Madre del Sur lying within the state of Guerrero. Their Prehispanic and Early Colonial history has been described in various pictorial documents, the Tlapanec Codices, which include the *Codex Azoyú 1*, the *Codex Azoyú 2*, and the *Lienzo de Tlapa-Azoyú*.

The first section of the *Codex Azoyú 1* records the annals of these groups from A.D. 1300 to 1565, according to the Tlapanec calendrical system. This document is located in the Pictographic Evidence Room of the library of the National Museum of Anthropology and History in Mexico City. It consists of thirty-eight accordion-pleated folios made of paper of the wild fig tree (*amate*). A layer of very fine plaster underlies the pictorial scenes but not the bands containing calendrical glyphs. The panels and the figures in them were outlined in black (lampblack); the figures were then decorated with colors: turquoise (Maya blue), carmine red (cochineal red), white (plaster), black and gray (lampblack), ocher yellow (*zacatlascale; Cuscuta* sp.), and light pink skin colors (*zacatlascale* mixed with cochineal red), according to Alejandro Huerta Carrillo's (1988) study of manufacturing techniques. All the materials were of Prehispanic origin.

THE READING OF THE GLYPHS

Before the folios were read, the glyphs were first surveyed and classified according to their elements: names of towns, calendrics, and Prehispanic and Colonial individuals. Among the Prehispanic personages represented are governors, warriors participating in sacrificial ceremonies during the Conquest, women, and commoners. Colonial personages include conquistadores, *encomenderos*, district civil officials such as *alcaldes mayores* and *corregidores*, ecclesiastical judicial authorities (vicars and *provisores bachilleres*), and tortured natives.

The identification and association of these elements permitted the reading of the folios, proceeding from earlier to more recent events and from left to right, as in contemporary writing. To describe each folio, the following

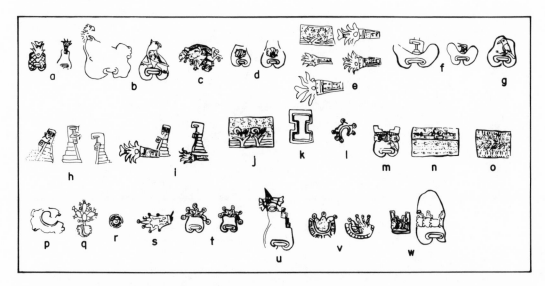

FIGURE 4-1. *Codex Azoyú*, toponymic glyphs: *a*, Tlachinolticpac 'The Town above the Burned Town', fols. 4, 24; *b*, Tototepec 'Place of the Birds', fols. 8, 30; *c*, Tecuanapan 'River of the Fierce' or 'River of the Cannibals', fol. 9; *d*, Tetzotzoncan or Tetzotzontepec 'Place of Those Who Work Stone', fols. 9, 10; *e*, Tlachinollan 'Place of the Burned Fields', fols. 16, 18, 22, 27, 38; *f*, Caltepemaxalco 'Place of the House on the Divided Mountain', fols. 17, 20; *g*, Huilotepec 'Dove Mountain', fol. 17; *h*, Caltitlan 'Beside the Houses', fols. 18, 26, 27; *i*, Tlachinollan and Caltitlan, fols. 18, 27; *j*, 'Cornfield (?)', fols. 18, 19; *k*, Tlachco 'Ball Court', fol. 19; *l*, Atliztaca 'Place of the Whiteness of the Water', fol. 19; *m*, Quecholtenango 'In the Walled Place of Flamingos', fol. 20; *n*, Totomixtlahuacan 'Plain of Bird Hunters', fol. 21; *o*, Petlacala 'In the House of the Woven Straw Boxes', fol. 22; *p*, Oztotzinco 'Small Place of the Cave (or Caves)', fol. 22; *q*, Tenochtitlan 'Near the Cactus with Red Fruit', fol. 24; *r*, Yoallan 'Place of the Divinity of Night', fol. 25; *s*, Atlimaxac 'Where the Water Divides', fol. 26; *t*, Atlitepec 'On the Hill of Water', fols. 28, 31; *u*, Xipetepec 'On the Hill of the God Xipe', fol. 30; *v*, Acocozpan 'Place of the Canals of Very Yellow Water', fols. 31, 38; *w*, Tetenanco 'In the Place Fenced or Walled with Stones', fols. 31, 32.

steps were taken: (1) the chronology was established; (2) the name of the town was deciphered; (3) the governors and the dates of their rule were identified; (4) other individuals were identified: warriors, sacrificial victims, commoners, conquistadores, *encomenderos*, and *alcaldes;* (5) the action portrayed was described: government, conquest and domination of a town, sacrificial ceremony, or migration; (6) the relationship of each folio with those preceding and following it was determined; (7) the document was read.

Toponymic Glyphs

This study began with the analysis of place-name glyphs, to establish the geographic focus of the document. The glyphs were identified by comparing them with those occurring on other documents from the region: *Azoyú 2, Lienzo de Tlapa-Azoyú, Lienzo de Totomixtlahuacan* (1974), *Codex Cualac* (Jacobs Müller 1958), *Lienzo de Chiepetlan 1* (Galarza 1972), *Veinte Mazorcas* (Barlow 1961), the *Matrícula de Tributos*, and the *Codex Mendoza* (1964). Karen Dakin (1983) wrote the etymological analysis and the corrected Nahuatl form.

The names of the recorded towns (Fig. 4-1) were Tlachinolticpac (*a*), Tototepec (*b*), Tecuanapan (*c*), Tetzotzoncan (*d*), Tlachinollan (*e*), Caltepemaxalco (*f*), Huilotepec (*g*), Caltitlan (*h*), Cornfield (?) Tlachinollan and Caltitlan (*i*), (*j*), Tlachco (*k*), Atliztaca (*l*),

35

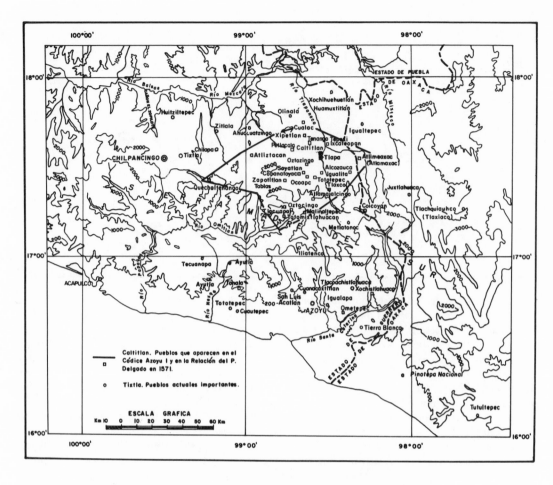

FIGURE 4-2. Towns and geographic regions in the Kingdom of Tlachinollan.

Quecholtenango (*m*), Totomixtlahuacan (*n*), Petlacala (*o*), Oztotzinco (*p*), Tenochtitlan (*q*), Yoallan (*r*), Atlimaxac (*s*), Atlitepec (*t*), Xipetepec (*u*), Acocozpan (*v*), and Tetenanco (*w*). Among those, the glyph that occurs most frequently is the one for Tlachinollan 'Place of the Burned Fields', which is now named Tlapa. Identifying the town has permitted us to locate this region in the east-central part of the Sierra Madre del Sur, in the state of Guerrero. It lies west of the Mixteca Alta of the state of Oaxaca (Fig. 4-2). In his 1571 enumeration of towns in this region, Fray Alonso Delgado (1904:97–107) listed both the principal towns with their respective tributary pueblos and the languages spoken, which were Tlapanec, Mixtec, and Nahua.

The Calendar

The *Codex Azoyú 1* contains thirty-eight folios, painted on both sides, with the chronology written on the right side and across the top; these sections are read from the bottom to the top and from right to left. Each folio records 7 years, each within a rectangular frame, producing a record of 266 years. The calendrical system has the following charac-

36

FIGURE 4-3. The year bearers of the Tlapanec solar calendar, *Azoyú 1*, fol. 13: *a*, 9 Movement; *b*, 10 Wind; *c*, 11 Deer; *d*, 12 Grass; *e*, 13 Movement; *f*, 14 Wind; *g*, 2 Deer.

teristics: the numbers are represented by dots; the years are counted from 2 to 14; and the names of the year bearers are Deer (Mazatl), Grass (Malinalli), Movement (Ollin), and Wind (Ehecatl) (Fig. 4-3).

Given the identities of the year bearers, it can be concluded immediately that this calendar belongs to Type II, which is considered to be of Teotihuacan origin, according to the studies of Munro S. Edmonson (1988a:241). Edmonson also documented at Teotihuacan the coefficients to record the years from 2 to 14. The number 14 was found, however, with the year Flint in a cartouche of the Mixtec Yucuñudahui style, which corresponds to the Type III calendar.

The foregoing implies that the Tlapanecan calendar inherited from Teotihuacan the use of the Type II bearers—Wind, Deer, Grass, and Movement—as well as, perhaps, the coefficients 2 to 14. According to the *Codex Azoyú 1*, these numbers were used to name the 365-day solar years, but so far no evidence corroborates their use in the 260-day calendar (*tonalpohualli*) during the fourteenth to the sixteenth centuries in this region.

Folio 32 of the codex reports that in the Tlapanec year 3 Wind a Spanish conqueror arrived in Tetenanco; this corresponds to the Aztec year 3 House. Both occur between May 1521 and January 1522, according to Edmonson's calendrical correlations. It is therefore proposed that the number 14 in the Tlapanec calendar corresponds to the number 13 in the Aztec thirteen-day count.

The Individuals

To define the function of Prehispanic and Colonial personages, their apparel and specific attributes have been analyzed and compared with those of similar individuals in other codices. Among the Prehispanic representations, those of the governors were the most important element for reconstructing the events that *Codex Azoyú 1* relates. As symbols of power they bear the fan and the bag of copal that invest them with the "functions of *alcaldes*, judges, ambassadors, military leaders, and priests" (*Codex Mendoza*, Fig. 69; *Codex Vaticano Latino 3738*, Fig. 48; *Codex Tudela*, fol. 50r) (Fig. 4-4). To identify the glyphs referring to individuals, the names of the Nahua nobility (*teuhtli*) recorded in the *Lienzo de Tlapa-Azoyú* and in the works of Alfonso Caso (1977; 1979) about Mixtec kings and their kingdoms were taken into consideration. Thus I reconstructed the genealogies of the Tlapanec-Nahua and Mixtec governors using calendar names (Table 4-1).

In the *Codex Azoyú 1* the warriors indicate their profession by wearing their hair tied at the top of their heads (Chimalpahin 1965:24, 27). The warrior with shaved hair in folio 32 belongs to the *quachic*, a military group of high status, since he also wears feathers on his head, clothing of netted fabric, and body paint decorated with half-moons, which also adorn his shield (Fig. 4-5). Antonio Peñafiel (1985:25, Fig. 36) called this shield, with its half-moons, *cuexyo-chimalli;* it was also carried by the jaguar knights at Tenochtitlan. Peñafiel also tells us that another warrior emblem was flags, called *macpamitl*, which war-

TABLE 4-1. Governors in the *Codex Azoyú 1*

	Mixtec Lineage		Tlapanec-Nahua Lineage	
Folio	Name	Dates	Name	Dates
1	10 Deer	1300–1307	Dead (Sun)	1300–1321
2	9 Alligator	1307–1314		
3	4 Eagle	1314–1321		
4	3 Jaguar	1321–1334	House	1321–1328
5			Tlaloc	1328–1335
6			Xipe	1335–?
			Shield	1335–?
7			Bird Alligator	1342–1362
8			Rabbit	1349–?
9				
10	2 Water-Arrow	1363–?		
	4 Alligator	1363–1370		
	6 Death	1363–?		
11	1 Dog with Serpent Decoration	1370–1376		
12			Cane Chilli	1377–1383
13			Cane Alligator	1384–1391
			Night Obsidian	1384–1391
14			Stone Flag	1391–1398
			Great Monkey	1391–1433
15			Lizard	1398–1421
16				
17				
18			Flag of Quetzal Feathers	1421–1454
19				
20				
21			Deer Antlers (?)	1440–?
22				
23			Tlaloc	1454–1477
24			Bee	1461–?
25				
26			Turquoise Serpent	1477–1496
27				
28				
29			Green Corn	1496–1517
30				
31	2 Deer	1510–1516	Dog	1510–?
			Jaguar	1510–?
			Eagle	1510–?
32			Flames	1517–1528
33			Rain on the Cultivated Field	1528–1533
34			House	1533–1538
35			Mace	1538–1541
			Jaguar	1542–1561
36			Butterfly	1545–1550
37				
38			Arrow	1562–?

FIGURE 4-4. Rulers: *a, Azoyú 1,* Tlapanec-Nahua lineage, Flag of Quetzal Feathers; *b, Azoyú 1,* Mixtec lineage, 4 Eagle; *c, Mendoza,* Pl. 69; *d, Vaticano Latino 3738,* Pl. 48; *e, Tudela,* fol. 50r.

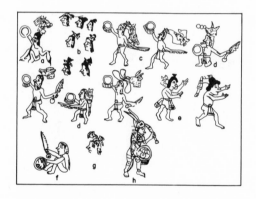

FIGURE 4-5. Warriors, *Azoyú 1: a,* warrior with his hair tied at the top of his head, *cuauhchimalli* (shield), and sacrificial knife, fol. 8; *b,* warriors with their hair tied at the top of their heads, fol. 8; *c,* warriors named Jaguar and Vampire, with *cuauhchimalli* (shield) and *macuahuitl* (mace), fol. 20; *d,* warriors named 3 Dog, Jaguar, Arrow (?), and Deer, with shield and mace, fol. 22; *e,* warriors with their hair tied and adorned with feathers, unarmed, about to be sacrificed, fol. 27; *f,* common man with weapons, fol. 30; *g,* warrior with hair tied at the top of his head, fol. 31; *h,* head of a warrior of *quachic* status, with shaved head and feathers, clothing of netted fabric, body paint, shield, and mace, fol. 32.

riors carried attached to their backs like ladders or frameworks called *cacaxtli,* at the end of one bar of which was the distinctive sign, and that when they began battles they carried small gold banners in their hands.

The *Relación de la Alcaldía Mayor de las Minas de Zumpango, Chilapa y Huitziltepec* (1582) describes how the natives of this region dressed and fought: "The fighting practices were those of all the land. The costume and dress that they had was to go naked, except for the captains and chiefs, who bore escutcheons made of cloth and cotton, backstitched, and shields made of thick cane and lined with cloth and cotton. For arms they carried maces like swords with points of stone blades; the rest of them carried bows and arrows" (Paso y Troncoso 1905:VI:318). We find the ceremony of sacrifice represented in this codex associated with events of conquest and the domination of towns. The personages who participate in the ceremony can be described as people sacrificed by heart extraction, as lying down or standing, as captives on the way to be sacrificed (Fig. 4-6), and as executioners. These participants are decorated with down feathers and flags.

We find similar representations in the *Codex Tudela,* on folio 51, where the victim and the executioner are participating in a ceremony presided over by the god Mictlantecuhtli. Folio 53 shows two victims with feathers on their heads and the executioner; folio 57 shows a victim with down on his head as the companion of an agent of his demise. On folio 54 of the *Codex Magliabechiano,* a victim adorned with down on his head is also a companion of high rank, and folio 58 exhibits two victims and a sacrificer. The following text accompanies them:

This is a staff superimposed by a cross-bar like the feathered ones they use here, which served as a flag for them and stood before the temple. When they sacrificed Indians . . . , since they took them to the top, they threw them on their backs over a stone and removed their hearts, and someone else seized them by the feet so they would not move. And this was a *tlamacaz,* which means the chief of these executioners, who killed. And to do this, they tied their heads and hair with a white cloth to remove their hearts to anoint the snouts of the demon.

(Nuttall 1903: fol. 58)

The similarity of the sacrificial ritual and clothing in these documents is obvious. The white cloth for covering the hair and the feather tassels are also used in the *Codex Azoyú 1*.

The feminine representations in this codex are accompanied by the glyphs for their names. They are seated on their haunches and are wearing skirts and *quechquemitl* (shawls). Their hair falls over their shoulders, and they are wearing earrings in the form of *chalchihuitl* (jade beads). They appear to be conversing. In the *Codex Magliabechiano*, folios 46 and 63, we see the goddesses Mayauel and the so-called Atlacoya also wearing *quechquemitl* and the female commoners wearing blouses without sleeves. Thus, these feminine figures in the *Codex Azoyú 1* correspond to the stratum of the nobles, *pipiltin*.

The common people, *macehualtin,* are represented in this document simply by their heads; the people of various towns are depicted, since one finds them next to toponymic glyphs.

I compared the Colonial figures with those in the *Codex Telleriano Remensis* and in the manuscript called the *Pintura del Gobernador, Alcaldes y Regidores* (Painting of the Governor, Mayors, and Aldermen), also known as the *Codex Osuna*, with the goal of defining their position and function in the Colonial political and economic organization. Individuals representing the Spanish ascendancy include conquerors, *encomenderos, alcaldes mayores, corregidores,* judges, and vicars (Fig. 4.7).

The *alcaldes mayores* or *corregidores* who are noted in the *Codex Azoyú 1* wear cloaks knotted at the shoulder; they are barefooted, seated on *icpalli* (woven straw seats), and they have the staff of authority in their hands. In the *Codex Osuna* (fol. v. 9-471), a scene is depicted in which the Viceroy confers the

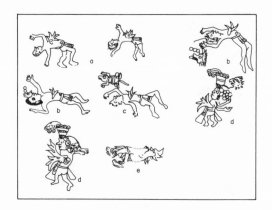

FIGURE 4-6. Sacrificed victims, *Azoyú 1: a,* victims with hearts extracted in ceremonies of conquest and domination of towns, fols. 8, 10; *b,* victims of Mixtec lineage named 3 Monkey and 2 Dog, fol. 17; *c,* sacrifice of the person named Stone Lizard, of Tlapanec Nahua lineage, fol. 22; *d,* sacrifice of two warriors adorned with feathers, fol. 27; *e,* victim in flames, fol. 26.

FIGURE 4-7. Colonial personages, *Azoyú 1: a,* Spanish conquistador, fol. 32; *b, oidor* (judge of *audiencia*), fols. 34, 35; *c, juez* (judge), fols. 35, 37; *d, provisor bachiller,* fol. 36; *e, encomendero,* fol. 37; *f, provisor bachiller,* fols. 37, 38; *g, alcalde* or *corregidor,* fol. 38.

40

staff of authority on the alcaldes of Mexico through an interpreter. The text says:

The custom that the Viceroy don Luis de Velasco had, in conferring the staffs on the *alcaldes alguaciles*, charging them with doctrine, policy, and the good treatment of the natives.

When he passes the *topilli* [staff of authority] to the *alcaldes* of Mexico, the Viceroy says to them: "You are now *alcaldes;* now the first thing is that you should speak widely about Christian doctrine, so that all of the people know and are familiar with the services of Our Lord God. And then you will talk about the services of our sovereign, His Majesty, about what is necessary for him. It is necessary that you charge yourselves well with speaking of that. All of the people, the commoners, will keep it well, will want it, will judge no one without a reason, and will carefully see to it that all of the people will work the land, that no one lives idle.

The representations of tortured natives in *Codex Azoyú 1* consist of the burning of feet with hot water or fire, the garrote, stocks, chaining, and hanging by the feet. The *Codex Osuna* (fol. v. 12-474), relates how Dr. Puga punished the *alcaldes mayores* and native *alguaciles* who committed abuses.

The representations of tortured natives in *Codex Azoyú 1* bear testimony to the existence of the *encomienda* system, as do those of the *alcalde mayor* and the vicar for the *corregimiento* system. Both were Spanish government institutions, one private and the other political, and they coexisted during the first fifty years of the colonial regime in New Spain (González de Cosío 1952:511, 512; Gibson 1967:62).

Reading the Folios

The folios of the *Codex Azoyú 1* can well be considered a documentary history that demonstrates the existence of the Kingdom of Tlachinollan, which resembles kingdoms in the Mixteca Alta. Its calendrical register, the names of the towns, the genealogies of its governors, warriors, priests, sacrificial victims, women, and commoners confirm the existence of Tlachinollan's territory, government, social stratification, ceremonies of conquest and domination, and tribute.

Alfonso Caso, in *Reyes y reinos de la Mixteca*, has this to say:

If we speak in the plural of kings, it is because the political organization of the Mixtec region, unlike that of the Zapotecs, did not consist of just one entity. We can speak of Mixtec culture, but the orography of a region where fertile valleys are separated by rough and sterile mountains gave rise to political separation among the small political units of the Mixtec valleys. They differed sharply from the Zapotec political unity, founded on the geographic integrity of the Central Valley of Oaxaca.

(Caso 1977:30)

Barbro Dahlgren de Jordán, in *La Mixteca: Su cultura e historia prehispánicas*, explains:

The Mixteca was basically divided into a large number of domains, each with a town and its immediate surroundings. In some cases such a unit was equivalent to a ceremonial center with its nearby farms. At the time of the Conquest, the majority of the settlements were grouped in a series of provinces or principalities of varying sizes, while others maintained their independence. The largest, such as Coixtlahuaca, Tilantongo, Tlaxiaco, and Tutepec, are mentioned in the chronicles as kingdoms. At the head of each of these polities was a city that, because of either its chiefs' prestigious lineages, its importance as a religious center, or simply its wealth or military strength, had succeeded in achieving hegemony over the neighboring domains. Wars, alliances, and marriages conserved and augmented the area under control. In addition, through feudal pacts powerful chiefs agreed to de-

41

fend smaller farming villages in exchange for tribute.

(Dahlgren 1979:167–168)

The following is the reading of the folios of the *Codex Azoyú 1*:

Folio 1
A.D. 1300–1306

The Kingdom of Tlachinollan Begins in 1300

The enumeration of years in this document begins in the year 3 Movement of the Tlapanec calendar, which, according to our chronological record, corresponds to A.D. 1300. The document also initiates here the list of genealogies of the governors of the Tlapanec-Nahua and the Mixtec lineages of the Kingdom of Tlachinollan. These were Lord Dead (Sun) and Lord 10 Deer, who were represented carrying a fan and a bag of copal, symbols of the functions of "*alcaldes*, judges, ambassadors, war captains, and priests" (Fig. 4-8). Lord Death Sun is accompanied by a sun drawn in the European style.

Folio 2
A.D. 1307–1313

Lord 9 Alligator Assumes Power

Lord 9 Alligator succeeds the governor of the Mixtec lineage and shares with Lord Dead (Sun) the functions of authority from 1307 to 1313.

Folio 3
A.D. 1314–1320

Lords Dead (Sun) and 4 Eagle Rule

The Mixtec Lord 4 Eagle takes the throne in 1314 and governs until 1320, also sharing power with Lord Death Sun.

Folio 4
A.D. 1321–1327

The Government is Established in Tlachinolticpac in 1321

FIGURE 4-8. *Azoyú 1*, fol. 1: *a*, Year 3 Movement, A.D. 1300; *b*, Lord Death Sun; *c*, Lord 10 Deer.

In the town called Tlachinolticpac 'The Town above the Burned Town', Lords House and 3 Jaguar govern from 1321 until 1327, succeeding Lords Death Sun and 4 Eagle.

According to the Tlapanec calendrical record, then, governors of the Tlapanec-Nahua and the Mixtec lineages ruled in the town of Tlachinolticpac from 1321 on.

Folio 5
A.D. 1328–1334

Lords Tlaloc and 3 Jaguar Rule

Lord Tlaloc follows Lord House and governs in the pueblo of Tlachinolticpac from 1328, sharing the power with Lord 3 Jaguar, until 1334.

Folio 6
A.D. 1335–1341

Two Tlapanec-Nahuas Govern in Tlachinolticpac

Around 1335, two governors of the Tlapanec-Nahua lineage ascend to power in Tlachinolticpac: Lord Xipe and Lord Shield. It is probable that Lord Xipe has principally religious attributes, since the god of this name has great importance among the Tlapanecs.

Folio 7
A.D. 1342–1348

Lord Bird Alligator Assumes Power

Lord Bird Alligator becomes governor in Tlachinolticpac in 1342. He carries only the bag of copal, indicating that his functions are religious. Thus, it is probable that he succeeds Lord Xipe and shares authority with Lord Shield during the period 1342–1348.

Folio 8
A.D. 1349–1355

Conquest and Control of Tototepec

Lord Bird Alligator,[1] governor of Tlachinolticpac, presides over the ceremony of conquest and control of the town of Tototepec 'Place of the Birds'. This ceremony of human sacrifice is carried out by a warrior with the sacrificial knife in his hand. Seven other warriors, their hair tied on top of their heads to indicate their status, take part in the ceremony.

In addition, an interview takes place between Lord Rabbit, who shares authority in the kingdom, and an individual from Tototepec, who explains his affairs. One unidentified person, as well as people named Flames, Bird, and Bee, accompany them.

Tototepec is the first town dominated by the governors of Tlachinolticpac.

Folio 9
A.D. 1356–1362

The Conquest of Tetzotzontepec

The principal scene of this folio is the domination of Tetzotzontepec 'Place of Those Who Work Stone', by the warriors of Caltitlan. Beside the glyph of Tetzotzontepec stands the sacrificer, with a flag in his hand and his hair covered and adorned with feathers. Beneath the glyph of Caltitlan are fifteen heads with

FIGURE 4-9. *Azoyú 1*, fol. 10: *a*, Year 14 Grass, A.D. 1363; *b*, Lord 2 Water-Arrow; *c*, 4 Alligator; *d*, 6 Death; *e*, ceremony of conquest and domination of Tetzotzontepec; *f*, Year 3 Movement, A.D. 1363; *g*, Teocuahuitl, the divine wood that represents the ceremony of the New Fire.

closed eyes and the flag of sacrifice. These people were probably sacrificed during the conquest of Tetzotzontepec.

Two noblewomen, named Cane and Flower, appear to depict what has happened to Lords 5 Eagle-Cane, Dog, Water, Serpent, Deer Foot, Bat, and other, unidentified, lords. The men are probably from the town of Tecuanapan 'River of the Fierce Women', and Cane and Flower are asking them to attend the ceremony of sacrifice. Governor Bird Alligator of Tlachinolticpac appears to remain on the outskirts of this conflict.

Folio 10
A.D. 1363–1369

The Mixtec Domination

Caltitlan lords of Mixtec lineage, named 2 Water-Arrow, 4 Alligator, and 6 Death (Caso 1979:151), preside over the ceremony of conquest and domination of Tetzotzontepec with the sacrifice of a man named 3 Movement (Fig. 4-9). With this sacrifice they take control. This ceremony takes place in the year 14 Grass, or A.D. 1363.

The divine wood (*teocuahuitl*) above the sacrificial victim indicates that this important festival resembles the Ceremony of New Fire, or the Binding of the Years. The *Codices Vaticano Latino 3738* (Fig. 121) and *Telleriano Remensis* (Part 4, Fig. 19) also represent in this way the important Dedication of the Great Temple at Tenochtitlan. Therefore I suggest that this festival is concerned with an important event in regional history: the Mixtec domination over the Tlapanec-Nahua from A.D. 1328 to 1362. This ceremony probably also had the function of dedicating a temple to a Mixtec god.

Folio 11
A.D. 1370–1376

The Continuation of the Mixtec Domination

This folio records for the first time the death of one of the Mixtec lords, Lord 4 Alligator, as indicated by the Death Bundle with his name. Lord 1 Dog with Serpent Decoration succeeds him. Thus, the Mixtec lords retain power until 1376, when the death of this last governor is mentioned.

The conversation between Lady Flower (Xochitl Cihuapilli) and someone named Dog, who is seated on a wooden chair, probably concerns the arrangement of a marriage between nobles.

Folio 12
A.D. 1377–1383

Tlapanec-Nahua Control Is Reestablished

Lord Cane Chilli of the Tlapanec-Nahua lineage governs from 1377 to 1383, when his death is recorded. This signifies that once again the Tlapanec-Nahuas control the region, with their capital at Tlachinolticpac.

Folio 13
A.D. 1384–1390

Tlapanec-Nahua Rule Continues

Lords Night Obsidian and Cane Alligator rule between 1384 and 1390. They face each other, carrying the fan and the bag of copal, sharing and discussing the policy of the Tlapanec-Nahua government.

Folio 14
A.D. 1391–1397

Lords Stone Flag and Great Monkey Take Power

The death of Lord Night Obsidian and the ascent to power of Lords Stone Flag and Great Monkey are recorded here. Thus, the Tlapanec-Nahua domination continues during this period.

A captive adorned with feathers on his head and a flag in his hand is going to be sacrificed, probably to celebrate the coronation of the new governors.

Folio 15
A.D. 1398–1404

Lord Lizard

Lord Stone Flag dies in 1398 and is succeeded by Lord Lizard, who probably shares power with Lord Great Monkey. The Tlapanec-Nahua rule continues in the region.

Folio 16
A.D. 1405–1411

A Ceremony in Tlachinollan

In Tlachinollan 'Place of the Burned Fields', a religious ceremony is carried out in which possibly Lord Lizard is invested as a jaguar. He uses a helmet representing this animal as he participates in a rain ceremony.[2] The captive is ready to be sacrificed, as his headdress and flag indicate.

The town of Tlachinollan was from this time on the capital of the kingdom. Probably this capital was moved to a nearby place, beneath the mountain and along the Tlapaneco River, where the present town of Tlapa is located.

Folio 17
A.D. 1412–1418

Ceremony of Domination in Huilotepec and Caltepemaxalco

In Huilotepec 'Dove Mountain' and in Caltepemaxalco 'Place of the House on the Divided Mountain', a conquest and domination ceremony takes place. Two Mixtec captives are sacrificed: 3 Monkey in Huilotepec, and 2 Dog in Caltepemaxalco. A priest presides over the sacrifice. In the conquered towns are rivers, palm groves, and cacao.

The kingdom has been integrated under the control of Lord Lizard and Lord Great Monkey.

Folio 18
A.D. 1419–1425

Consolidation of the Kingdom of Tlachinollan

Lord Lizard dies in 1421 (identified as the year 7 Wind), and he is followed by Lord Flag of Quetzal Feathers from the towns of Tlachinollan and Caltitlan, which have united for the first time to form the capital of this kingdom (Fig. 4-10). This person governs thirty-three years and carries out conquests that mark a period of expansion for the kingdom. In front of him is a town glyph that has not been identified (possibly Cornfield).

The name of this lord, Flag of Quetzal Feathers, signifies that he was a great warrior, and his emblem shows his high rank (Peñafiel 1985 : Plate 73B).

Folio 19
A.D. 1426–1432

The Expansion Begins

During the years 1426–1432, the towns of Atliztaca 'Place of the Whiteness of the Water' and Tlachco 'Ball Court' are taken over, perhaps pacifically. Both are in front of the glyph of Cornfield (?).

The ceremony of domination is celebrated in Tlachco, where the feather-covered head of the sacrificial victim is seen. This occurs during the government of Lord Flag of Quet-

FIGURE 4-10. *Azoyú 1*, fol. 18: *a*, Year 5 Grass, A.D. 1419; *b*, Lord Lizard; *c*, Year 7 Wind, A.D. 1421; *d*, Lord Flag of Quetzal Feathers; *e*, glyphs of Tlachinollan and Caltitlan; *f*, Cornfield (?).

zal Feathers, who probably still shares power with Lord Great Monkey.

Folio 20
A.D. 1433–1439

Conquest and Subjugation of Quecholtenango and Caltepemaxalco

During this period, under the government of Lord Flag of Quetzal Feathers, the town of Quecholtenango 'In the Walled Place of Flamingos' is conquered. Caltepemaxalco, which was occupied between 1412 and 1418, is reconquered. Beside the governor is seen an individual with two flags, one on his back and one in his right hand, in the process of leading warriors named Vampire and Jaguar. Above the glyphs of the conquered pueblos appear the heads of two people who do not face the warriors. This could signify that they surrendered without offering resistance.

Folio 21
A.D. 1440–1446

Occupation of Totomixtlahuacan

In this folio Lord Deer Antlers (?) is above both the name of the pueblo of Totomixtla-

45

huacan 'Plain of Bird Hunters' and a field planted in cacao. Thus, this town peacefully becomes part of the Kingdom of Tlachinollan between 1440 and 1446, during the reigns of Lords Branches (?) and Flag of Quetzal Feathers.

Folio 22
A.D. 1447–1453
Conquest and Occupation of Oztotzinco and Petlacala

During the administration of Lord Flag of Quetzal Feathers, the towns of Oztotzinco 'Small Place of the Caves' and Petlacala 'In the House of the Woven Straw Boxes' are also conquered and occupied. Four warriors, 3 Dog, Deer, Arrow, and Jaguar, represent the warriors of the winners of Tlachinollan, who carry out the ceremony of domination in Oztotzinco by sacrificing a man named Stone Lizard, who was probably one of the defending soldiers.

Folio 23
A.D. 1454–1460
End of the Government of Lord Flag of Quetzal Feathers

In the year 2 Cane (1455) the New Fire is celebrated in Tenochtitlan (*Codex Telleriano Remensis*, Part 4, pl. 8). It should have been recorded in the year 2 Grass of the Tlapanec calendar.

Here ends the government of Lord Flag of Quetzal Feathers, who expanded the Kingdom of Tlachinollan by adding the pueblos of Atliztaca, Tlachco, Cornfield (?), Quecholtenango, Caltepemaxalco, Totomixtlahuacan, Oztotzinco, and Petlacala. Lord Tlaloc succeeds him in the government; his name indicates that he may have enjoyed great religious power.

This folio also includes several names of towns and other words between the calendrical glyphs. The names are Tliltepec, Tlacuilotepec, Momohtitla, Istacpopotitla, Hui-

tzicalepec, Amaxac, Xocotepec, Cucutepec, Atlatepec, and Aticapa.

Folio 24
A.D. 1461–1467
Beginning of Mexica Rule

Lord Tlaloc appears, carrying the royal diadem of the Mexica lords as a symbol of domination. The glyph of Tenochtitlan, the capital city of the Mexica empire, is in front of him, and the name Montecsuma[3] is written above his head. This scene marks the beginning of the Mexica rule over the Kingdom of Tlachinollan, during the reign of Lord Tlaloc.

Facing Lord Tlaloc is Lord Bee from Tlachinolticpac (the ancient name of Tlachinollan), with a mantle decorated in a style resembling that of Tenochtitlan. The word sign in front of Lord Bee indicates that he is informing or petitioning Lord Tlaloc about (probably) the antiquity of his lineage. Lord Tlaloc will likely designate him to collect tribute. Various nobles, including one named Deer, accompany Lord Bee.

This folio also contains place names intercalated between the year glyphs: Chichihualtepec, Tlauancatepeltitla, Amatitla, Mi...tepec, Cuausauatitlan, Atitlapano, Cuitepantli, Ysauxilotl, Tlancoliami, and Tenochtitlan.[4]

Folio 25
A.D. 1468–1474
Yoallan Is Overpowered

Yoallan 'Place of the Divinity of Night' is conquered at the end of the reign of Montecsuma I in 1468, during the government of Lord Tlaloc of Tlachinollan. Beside the name of this town appear three bundles containing three human bodies and bearing the names of the dead, probably some of the warriors who defended Yoallan. Lady Rattlesnake Skirt (Coua Cuey Ciuapilli) is talking with a lord named Fish, probably to arrange a marriage.

Folio 26
A.D. 1475–1481

Lord Turquoise Serpent Takes the Throne in Caltitlan

Lord Tlaloc from Tlachinollan dies in 1477 (7 Wind in his calendar), and Lord Turquoise Serpent takes power in Caltitlan, one of the capitals of this kingdom. The ceremonial festivities include a sacrifice by fire and a jaguar fight, which culminates with the defeat of one of the jaguars. Probably both were from Atlimaxac 'Where the Water Divides'.

During this same period, people migrate, as is indicated by the footprints, probably leaving Tlachinolticpac and Yoallan in 1481. The cause may have been the pressure of Mexica rule, which had started under the government of Montecsuma I. Three persons wearing knotted ribbons at the throat talk with others who have no such accessories. The conversation between Lords Serpent and 9 Jaguar is a focal point of the page.

Folio 27
A.D. 1482–1488

Burning of Tlachinollan and Caltitlan in 1486

In the year 7 Deer of the Tlapanec calendar, which ran from 11 May 1486 to 10 May 1587, the kingdom of Tlachinollan falls under the sway of the Mexicas. The ceremony of Mexica conquest and domination is represented by the burning of Tlachinollan and Caltitlan and by a great ceremony sacrificing two important warriors to Tlaloc.

Facing the glyph of Caltitlan is a captive with his hair covered by large feathers and with two flags in his hands. He seems to be surrendering the flags to two warrior princes, who wear their hair tied at the nape of their necks. Glyphs indicate their names, one of which is Arrow.

Below the glyph of Tlachinollan is the priest in charge of the sacrifice; facing him are the victims, with large headpieces and numerous plumes. They are standing up at the time of their sacrifice, presumably to indicate their valor in the defense of the kingdom. One is probably an eagle knight.

The Kingdom of Tlachinollan becomes the Tributary Province of Tlapan, according to its registry in the *Matrícula de Tributos*, folio 10R.

Folio 28
A.D. 1489–1495

The Mexica Domination Continues

The town of Atlitepec 'On the Hill of the Water' is taken during this period. An individual named Deer, probably a warrior, carries flags and is followed by two similar people. He achieves the conquest of the village, during which five leaders die, one woman and the Lords Deer, Spine, Serpent, and Big Feather.

Atlitepec is overcome by the Mexicas after the fall of Tlachinollan and Caltitlan, in the time of governor Ahuizotl of Tenochtitlan.[5]

Folio 29
A.D. 1496–1502

Lord Green Corn Assumes Power

Lord Turquoise Serpent from Caltitlan dies, after reigning from 1477 to 1496. He is succeeded by Lord Green Corn (Xilomatzin Teuhtli), who governs until 1517.

Folio 30
A.D. 1503–1509

Xipetepec and Tototepec Become Part of the Tributary Province of Tlapan

During this period, during the government of Lord Green Corn from Caltitlan, the towns of Xipetepec 'On the Hill of the God Xipe' and Tototepec 'Place of the Birds' are conquered. Facing the glyphs of these towns is a seated warrior, which probably signifies that the conquest was peaceful.

In 1507 the last binding of the year is commemorated through the Ceremony of the New Fire in Tenochtitlan, as is recorded in the *Codex Telleriano Remensis* (Part 4, Pl.

25). It should have been celebrated in the year 2 Grass of the Tlapanec calendar. Montecsuma II rules in Tenochtitlan.

Folio 31
A.D. 1510–1516
Atlitepec, Acocozpan, and Tetenanco Are Conquered

This folio shows the conquest and occupation of the towns of Atlitepec, Acocozpan 'Place of the Canals of Very Yellow Water', and Tetenanco 'In the Place Ringed or Walled with Stones' in the year 10 Grass of the Tlapanec calendar, or A.D. 1515.

The conquest is indicated by a warrior with his hair tied high on his head; the occupation is represented by the royal diadem and a chair with a back like those used by Mexica governors. This portrayal of the lord of Acocozpan implies that he is a noble of Mexica origin, sent to control the region.

In contrast, in Atlitepec the signs of power fall on Lord Dog and Lord 2 Deer. The first carries the traditional insignia—fan and bag of copal—as well as the turquoise diadem in his name glyph. In Tetenanco, Lord Dog and Lord Eagle govern, wearing the royal diadem. This means that Mexicas dominated these three pueblos.

Folio 32
A.D. 1517–1523
The Conquistador Reaches Tetenanco

Lord Green Corn dies, having ruled from 1496 to 1517, according to this record. Lord Flames assumes power in Caltitlan, wearing an embroidered mantle and seated on a chair with a back, like those of the Mexica *tlatoani* (compare Figs. 4-11 and 4-12). The hairdo indicates that this is a prince jaguar knight, probably so designated by Montecsuma II.

In the Year 3 Wind, or A.D. 1521, the Spanish conquistador arrives at Tetenanco. The occupation of this Mexica garrison is represented by chains over the glyph for the town name. In front of the glyph is a defend-

FIGURE 4-11. *Azoyú 1*, fol. 32: *a*, Year 12 Wind, A.D. 1517; *b*, Death Bundle of Lord Green Corn; *c*, Lord Flames; *d*, Year 3 Wind, A.D. 1521; *e*, Spanish conqueror; *f*, glyph of the town of Tetenanco with chains to indicate its domination; *g*, *quachic* warrior; *h*, footprints on the road; *i*, native warrior accompanying a conquistador.

FIGURE 4-12. *Azoyú 1*, fol. 36: *a*, Year 14 Wind, A.D. 1545; *b*, Lord Butterfly; *c*, Year 6 Deer, A.D. 1550, death of Lord Butterfly; *d*, Lord Jaguar, invested as chief.

48

ing warrior, possibly the governor, Flames. The warrior has the shaved head with feathers of the *quachic,* wears mesh clothing and body paint, and carries a mace (*macuahuitl*).

The folio also records a migration to this place, indicated by footprints in a river. Probably warriors are arriving from neighboring pueblos to defend Tetenanco. The conqueror is preceded by a native warrior, perhaps a Tlaxcaltec.

Tetenanco surrendered, according to this codex, in the same year as the taking of Tenochtitlan, which occurred on 13 August 1521, or in the Aztec year 3 House (Caso 1967 : 48, 51, 52, Tables 4–6). Thus, this event could have happened between September 1521 and April 1522, which would correspond to the year 3 Wind in the Tlapanec calendar.

Folio 33
A.D. 1524–1530

The Indigenous Nobles Rule

Lord Flames from Caltitlan dies in the Tlapanec year 10 Movement, A.D. 1528, and Lord Rain on the Cultivated Field assumes power. He uses the seat and the mantle of the Tenochtitlan lords but he does not wear the royal diadem. This may signify the loss of Mexica control and primacy.

Folio 34
A.D. 1531–1537

Oppression by the *Encomendero*

Lord Rain on the Cultivated Field, of Caltitlan, dies and is buried in the Christian way, as is indicated by his burial wrap. Then begins the government of Lord House in the province of Tlapan. He is shown invested with the mantle and seat of the Mexica tradition, in the year 2 Wind, or A.D. 1533.

During the rule of these governors, the Spanish domination becomes clear in the personage of the *alcalde mayor,* who has a staff of command and orders vile tortures by the iron collar, boiling water, hangings, and chainings of natives who have opposed his commands.

Folio 35
A.D. 1538–1544

The Beginning of the *Corregimientos*

Lord House from Caltitlan dies in 1538 and receives a Christian burial. Lord Mace succeeds him; he is shown with a decorated mantle and seated on a chair with a back. Lord Mace dies in 1541, or 10 Wind. He is followed in 1542 by Lord Jaguar, who is portrayed interviewing native functionaries while holding a staff of authority. These are probably *alcaldes* serving as judges and are accompanied by two lords, named Mace and Arrow, accusers of Lady 4 Rain, who is viciously tortured with the garotte as punishment.

The *corregidor* carries on his head a gourd with *pulque,* probably indicating that he frequently became inebriated.

Folio 36
A.D. 1545–1551

The Chiefs Butterfly and Jaguar

Lord Butterfly assumes power in 1545 and dies in 1550, or the year 6 Deer. He also wears a decorated mantle and uses a traditional Mexica seat (Fig. 4-12). Lord Jaguar appears next, invested as a chief with a Spanish tunic; he is seated on a chair such as those used by friars, but retains the customary Tlapanec fan signifying "functions of *alcalde,* judge, ambassador, and military leader."

Folio 37
A.D. 1552–1558

The Punishment of the *Encomendero*

A native chief named Jaguar talks with two *alcaldes,* serving as judges, about the excesses of the *encomendero,* who is being tortured by the garotte. His hands are chained, also a sign of control and disagreement with his activities. Above the name of Lord Jaguar is an arm bent at a right angle, indicating his accusation of this *encomendero.*

Folio 38
A.D. 1559–1565

The Last Native Chiefs

The governor's chair of the *cacicazgo* of Tlachinollan is empty in 1559. In front of it now stands the figure of the *corregidor*. The authority of the Spanish government over the province of Tlapa is complete.

The death of Lord Jaguar in 1561—the year 4 Wind—is nonetheless recorded, and he is buried in a wooden box. After three moons, which represent ninety days or approximately one quarter of the year 5 Deer (1562), Lord Bird also dies. Only Lord Arrow from the pueblo of Acocozpan remains, seated on an armchair of the type used by the friars and carrying a fan. He shares official duties with the *corregidor* of Tlapa.

Thus ends the record of the governors in 1559, the year in which the Ceremony of the New Fire would have been celebrated. In 1565, the history of the Kingdom of Tlachinollan comes to an end.

HISTORY ACCORDING TO THE CODEX AZOYÚ 1

According to the Tlapanec annals in the *Codex Azoyú 1*, the Kingdom of Tlachinollan was located in the eastern region of the Sierra Madre del Sur, between the towns of Chiepetlan in the north, Totomixtlahuacan in the south, Atlimaxac in the east, and Quecholtenango in the west. The ancient towns of Tlachinollan and Caltitlan served as capitals of the zone. Tlapa is currently the capital. At the beginning of the sixteenth century the following principal towns were subjects: Tototepec, Tecuanapan, Tetzotzoncan, Caltepemaxalco, Huilotepec, Tlachco, Atliztaca, Quecholtenango, Totomixtlahuacan, Oztotzinco, Petlacala, Yoallan, Atlimaxac, Atlitepec, Xipetepec, Acocozpan, and Tetenanco.

The genealogies of the governors and the record of important events in their reigns have permitted us to outline the stages of development in this area.

Formation of the Kingdom of Tlachinollan

The Kingdom of Tlachinollan was formed, according to the *Codex Azoyú 1*, between 1300 and 1421. The coexistence of Tlapanec, Mixtec, and Nahua groups in the same territory, with a dual government, characterized this period. The battle for political and religious control of these ethnic groups is revealed mainly through the lineages of the governors. Territorial and political unification was achieved, a capital was established, and several conquered towns probably paid tribute.

The first governors, Lord Death Sun and Lord 10 Deer, did not have a permanent residence. It is probable that they were mythical personages. Around 1321, government was established in the town of Tlachinolticpac, under Lords House and 3 Jaguar. In 1335, a brief Tlapanec-Nahua rule began, culminating with the conquest and occupation of the pueblo of Tototepec.

About 1363 a period of Mixtec occupation began during which Caltitlan and Tetzotzontepec were conquered. Lords 2 Water-Arrow, 4 Alligator, and 6 Death presided over an important festival celebrating the event. In 1377, government by lords of the Tlapanec-Nahua line resumed. Under the government of Lords Great Monkey and Lizard, Huilotepec and Caltepemaxalco were conquered. The inauguration of Lord Flag of Quetzal Feathers in Tlachinollan and Caltitlan in 1421 culminated the integration of this kingdom. These last towns were united here for the first time and constituted the capital and seat of government.

During this period of formation and consolidation, the kingdom controlled the following towns: Tototepec, Tetzotzontepec, Tecuanapan, Huilotepec, Caltepemaxalco, and Cornfield (?). Tlachinollan and Caltitlan served as capitals; these are now *barrios* of Tlapa.[6]

Expansion

The period of expansion extended from 1421 until 1461, when Mexica domination began in this region, according to the *Codex Azoyú*

1. Lord Flag of Quetzal Feathers governed thirty-three years, from 1421 to 1454, sharing power with only two other nobles of the Tlapaneca-Nahua lineage. Political and economic control seems to have been absolute during his reign. He conquered the pueblos of Atliztaca, Tlachco, Quecholtenango, Caltepemaxalco, Totomixtlahuacan, Oztotzinco, Cornfield (?), and Petlacala, some of which may have been annexed peacefully. The geographic location shows that the territory of this kingdom extended principally south and west of the capital, in an area now lying between the towns of Tlapa and Chilapa.

The Mexica Domination

The period of Mexica domination of the Kingdom of Tlachinollan began in 1461 with incursions by Montecsuma I, Lord of Tenochtitlan, and ended with the arrival of the Spanish conqueror in the last months of 1521 or the beginning of 1522. It started with the gradual conquest of some of the towns, followed by the designation of tribute collectors. This function may have fallen to local governors, who are portrayed with emblems of the Mexica *tlatoani*: royal diadems, embroidered tunics tied at the shoulder, and chairs with a back. From this point on, illustrations use a speech scroll to indicate conversation.

According to *Codex Azoyú 1*, Montecsuma I probably named a noble of ancient Tlapanec-Nahua lineage from Tlachinolticpac as his representative and tribute collector. After that, in 1468, he conquered the pueblo of Yoallan, which has been identified as Igualita, located south of Tlapa. These events developed during the government of Lord Tlaloc of Tlachinollan.

In 1481, during the government of Lord Turquoise Serpent from Caltitlan, a migration from Tlachinolticpac and Yoallan took place, probably caused by the pressure of the Mexica occupation. The *Codex Azoyú 1* records the great fall and burning of Tlachinollan and Caltitlan, capitals of the kingdom, in the year 7 Deer of the Tlapanec calendar, between 11 May 1486 and 10 May 1487. This corresponds to the inauguration of the government of the sovereign Ahuitzotl of Tenochtitlan, who conquered Atlitepec in 1493.

Montecsuma II, lord of Tenochtitlan, took over Xipetepec and Tototepec between 1503 and 1507. In 1515, he reconquered Atlitepec and occupied Acocozpan and Tetenanco. Peter Gerhard (1972:321) says that from the end of the fifteenth century Tetenanco and Chipetlan had Nahuatl-speaking *tlatoque* (chiefs).

The Spanish Conquest

The Spanish Conquest is recorded in this document from 1521 until 1565. During the government of Lord Flames from Caltitlan, in the year 3 Wind of the Tlapanec calendar, the Spanish conqueror reached Tetenanco. The fall of Tenochtitlan to the Spanish occurred on 13 August 1521. Thus, the entry of the Spaniards into the province of Tlapa could have taken place between the end of 1521 and the beginning of May 1522, as 3 Wind ran from 3 May 1521 until 2 May 1522 (Edmonson, personal communication). This codex ends in 1565 with the presence of the *corregidor* in Tlapa, ancient capital of the Kingdom of Tlachinollan.

This last period is characterized in the codex by Colonial political and administrative figures, as well as by the *encomenderos'* oppression of the natives. Also recorded are the judgments against the excesses of the *encomendero*, signaling the beginning of viceregal authority.

The political and administrative organization here is shared in the codex by Spanish *alcaldes mayores* and *corregidores*, who carry the staff of authority, and the native chiefs, who bear the mantle and chair of the Mexica *tlatoani* but lack the royal diadem. Some of them retain the fan belonging to the *teuhtli* of this kingdom, which endows them with the "functions of *alcaldes*, judges, ambassadors, and military leaders." The total absence of the bag of copal indicates that the native religious functions have been officially suppressed.

According to the *Codex Azoyú 1*, in the province of Tlapa the *alcaldes mayores* or *corregidores* assumed their roles in 1531. In the same year abuses by the *encomenderos* are noted. An indication of Spanish evangelism is the burial of nobles in the Christian manner: shrouded in an extended position. In 1538, the native chiefs appear to be sharing political and administrative functions with Spanish *alcaldes*, and by 1545, they are wearing the Spanish tunic and sitting on a European-style chair, although they still carry the fan as the last indigenous element of prestige.

By 1565, the last year mentioned in this codex, no more indigenous governors exist. The *corregidor* of Tlapa is the only authority illustrated.

FINAL CONSIDERATIONS

Codex Azoyú 1 shows a cultural area that, because of its geographic location and its historical development, remained principally under the cultural and political influence of the Mixteca and of the Valley of Mexico.

Because (1) the native inhabitants are Mixtec and Tlapanec, (2) the formation of the Kingdom of Tlachinollan stretches from 1300 to 1421, and (3) the expansion culminates in 1464, we can conclude that during this formative epoch, the political and social organization was related more to the Mixtec kingdoms. Mixtec culture began in the tenth century, according to Ronald Spores (1967:102).

The period of Mexica domination over this kingdom began in 1461 with Montecsuma I and ended in 1521 with the arrival of the Spanish conqueror. During this stage, the Triple Alliance collected tribute, designating collectors but respecting the local religious organization. The Spanish hegemony, according to this document, started in the months immediately after the fall of Tenochtitlan.

NOTES

1. The name of the governor Bird Alligator seems to be separate. The Bird glyph is beside the individual in the upper left corner.

2. The battle of the jaguars (*tecuanes*) is still carried out during the rain ceremony, at the beginning of May, in Acatlan, Guerrero, according to my 1987 field notes.

3. According to Nigel Davies (1973:305), Montecsuma I governed in Tenochtitlan from 1440 to 1468, and Montecsuma II from 1502 to 1520.

4. Karen Dakin (1986:314) considers that probably a scribe altered Folios 23 and 24 of the *Codex Azoyú 1*, adding in Latin letters the place names that he could read from the back. This may have occurred after the codex had begun to deteriorate.

5. Ahuizotl, Lord of Tenochtitlan, defeated the Tlapanecs in the year 7 Rabbit (1486), according to the *Codex Chimalpopoca* (1945:57).

6. Tlachinollan is currently in the oldest *barrio* of Tlapa and Caltitlan, on the former Hacienda de Santa Ana.

5. Aztec Writing

HANNS J. PREM

INTRODUCTION

THE WRITING SYSTEM used in late Post-classic times in the Basin of Mexico and its immediate surroundings was fairly standardized. Although this system has been used in various political entities and by various ethnic groups, it will here, for the sake of convenience, be called "Aztec."

AZTEC WRITING

Of all writing systems of western Mesoamerica, only Aztec writing can be considered well known. This is due to its relatively long survival into Colonial times and its intensive use in documents prepared for the Colonial administration. Glosses in European characters have been added to many of the Colonial documents, which provide a more or less authentic transcription.

This situation greatly facilitated modern analysis of the writing system, which began in the middle of the nineteenth century (Aubin 1885). A large number of accurate, though superficial, descriptions of Aztec writing can be found in a wide range of modern publications on Central Mexican civilization. This does not mean, however, that the reading of Aztec inscriptions and manuscripts is beyond any doubt in every case. The remaining ambiguities do not result, at least in the majority of cases, from insufficient knowledge of the system but from the peculiarities of the writing system itself, which does not permit more precision. Consequently, although the general outlines of the writing system have been aptly presented in an earlier volume of the *Handbook* (Dibble 1971), the present discussion will be focused rather on its functional limitations, which may throw a stronger light on its many peculiarities (Prem 1970; 1979).

Writing, which can be considered as the graphic representation of messages, was in ancient Mesoamerica, and especially so in its western half, a combination of two independently working but related and cooperating subsystems. I shall call them "narrative pictography" and "hieroglyphic writing." Each was specialized for types of information that could not be satisfactorily recorded by the other.

Narrative Pictography

Narrative pictography has been given various names (Dibble 1971:324). In principle, this type of graphic representation registers certain information not by recording the verbal form of the message but by interpreting and depicting its content. What will here be called "depiction" distinguishes itself from photographic portrayal in two respects: it emphasizes characteristic details which help to identify the depicted object more precisely; and it ignores others which in the given context are less relevant. "Depiction" in the present sense also utilizes some sort of coding, which means the employment of agreed-upon standards of graphic representation.

Pictography should not be considered a defective method, since it has undeniable advantages, the most important of which is that pictographic recording is not confined to a particular language but resembles in many respects a language of its own. Every story rendered in narrative pictography can be retold verbally in virtually any spoken language—certainly quite a useful feature in multilingual ancient Mexico. Even a modern reader can at least vaguely trace the complex scenes of unknown rituals, such as those depicted in the *Codex Borgia,* even though the language of its painter remains unknown. The second advantage has been less noted until now: narrative pictography allows readers to vary the length of their verbal renditions. This stands in contrast to textual writing, where the reading of a coherent story can be modified neither in wording nor in completeness.

On the other hand, these very characteristics of narrative pictography adversely affect the quality of transmission: because the record is restricted largely to the visible content of a possible verbal message, all details which escape direct depiction are lost. This applies, among other things, to attributes of certain objects, to temporal relations, to causalities, to matters as simple as negations, and above all to abstract ideas. For some abstract ideas, circumlocutory solutions have been developed and established by convention. The basis of these is predominantly metaphorical: the well-known representation of water and burned fields corresponds to the common verbal metaphor *atl tlachinolli* (literally, 'water [and] burned-off land') for war. Some are symbolic in the sense that a relationship was established culturally between an action or situation suited for depiction and the abstract meaning which was to be recorded. Without knowledge of this code, understanding is impossible, as is the case with the ritualistic chapters of manuscripts like the *Codex Borbonicus* (see the schematic interpretation of such manuscripts in Nowotny 1961).

GRAPHIC REPRESENTATION CODE. As already stated, in narrative pictography, a photographic type of depiction was not attempted, nor would it have been useful. A conventionalized formula was applied which permitted relatively quick drawing and easy recognition. The same principles were also used in hieroglyphic writing.

Abbreviation. A depiction was reduced to the essential outline, in many cases dispensing with the realistic rendition altogether. Details that were not needed for precise identification were generally omitted. Characteristic traits were emphasized, even exaggerated. The *pars pro toto* principle, by which an item is rendered by a prominent part of the whole, such as the head of an animal for the entire beast, was often applied.

Standardization. To improve precision and to make a depiction as distinctive as possible, it is necessary to reduce the range of graphic variation of every representational unit. In many cases, a simple but unambiguous graphic form was developed at the cost of an easily recognizable relationship between form and referent. This is the case with the simple graphic form of a scroll, which had three standardized meanings. Placed horizontally, as shown in front of the mouth of a Tenochtitlan ruler (Fig. 5-1a), it indicates 'speech' (very likely depicting the, in fact, invisible aspiration) and perhaps also refers to the office of *tlatoani* 'speaker'. Pointing up-

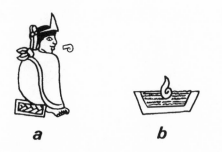

a   **b**

FIGURE 5-1. Standardized signs: Scroll for 'speech, speaker' in *a*, ruler (*tlatoani*) of Tenochtitlan (*Codex Mendoza*, fol. 5v and passim); and for 'excrement' in *b*, the place name Cuitlahuac (*Codex Mendoza*, fols. 2v, 6, 20v, 39).

ward, the same scroll represents 'smoke' (*Codex Boturini*), whereas a very similar scroll pointing down is a rather naturalistic representation of 'excrement' (Fig. 5-1*b*).

Trait Saturation. Significant elements were depicted even if they were not visible from a single angle, which means that a certain degree of distortion was accepted. Thus, men were shown in profile with only the part between neck and hips turned into a frontal view. Another typical example is the representation code for "house," which combines a partial front view with a section of a building with a flat roof.

Imaginative Representation. In many instances, elements of objects were depicted which are, at least under normal circumstances, invisible but which were considered essential constituents of the object. Well-known examples are the depiction of the roots of a tree and the bases of a mountain, which were invariably added to the depiction of the visible parts.

Certain additional information that normally escapes naturalistic depiction could be included in the pictographic record. This refers, among other things, to the qualities of objects: the rough surface of a stone or mountain was expressed by a special combination of three volutes on its outer border, and even minute differences in soil type could be indi-

cated when necessary (Williams 1980).

SPATIAL ARRANGEMENT. Narrative pictography was used to render complex, coherent, and often long stories, such as that of the Aztec migration in the *Codex Boturini*. Narrations of this type tend to be arranged chronologically, often closely following a band of year signs. But narrative pictography does not need to be one-dimensional like speech, in which the sequence of narrative details, once uttered, cannot be changed. Narrative pictography is really capable of two-dimensional recording, where the reader has to design the narrative path to be followed. This is especially obvious in cartographic-historical documents (according to the classification in volume 14 of the *Handbook* [Glass 1975]), for example, in the *Codex Xolotl*.

Pictography in a noncoherent form is to be found predominantly on stone monuments, but it also occurs in manuscripts, as in the *Códice en Cruz*, where isolated events are rendered by a single short graphic scene. In many cases, this scene could be described in Nahuatl by a single word. The shorter and less complex a graphic representation was, the greater its link to the spoken version, and the closer it comes to hieroglyphic writing.

Hieroglyphic Writing

Because of its rather restricted capabilities, narrative pictography cannot render the exact wording of a message, which is especially important when details such as names are to be expressed. In Aztec writing, verbal messages (i.e., messages in their linguistic form) were transmitted by hieroglyphic writing.

In Mesoamerican epigraphy, a hieroglyph is considered a sign, which itself may be a combination of signs, forming a unit of writing employed to record unambiguously a linguistic unit, usually a word, in a verbal message. The term "hieroglyphic writing" does not say anything about the specific technique employed or the graphic forms involved. A sign will be referred to as a graphic representational unit with an obvious (directly intelligible) or conventionally established meaning.

In Aztec writing, the hieroglyphic subsystem is more closely tied to speech than pictography is. Thus, a considerable number of the signs cannot be understood without a thorough knowledge of the language. This precondition (which impedes translation of hieroglyphs in other Mesoamerican languages) is favorable in the case of Nahuatl because of the attention paid by Colonial institutions. Full understanding of a hieroglyphic system is facilitated when bilingual data are available. Such data are provided primarily by administrative documents from the sixteenth century in which the hieroglyphic data were transliterated and annotated in the European script. In the present chapter, most examples are taken from such documents, above all from the *Matrícula de Tributos* (composed only a short time after the Conquest) and its derivative, the *Codex Mendoza*.

TYPES OF HIEROGLYPHIC WRITING. Aztec hieroglyphic writing is not a homogeneous system. It combines different approaches which customarily are grouped into two main categories: ideographic and phonetic writing. Both types of writing employ the same graphic representation code and can only be distinguished according to the method of encoding employed. Because hieroglyphic writing is primarily used for verbal messages, the distinction depends upon the degree to which language is retained as a coding system. Which type is present in a given hieroglyph cannot be determined before the hieroglyph has been properly read.

In ideographic writing, the language code of a message is abandoned and replaced by a graphic representation code that refers to the meaning of a message. The message is thus encoded at one level only. In this regard and in many details, ideographic writing is very close to narrative pictography.

Phonetic writing uses the language code of a message and transposes phonetic units into graphic ones, regardless of meaning. The graphic representation code is applied to the

verbal code, which means that the message is encoded twice.

Although the distinction seems rather clearcut at first glance, the types are not always easy to discern. The differentiation of the types of writing is in every case, however, indispensable for precise reading. Already in Early Colonial times, persons well trained in the autochthonous writing tradition struggled with these problems and produced reading errors. It is highly revealing to study those instances in which indigenous readers arrived at different readings of the same hieroglyph. Many of them can be deduced from discrepancies between hieroglyphic sources and textual ones which are derived from pictorial manuscripts.

Ideographic Writing

In ideographic writing, a message is recorded by graphically depicting its meaning and neglecting its verbal expression. The method rests on the assumption that the reader will verbalize the ideographically expressed content of a message in roughly the same form as intended by the writer. Obviously, this system can work only for isolated words, and only when the reader is familiar with them, but even then a wide range of ambiguity cannot be avoided.

LOGOGRAPHIC WRITING. Only when an ideographically rendered meaning can be expressed by one word exclusively will reading ambiguity be avoided. In this case, where a direct correspondence between a word and its graphic expression is established, the graphic expression becomes a logogram. Thus the word *ozomatli*[1] will be written exclusively by the graphic depiction of a monkey, which will not be used for any other word. This unique correspondence can be automatic, when there is no other word with the same or similar meaning, but can also be created conventionally when the sign is not used for another possible word and vice versa. A nearly perfect example of a conventional logogram is the depiction of a jar, which corresponds in nearly all cases to *comitl*, in only a few instances to *xoctli* (*Matrícula de Huexotzinco*), but in no known example is read as *chachapatli*, although all three of these words mean '(earthenware) jar'.

Logograms tend to show a more standardized graphic representation than other hieroglyphs. Among the most standardized signs are those for *chalchihuitl* ('precious green stone', in the name Chalco [Fig. 5-2*a*]), *xihuitl* ('turquoise', 'grass', in the name Xiuhhuacan [Fig. 5-2*b*]), *oztotl* ('cave', the face of a terrestrial monster [Fig.5-2*c–d*], in both cases for the name Oztoman), and *tenamitl* ('wall', showing a section of wall with parapets, in the name Tenanco [Fig. 5-2*e*]). Aztec day signs are the most frequently used logograms. Logograms are best suited for employment in phonetic writing based on homonymy (see below).

RESTRICTIONS OF IDEOGRAPHIC WRITING. Logograms, especially conventional logograms, are not very frequent in Aztec writing. Most ideograms are not free of ambiguity.

Synonymous Designates. The most common reason for ambiguities in ideographic writing is that more than one word corresponds to the graphically expressed meaning (synonymy). Thus, because in Nahuatl a dog can be called *chichi* as well as *itzcuintli*, the drawing of a dog (in any form whatsoever) can be read with either of these two words.

True synonyms, however, are by no means frequent. Normally, their meanings are not wholly identical but differ in certain details or aspects. Depiction of the corresponding tiny distinctive details—if it is at all possible—generally conflicts with the graphic representation code. But even if the small differences of meaning could have been expressed by meticulous drawing, there was no means to let the reader know that the detail in question was not a superfluous embellishment but a distinctive trait. In the reverse instance, the reader was unable to decide whether a certain virtually distinctive detail was omitted intentionally or carelessly. This dilemma can

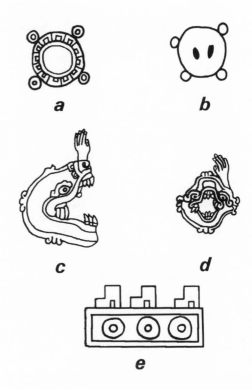

FIGURE 5-2. Logographic writing: *a*, the sign for 'jade' in the place name Chalco (*Codex Mendoza*, fol. 3v and passim, and *Matrícula de Tributos*, fol. 11); *b*, the sign for 'turquoise' in the place name Xiuhhuacan (*Codex Mendoza*, fols. 13, 38); *c–d*, the signs for 'cave' in the place name Oztoman (*Codex Mendoza*, fols. 18 and 10v); *e*, the sign for 'wall' in the place name Tenanco (*Codex Mendoza*, fol. 7v).

be seen in the graphic representation of different but similar objects (for example, different species of animals and plants). The drawing of a corncob corresponds to the words *elotl* 'ear of fresh young maize', *centli* 'dried ear of maize', or even *olotl* 'corncob with kernels removed' or *xilotl* 'tender ear of green maize'. There is normally no way of distinguishing among these slightly different meanings in the reduced space available for a single hieroglyph. The reader confronted with the drawing of an ear of maize cannot know which word is intended and has to choose on the basis of additional information.

Generic Words. Graphic representation is clearly confined to definite objects and cannot depict generalizations. The drawing of a human adult will show either the characteristic hairstyle and garment of a man (*oquichtli, telpochtli*) or of a woman (*cihuatl, ichpochtli*). Leaving out the distinctive elements of gender would make the drawing incomprehensible. Thus, there is no way of making clear when *tlacatl* 'human being' is intended. The same problem arises with the word *tototl* 'bird', because it is virtually impossible to show a bird that does not exhibit elements characteristic of a particular species (such as *cuauhtli* 'eagle', *tzopilotl* 'buzzard', *chichtli* 'owl', or *chicuatli* and *huitlalotl* 'barn owl').

The town of Tototepec is mentioned in the *Anales de Tlatelolco* as having been conquered by Motecuzoma. Robert H. Barlow (1946:212) identified this place with that given by the *Codex Mendoza* (see Fig. 5-3*b*) as Huilotepec (*huilotl* 'dove'). One is able to recognize a dove in the drawing because it really does look like that bird. But, as discussed above, how could the painter have written Tototepec by drawing a bird neutral enough not to resemble a specific one?

Words for Actions. Up to now, only nouns have been mentioned as the spoken referents of hieroglyphs. Verbs that describe actions or processes (e.g., *patlani* 'fly') can be depicted best by the individual or animal performing the act, e.g., flying via a bird with extended wings. Similarly, others can be illustrated by a depiction of their result, for example, *poztequi* 'break' by a broken object, *xima* 'shave' by a bald head, *paina* 'walk' or *pano* 'cross a river' by footprints. Ambiguity arises from the fact that the same graphic depictions can at least potentially be used to render the object itself. This problem can be illustrated once again by discrepant data in autochthonous sources, this time in the list of Tizoc's and Ahuitzotl's conquests. One of them is the town of Tlapan, sometimes also spelled Tlauhpan without assimilation. The graphic representation shows a circular field

a   **b**

FIGURE 5-3. Generic words: representation of 'bird' (*tototl*) versus certain species such as 'dove' (*huilotl*): *a*, the place name Tototepec (*Codex Mendoza*, fol. 13); *b*, the place name Huilotepec (*Codex Mendoza*, fol. 15v).

FIGURE 5-4. Graphic representation of verbs: the action 'walking' in the place name Tlapan (*Matrícula de Tributos*, fol. 10, and *Codex Mendoza*, fols. 12, 39). Sometimes misunderstood for object 'foot' (*Anales de Tlatelolco* 1939:93).

painted red (*tlahuitl* 'red paint') with a footprint inscribed, which is the result of the action 'walking' (*paina*) (Fig. 5-4). The author of the *Anales de Tlatelolco* (1939:93) twice mistook the drawing in his source for the representation of the foot itself and read Tlatlauquiicxic (*tlatlauhqui* 'red', *icxitl* 'leg').

The reverse is found in the case of the town of Tototepec, which is mentioned in the *Codex Mendoza* (Fig. 5-3*a*) as having been conquered by Ahuitzotl. The glyph shows a bird (*tototl*) atop a hill (*tepetl*). In the corresponding section of the list of conquered towns in the *Anales de Tlatelolco*, a place name, Patlanalan, occurs (identified by Peter Tschohl 1964:58, 63), which can be shown to be a different reading of the same hieroglyph.

FIGURE 5-5. Scale of graphic representation: A certain 'wild bee' (in the place name Pipiyoltepec [*Codex Mendoza*, fol. 16]) has also been misinterpreted as a larger one ("Xicotepec").

a   **b**

FIGURE 5-6. Representation of ethnonyms via characteristic elements of dress: *a*, the ethnic name Tlaxcaltecatl (*Codex Mendoza*, fol. 42); *b*, the place name Yopico (*Codex Mendoza*, fol. 20).

This reading corresponds more precisely to the drawing because the bird has its wings opened and is thus considered to be representing its characteristic action, i.e., 'flying' (*patlani*). Tototepec and Patlanalan are both ·well documented as place names.

Representation of Size. In certain cases, objects can only be differentiated by their size. But because hieroglyphic representation always involves a reduction in scale, size cannot reflect real proportions (but see below). A human figure of the same size may denote *tlacatl* 'man' or *tzapatl* 'dwarf'. This difficulty even caused errors among native readers: In its list of Motecuzoma II's conquests, folio 16 of the *Codex Mendoza* depicts a bee on a hill (Fig. 5-5); the gloss is

'Pipiyoltepec', corresponding to the glyphic elements *pipiyolin* 'wild bee' and *tepetl* 'hill'. The same conquest is referred to in the *Anales de Cuauhtitlan* (1938:318) as pertaining to Xicotepec. One has to assume that the native author interpreted the distinctive part of an identical hieroglyph in his pictorial source as *xicotli* 'large bee' and consequently read Xicotepec (Barlow 1946:210). On the other hand, size differentiation of hieroglyphs serves to indicate the adjective *huei* 'big', which is attested in several place signs (Whittaker 1980:66).

Ethnonyms. Not every word has a meaning that can be depicted easily, for example, the names of ethnic groups such as Tlaxcalteca, Huexotzinca, and Huaxteca. Some of them can be distinguished by certain depictable characteristics of dress, e.g., the headdress of the Tlaxcalteca (Fig. 5-6*a*) and the lip-plug of the Huexotzinca (*Codex Mendoza*, fol. 42). However, all of these characteristic elements of dress have their own names, which can be the intended meaning as well, e.g., *tenzacatl* (*Matrícula de Huexotzinco*), a certain kind of lip-plug, and *yacametztli*, a certain kind of nose-plug. The same is true with regard to the word *yopi*, which designates an ethnic group. The characteristic ornament that is used to write the name of Yopico, a settlement in the Valley of Mexico (Fig. 5-6*b*), serves also to indicate the month of Tlacaxipehualiztli (*Codex Mendoza*, fol. 47), the ceremonies of which were intimately related to the god Xipe Totec, who wears the *yopi* garment.

DERIVED LOGOGRAMS. Words that do not refer to concrete objects cannot be rendered directly in ideographic writing, but only by using a chain of associations. A frequently employed associative link is to write a word for a quality (in English, usually an adjective) by depicting an object that characteristically possesses the quality. Once graphically depicted, however, the reference to a certain quality cannot be differentiated from the depicted object itself. For example, the derived meaning is employed in the case of

a   *b*

FIGURE 5-7. Derived logograms: the quality 'new' (*yancuic*) represented by a new-looking object (a blanket): *a*, the place name Yancuitlan (*Codex Mendoza*, fol. 43, and *Matrícula de Tributos*, fol. 12r); *b*, the place name Yancuitoch (*Codex Xolotl*, fol. 2 fragment; drawing in part after McGowan and Van Nice 1979:104).

yancuic 'new'. This word has been expressed by the depiction of a (new) blanket (Yancuitlan [Fig. 5-7*a*–*b*]). The author of the *Anales de Tlatelolco* (1939:93), who obviously was not very familiar with the names of distant places, mistakenly called the town Yancuitlan "Tilmatlan" (*tilmatli* 'blanket, men's garment'), taking the direct meaning of the displayed object when he transformed a pictorial list of Tizoc's conquests into his textual version.

FURTHER SOURCES OF ERRORS. An unknown but presumably considerable number of reading errors in written sources result from a mistake not considered so far. A native reader who is not familiar with a certain name cannot translate the graphic representation but, rather, is forced to describe it. Such descriptive pseudo-names often can be recognized by their verbal structure, even if the hieroglyph involved is not recorded. Thus, Itzomitenxayacatzin 'Face with Lips Which Are Pointed like a Bone' is mentioned by Chimal-pahin (seventh *relación,* Zimmerman 1963:62) as an alternative name for a person called Ecaxayacatzin, the hieroglyph for whom must have consisted of a face, *xayacatl*, with protruding lips characteristic of Eecatl, the

wind god. Another similar case in Chimalpahin (seventh *relación,* Zimmerman 1963:63) results in the names Tlacochimalpopocatzin 'He Smokes like Spear and Shield' and Toyaotzin 'Our Enemy' for the same person. The first name is a more descriptive but probably less accurate reading of a hieroglyph that must have consisted of the weapons and smoke, a regular convention for the not-directly-expressible concept 'enemy'. A similar misinterpretation was committed by Ixtlilxochitl (1977:10), who called a person whose hieroglyph must have consisted of a red thorn "Tlapalhuitz" (*tlapalli* 'red color', *huitztli* 'thorn'). An alternative reading provided by Ixtlilxochitl in a parallel version (1975:397) is "Tlapalmetzo(l)tzin," which the historian arrived at by interpreting the thorn as standing for *metzolli* 'maguey pith' (Whittaker, personal communication). In this particular account, there are also similar discrepancies in other names. An even more disparate reading can be found in the *Anales de Tlatelolco* (1939:93), where the name Occentepetl (literally, 'one more mountain') occurs twice in the list of Tizoc's conquests, indicating that the author recognized only the determinative for place, a mountain, but was unable to read the sign.

Phonetic Writing

Phonetic writing is a synthetic method. Elements of speech (words, morphemes, syllables, sounds) are expressed graphically. In Aztec hieroglyphic writing, the phonetic designate of signs is established either by convention or by the employment of homonyms.

If a hieroglyph consists only of a single representational unit (i.e., the depiction of only one object, action, or the like), it is necessarily either ideographic writing or phonetic writing by homonymy (apart from the possibility of an incomplete writing). It does not make any difference whether the word to be written is simple or compound. The well-known sign for the head of an eagle uniquely corresponds to the word (and name) *cuauhtli*.

60

And another (in most cases) simple sign corresponds to the compound word *cozcacuauhtli* 'king vulture'.

Composite hieroglyphs which consist of more than one representational unit and which denote only one noncompound word always contain at least one phonetic component. With composite hieroglyphs denoting compound words it is, in contrast to common understanding, often the case that the distinction between ideographic and phonetic writing blurs. Classification depends on how closely the graphic representation mirrors the etymological construction of the word, which, especially in the case of proper names constituting the majority of hieroglyphic examples, is not always beyond any doubt. Thus, to write the word *tototetl* 'egg', two methods have been used (*Matrícula de Huexotzinco*, fols. 677r, 781v). The first consists of depicting a bird's nest with a few eggs and a bird, which designates the compound as a whole and has to be considered ideographic writing. But the question is whether the second method, a compositional writing by means of the signs for *tototl* 'bird' and *tetl* 'stone or any solid discrete element' (Karttunen 1983:235), should be considered as composed of representations of sounds (phonetic writing) or meanings (ideographic).

WRITING VIA HOMONYMS. The simplest method of phonetic writing is the employment of homonyms. Thus the words *cuauhtli* 'eagle' and *cuahuitl* 'tree' are interchangeable at times: the place names Quauhtitlan and Quauhtlan, both most probably meaning 'Near the Wood', are expressed by representations of a tree and an eagle, respectively (Fig. 5-8).

The very common personal name Coatl (208 attestations in the *Matrícula de Huexotzinco*), is exclusively expressed by means of a drawing of a snake (*coatl*). But it is at least equally possible that the personal name is not to be connected with this meaning but with the homonym 'twin, companion' or possibly another with unknown meaning (Bierhorst 1985:89). In the latter cases this would be

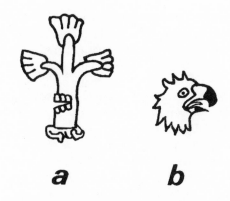

FIGURE 5-8. Use of homonyms: *a*, the place name Quauhtitlan (*Codex Mendoza*, fol. 5v); *b*, the place name Quauhtlan (*Codex Mendoza*, fol. 24v, and *Matrícula de Tributos*, fol. 4).

phonetic writing via homonymy.

Full homonyms are not really frequent in Nahuatl. Spellings also make use of near-homonyms. In Huexotzinco the most frequent personal name, Yaotl 'enemy' (505 attestations in the *Matrícula de Huexotzinco*), is exclusively expressed by means of the shell of a tortoise (*ayotl*). This particular logogram is not known from documents from other places, where the same name is expressed by a shield and a club.

WRITING BY PHONETIC COMPOSITION. Two types of such writing can be distinguished. In the first type, the word is written exclusively by signs that do not have anything to do with the meaning of the word, the name, or the like.

This method is not clearly attested for Preconquest times. There are, however, indications of its use, for example, in the hieroglyph for the place name Tzompanco 'At the Skull Rack'. The skull rack is depicted in one attestation of the place name (Fig. 5-9*a*), but on another occasion (Fig. 5-9*b*), the name is rendered phonetically exclusively by the glyphic signs for hair (*tzontli*) and flag (*panitl*).

In the second type of phonetic composition, the phonetic element serves to support a specific reading of an ideogram or a homonymic logogram. The most famous examples are the place names Acolhuacan (Fig. 5-10*a*) and Acolman (Fig. 5-10*b*), where the sign for *atl* 'water' is added to the sign for *acolli* 'arm'. The vowel length in the place names (the first two vowels are long) and the absence of the glottal stop show that neither derives its meaning from *acolli* (both vowels are short with a glottal stop after the first). The drawing of the shoulder serves exclusively to give the sound, not the meaning of the place names. The sign *atl* further corroborates the phonetic reading by stressing the vowel *a* (long in this word). The names are slightly differentiated from one another by the position of the sign for 'water' in relation to the sign for 'arm'. One cannot decide, however, if this is sufficient to distinguish the reading.

In rare cases, the distinctive part of the name is written twice. The hieroglyph for the place name Cuahuacan (Fig. 5-11*a*) consists of the drawing of an eagle (*cuauhtli*) and a tree (*cuahuitl*). It is more likely that the first sign corroborates the second one phonetically; the second one corresponds to the meaning of the place name and is therefore ideographic. More frequently, the phonetic part stresses only a part of the ideographic reading. This is the case with the place name Ahuehuepan (Fig. 5-11*b*), in which the ideographically employed sign for 'cypress tree' (*ahuehuetl*) is nearly reduplicated by the phonetically used sign for 'drum' (*huehuetl*).

WRITING OF SUFFIXES. In most cases, the specific locative suffixes of place names are not recorded in hieroglyphic writing. There are exceptions with certain suffixes. The suffix *-tlan* is frequently indicated phonetically by the drawing of two teeth (*tlantli*), as in Petlatlan, Huehuetlan, and Iztatlan (Fig. 5-12*a*–*c*). The last hieroglyph shares the dominant sign with Iztapan (Fig. 5-12*d*), the differing suffix being indicated by a footprint (*paina* 'walking'). In other pictorial documents (for example, *Codex Xolotl*), the suffix is represented by a flag (*panitl*). Other common place-name suffixes are *-tzinco*, expressed

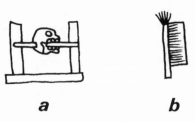

a **b**

FIGURE 5-9. Phonetic composition: *a*, ideographic writing in the place name Tzompanco (*Codex Mendoza*, fol. 17v); *b*, phonetic writing of *tzompantli* 'skull rack' in the place name Tzompanco (*Codex Mendoza*, fol. 24v; cf. *Matrícula de Tributos*, fol. 4).

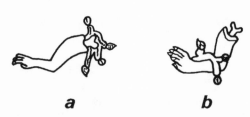

a **b**

FIGURE 5-10. Phonetic writing in support of ideographic writing represented by the sign for *atl* 'water': *a*, the place name Acolhuacan (*Codex Mendoza*, fols. 3v, 5v, 21v, and *Matrícula de Tributos* [mistakenly read as Acolman]); *b*, the place name Acolman (*Codex Mendoza*, fol. 3v).

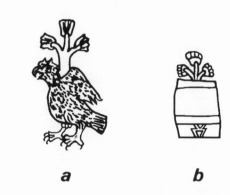

a **b**

FIGURE 5-11. Phonetic repetition of an ideographic expression: *a*, the place name Cuahuacan (*Codex Mendoza*, fol. 5v; cf. *Codex Mendoza*, fol. 32, and *Matrícula de Tributos*, fol. 6v); *b*, the place name Ahuehuepan (*Codex Mendoza*, fol. 24v and *Matrícula de Tributos*, fol. 4).

by the homonymous *tzintli* 'lower part of the body', *-yacac* by the related *yacatl* 'nose', *-nahuac* by the homonymous *nahuatl* 'clear sound'.

WRITING ECONOMY. Writing Aztec hieroglyphs was time-consuming for several reasons. The lack of standardized abbreviated signs made elaborate drawing unavoidable. Writing all elements of a complex place name, for example, also required considerable space. Consequently, there is a strong tendency toward representation of only the most crucial elements of a name. This did not in every case result in great ambiguity if the reader was familiar with most of the possible names. Native readers did not expect signs to reflect the respective designates completely and were prepared to provide additional data, even if unnecessary and incorrect.

The *Codex Mendoza* (Fig. 5-13) has an identical hieroglyph depicting a mirror (*tezcatl*) on the top of a hill in two tribute provinces, Axocopan and Hueypochtlan. In both provinces, settlements with the name Tezcatepec existed or still exist. But the commentator of the *Codex Mendoza*, without any glyphic or empirical reason, named one of them Tezcatepetonco, to be understood as Little Tezcatepec.

TYPES OF CONCATENATION. For phonetic writing, words were divided into suitable segments of varying length (vowel, consonant + vowel, consonant + vowel + consonant, and sometimes even more). In most cases, these segments were arranged in sequential order without leaving intermediary sounds unexpressed. Sometimes, however, the segments seem to be taken only casually and incompletely.

Cases of metathesis, where one of the phonetically expressed words corresponds in part to the beginning and in part to the end of the name while another corresponds to the middle part, are rather rare. H. B. Nicholson (1973:17) cites Karl A. Nowotny for such a case with the Nahuatlized foreign place name Tamapachco (Fig. 5-14*a;* see below). Other purely Nahuatl examples were not recognized by Nowotny (1959): Axocopan (Fig. 5-14*b*),

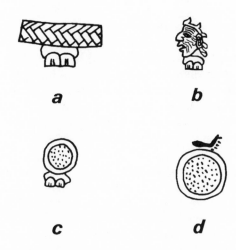

FIGURE 5-12. Phonetic writing of suffixes: the suffix *-tlan* in *a*, the place name Petlatlan (*Codex Mendoza*, fol. 38, and *Matrícula de Tributos*, fol. 9v); *b*, the place name Huehuetlan (*Codex Mendoza*, fol. 13v); *c*, the place name Iztatlan (*Codex Mendoza*, fol. 13v); the suffix *-pan* in *d*, the place name Iztapan (*Codex Mendoza*, fol. 38, and *Matrícula de Tributos*, fol. 9v).

FIGURE 5-13. Omission of distinctive elements: the place names Tezcatepec and Tezcatepetonco are expressed by identical hieroglyphs (*Codex Mendoza*, fols. 27, 29; cf. *Matrícula de Tributos*, fol. 5).

expressed by *apantli* 'canal' and *xocotl* 'plum tree', and Acocozpan (Fig. 5-14c), also composed of *apantli* 'canal' with *coztic* 'yellow'.

As a rule, there was no way to indicate in which way and to which degree a given hieroglyph expressed a word phonetically. In any case, it was left to the reader to detect how the original form should be reassembled.

READING ORDER. A fixed reading order is an indispensable prerequisite for the unambiguous reading of complex hieroglyphs with more than one element. Aztec writing did not have such a reading order, perhaps because of the very free assembly of individual hieroglyphs. This can be seen in the place names Acuitlapan (Fig. 5-15a) and Cuitlahuac (Fig. 5-15b), both consisting of the same spatial arrangement of the identical representational units, i.e., the conventionalized sign for *cuitlatl* 'excrement' and one that in the *Codex Mendoza* has been used for *atl* 'water' or *apantli* 'canal'.

In many cases, a sequence from top to bottom has been maintained, for example, in Itzteyocan (Fig. 5-16a), where the signs for *itztli* 'obsidian', *tetl* 'stone', and *otli* 'path' are arranged in this order. Another hieroglyph for the same name (Fig. 5-16b) omits the last sign, however. In other examples, the order from top to bottom is not followed; for instance, the place name Itzmiquilpan (Fig. 5-16c) is written from top to bottom with the signs *itztli* 'obsidian', *quilitl* 'greens', and *milli* 'field'.

Even indigenous authors raised in the autochthonous writing tradition differed as to the correct order of elements. For example, the name of the town of Quauhnacaztlan, conquered by Ahuitzotl, is written in the *Codex Mendoza* (Fig. 5-17) with the conventionalized drawings of a tree (*quahuitl*) and a man's ear (*nacaztli*). Although this seems to be the correct name (see Karttunen 1983:156: -*nacaztlan* 'next to'), the name can be found in the *Anales de Tlatelolco* with the order of elements reversed: Nacazquauhtla (for identification, see Tschohl 1964:58, 66).

TYPES OF GRAPHIC ARRANGEMENT. The most common form of graphic arrangement is

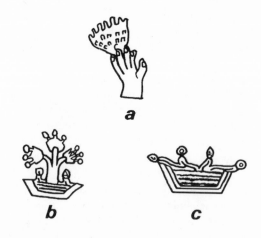

FIGURE 5-14. Phonetic expression with metathesis of elements: *a*, the place name Tamapachco (*Codex Mendoza*, fol. 12); *b*, the place name Axocopan (*Codex Mendoza*, fol. 8); *c*, the place name Acocozpan (*Codex Mendoza*, fol. 39, and *Matrícula de Tributos*, fol. 10).

FIGURE 5-15. Scrambled reading order (i.e., identical arrangement of hieroglyphic elements for different names): *a*, the place name Acuitlapan (*Codex Mendoza*, fol. 39, and *Matrícula de Tributos*, fol. 10); *b*, the place name Cuitlahuac (*Codex Mendoza*, fols. 2v, 6, 20).

a more or less linear sequence of signs without further linking (see the example for Itzteyocan above).

The next most important type is incorporation. One sign is not added to another but expressed through modification of the shape or design of another sign, set as a whole into an empty or uniform space within the other, or attached to the other's contour. Modification of shape can change the whole appearance of a sign. In the hieroglyph for Tepemaxalco (Fig. 5-18a), the mountain (*tepetl*) appears

64

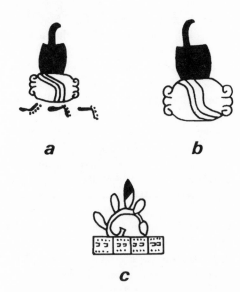

a **b**

c

FIGURE 5-16. Top-to-bottom reading order: *a*, the place name Itzteyocan (*Codex Mendoza*, fol. 48, and *Matrícula de Tributos*, fol. 13v); *b*, the place name Itzteyocan (*Codex Mendoza*, fol. 17v); *c*, place name Itzmiquilpan (*Codex Mendoza*, fol. 27).

FIGURE 5-17. Misreading because of uncertain reading order: the place name Quauhnacaztlan (sometimes also read Nacazquauhtla [*Codex Mendoza*, fol. 13v]).

doubled (*maxalli* 'forked'); in Tepexic (Fig. 5-18*b*), the mountain is split (*xini* 'collapse as of a mountain'); in Tepetlhuiacan (Fig. 5-18*c*), the mountain is enlarged (*huei* 'large'); in Tizatepec (Fig. 5-18*d*), it is filled with dots indicating dust or sand (*tizatl* 'chalk'; cf. Tizayocan [Fig. 5-18*e*]). Incorporation can also

include the graphic addition of terms for color or texture (see Acocozpan above). Obviously, incorporated elements cannot correspond to a linear reading order.

DETERMINATIVES. Determinatives are signs that do not contribute directly to the reading of a certain hieroglyph but convey

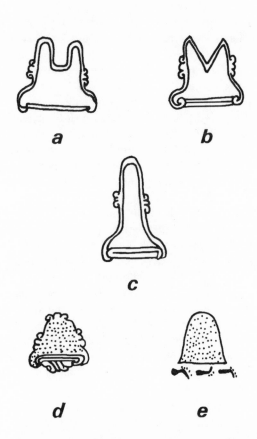

a **b**

c

d **e**

FIGURE 5-18. Spatial arrangement of graphic elements. Incorporation (modification of shape) in *a*, the place name Tepemaxalco (*Codex Mendoza*, fol. 33, and *Matrícula de Tributos*, fol. 7); *b*, the place name Tepexic (*Codex Mendoza*, fol. 42, and *Matrícula de Tributos*, fol. 11v); and *c*, the place name Tepetlhuiacan (*Codex Mendoza*, fol. 33, and *Matrícula de Tributos*, fol. 7). Modification of texture in *d*, the place name Tizatepec (*Codex Mendoza*, fol. 21v, and *Matrícula de Tributos*, fol. 3 [partially restored]), and *e*, the place name Tizayocan (*Codex Mendoza*, fol. 22, and *Matrícula de Tributos*, fol. 7).

65

additional information indirectly, in most cases signaling the category to which a written word belongs, e.g., place names or personal names. This application of the term "determinative" differs from that of Charles E. Dibble (1971:328).

Some of the determinatives are easily understood: a man's head indicates the name of a male person, a head with the characteristic hairstyle of women, the name of a female person. If the face has wrinkles, the person belongs to the category 'old', and if the eyes are closed, the person is dead.

The meaning of other determinatives is less obvious. In most pictorial sources, a mountain indicates that the name belongs to a place. There is no way of determining whether this is an inhabited place, i.e., a town or village (for example, in tribute lists), or a mountain (in cartographic documents indicating boundary points). It has frequently been suggested that the determinative 'mountain' corresponds to the Aztec term for 'town', *altepetl*. Although this interpretation cannot be discounted completely, the use of this determinative for places that would not be called *altepetl* in Nahuatl challenges this view.

The historical portion of the *Codex Mendoza* consistently shows a determinative for 'conquered town' in the form of a burning and collapsing house. This is usually understood by modern scholars as the representation of a temple, the burning of which marked the conquest of a town.

Another type of determinative has not been recognized thus far: signs that indicate the ethnic or linguistic region to which a town belongs. In the *Codex Mendoza* a number of hieroglyphs for towns in the Huaxteca include the head of a male person with a pierced nose and (sometimes) bristly hair. The wide range of corresponding names—that is, Tamuoc, Tenexticpac, Miquetlan (actually spelled Miquiyetlan [Fig. 5-19*a*]), Xochitlan (Fig. 20*a*)— is evidence that this sign has no phonetic designate. The identical sign has been used, however, to express ideographically the personal name Tohueyo 'stranger, especially in-

habitant of the Huaxteca' (Fig. 5-20*b*). In addition to the perforated nose, the head exhibits additional characteristic elements of Huaxtec dress (tattooing and headdress [Seler 1961:157–158]). The same sign (with the representation of tears added) is traditionally interpreted as the place name Cuextecatl ichocayan 'Where a Huaxtec [customarily] weeps' (*Codex Boturini*), although this reading may not be the real name but merely a description of the hieroglyph.

The conventional depiction of a river cannot be called a determinative, because names of watercourses were normally not recorded in Nahuatl documents.

THE SIGNIFICANCE OF CONTEXT. Context is of crucial importance in defective and ambiguous writing systems. Additional information is taken from the reader's knowledge, the type and content of the document, and from data transmitted independently.

Additional data will be considered here only if expressed by graphic information. For example, the name of the town Miquetlan in the Tochpan province had to be differentiated phonetically from that of another town called Mictlan (see Whittaker 1980:77–80). Differentiation from the place name Mictlan (mummy bundle and skull expressing *micqui* 'dead person' [Fig. 5-19*b*]) has been achieved by phonetically expressing the distinguishing sound through adding the drawing of a bean (*etl*; *Codex Mendoza*, fol. 52). In another case, this was done by simply using a determinative to supply the additional datum that the town was situated in the Huaxteca region (Fig. 5-19*a*). It is interesting to note that in the case of Miquetlan, the commentator of the *Codex Mendoza* overlooked the additional phonetic sign indicating *e* and mistakenly read Mictlan.

NUMBERS. It is well known that a series of ideographic signs has been used for the vigesimal units, i.e., a dot or a short vertical line for '1', a flag (*panitl*) for '20', a bristly element (*tzontli* 'bristles, head of hair') for '400', and a *copal* (incense) bag (*xiquipilli*) for '8,000'. Multiples of these units are expressed

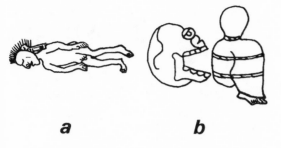

a　　　　*b*

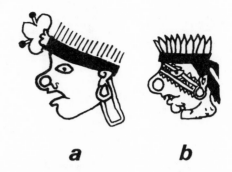

a　　　　*b*

FIGURE 5-19. Use of determinative for differentiating names of ethnic groups: *a*, the place name Miquiyetlan (in the Huaxtec region [*Codex Mendoza*, fol. 10v]); *b*, place name Mictlan (in Oaxaca [*Codex Mendoza*, fol. 43]).

FIGURE 5-20. Determinative for an ethnic group (Huaxtec): *a*, the place name Xochitlan (*Codex Mendoza*, fol. 13); *b*, the personal name Tohueyo (*Codex Kingsborough*, fol. 210v).

by repeating the signs as required. In Huexotzinco, the units for '10' and '15', mirroring the respective units in speech, were also used, but without multiplication. A similar system was used in Colonial cadastral documents to give the lengths of sides and surfaces of field plots (Williams 1984). It can be assumed that specialized signs also existed in other types of records.

Sign Inventory

I have already mentioned that a large proportion of the standardized signs developed into logograms. But many retained a rather wide range of designates. A good example is the conventionalized representation of 'soil' (best seen in Tlalcozauhtitlan [Fig. 5-21*a*]). The design, not the shape, is essential. It is read as *tlalli* 'soil', *ixtlahuatl* 'savanna' (Coaixtlahuacan [Fig. 5-21*b*]); *milli* 'field' (Amiltzinco [Fig. 5-21*c*]; Xochimilco [Fig. 5-21*d*]; Tecmilco [Fig. 5-21*e*]); and, less obvious, *chia(n)* or *chie(n)* 'chia plant and seed' (Chiapan [Fig. 5-21*f*]; Chietlan [Fig. 5-21*g*]) (see Whittaker 1980:81).

Colonial Development of Aztec Writing

The use of Aztec writing in Early Colonial times for Spanish names shows its versatility. Both of the already-existing methods of writing, ideographic and phonetic, were employed, though phonetic writing prevailed, as in the Precolonial writing of non-Nahuatl Indian names (Nicholson 1973:18). Ideographic writing was limited to a few instances of Christian names where Christian symbols were employed (e.g., Peter's key for Pedro and the Saint Andrew's cross for Andrés). Others were expressed phonetically by single signs (for instance, María by *malinalli* 'grass', or Gregorio by *coltic* 'bent') or compounds only approximating the sound (e.g., Antonio by *atl* 'water' and *tototl* 'bird', or Luis by *olotl* 'maize cob' and *ixtli* 'eye'). For more on this subject, see Joaquín Galarza (1966; 1967) and Dibble (1960).

Hieroglyphic expression of Spanish names was of necessity either more defective or more complex. The hieroglyphs chosen for Zorita (*zolin* 'quail') and Zaragoza (*zacatl* 'grass'), both attested in the *Codex Osuna* (Fig. 5-22*a*–*b*), and Vaca (*cactli* 'sandal') provide only a defective representation of the phonetic values involved (some of them, e.g., [r] and [g], being unknown to Nahuatl-speaking people). More complete is the rendition of Miguel (Díaz), which is composed of *mitl* 'arrow', *micqui* 'dead person', and *etl* 'bean' (the

67

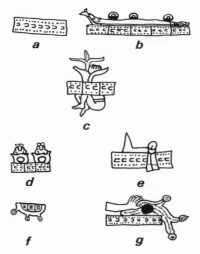

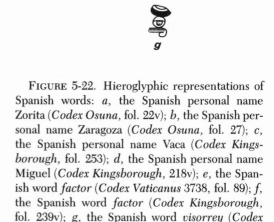

FIGURE 5-21. Signs with several referents: *milli* 'field' and related objects: *a*, the place name Tlalcozauhtitlan (*Codex Mendoza*, fol. 40v); *b*, the place name Coaixtlahuacan (*Codex Mendoza*, fol. 7v, and *Matrícula de Tributos*, fol. 12); *c*, the place name Amiltzinco (*Codex Mendoza*, fol. 25); *d*, the place name Xochimilco (*Codex Mendoza*, fols. 2v, 6; cf. Xochimilcatzinco in *Codex Mendoza*, fol. 24v, and *Matrícula de Tributos*, fol. 4); *e*, the place name Tecmilco (*Codex Mendoza*, fol. 41, and *Matrícula de Tributos*, fol. 11); *f*, the place name Chiapan (*Codex Mendoza*, fol. 13); *g*, the place name Chietlan (*Codex Mendoza*, fol. 42, and *Matrícula de Tributos*, fol. 11v).

FIGURE 5-22. Hieroglyphic representations of Spanish words: *a*, the Spanish personal name Zorita (*Codex Osuna*, fol. 22v); *b*, the Spanish personal name Zaragoza (*Codex Osuna*, fol. 27); *c*, the Spanish personal name Vaca (*Codex Kingsborough*, fol. 253); *d*, the Spanish personal name Miguel (*Codex Kingsborough*, 218v); *e*, the Spanish word *factor* (*Codex Vaticanus* 3738, fol. 89); *f*, the Spanish word *factor* (*Codex Kingsborough*, fol. 239v); *g*, the Spanish word *visorrey* (*Codex Osuna*, fol. 21).

last two examples come from *Codex Kingsborough* [Fig. 5-22*c*–*d*]).

This type of writing was not restricted to proper names. The office known in Spanish as *factor* was expressed either by a Nahuatl near-homonym, *patolli* 'a certain game performed with beans' (Fig. 5-22*e*), or by the same word with the addition of *panitl* 'flag' and *tolin* 'bullrush' (Fig. 5-22*f*). Similarly, in the *Codex Osuna*, the Spanish word *visorrey* was expressed by means of *ixtli* 'eye' and *etl* 'bean', with a third element that is not well understood (Fig. 5-22*g*). Many of the hieroglyphs for Spanish names cannot, however, be understood (Seler 1961:162–163).

CONCLUDING REMARKS

In principle, writing is to be seen as an independent coding system. It is, therefore, ill advised and a confusion of coding levels to use the composition of hieroglyphs as a clue to the correct etymology of names. This is evident in the perhaps not insignificant number of place names that obviously are Nahuatlized adaptations of names in other Indian languages. Thus, the Tarascan place name Taximaroa[2] was in all likelihood phonetically modified and superficially Nahuatlized as Tlaximaloyan. Although its language of origin is unknown, the name Teotihuacan seems to belong to the same category (the type of locative does not correspond to nonactive voice). The incorrect, though popular, interpretation 'Place Where One Becomes a God' is not suited for precise hieroglyphic writing. The extant attestations of the glyph show a solar face, which is a common logogram for *teotl* 'god'. Nicholson (1973:14–18) discusses other examples of hieroglyphs for place names of non-Nahuatl origin, among others, Coyocac, written with the signs for *coyotl* 'coyote' and *cactli* 'shoe', or Tamapachco, expressed by *tapachtli* 'red shell' and *maitl* 'hand' (see also Whittaker 1980:108; 1982:56, for an extreme case in which a Nahuatl place name would seem to derive from the Spanish translation of a Zapotec name).

In spite of its capacity to express words even in foreign languages, Aztec writing has to be considered a largely defective system that was inferior to the European script in nearly every respect. This was also the impression of the contemporary Indians, who, in spite of all the efforts by Spanish missionaries to employ pictographic and, to a lesser degree, hieroglyphic writing, quickly adopted the European system and made ample use of its advantages.

NOTES

1. Glottal stops and vowel length are not indicated in Nahuatl transcription, in accordance with the traditional spelling conventions of Nahuatl outside of actual texts. In many instances, these features cannot be reconstructed with certainty, and in any case, they have only a limited bearing on the writing system.

2. No Tarascan etymology seems to be available (Robelo 1962:180, 187).

6. Noun and Verb Morphology in the Maya Script

VICTORIA R. BRICKER

Introduction

VOLUME 3 of the *Handbook of Middle American Indians* contains a chapter by the eminent Maya epigrapher J. Eric S. Thompson entitled "Maya Hieroglyphic Writing." In 1965, when Volume 3 was published, there was already good evidence that the Precolumbian Maya script employed both logographic and syllabic signs. Yuri Knorozov's (1958a; 1958b) demonstration of the syllabic component of Maya writing was well known in scholarly circles at that time (see Kelley 1962b, for a history of the decipherment of Maya hieroglyphs). However, Thompson was unwilling to contemplate the possibility that the Maya script might contain syllabic signs, and his discussion of Maya writing in the *Handbook* article is essentially a diatribe against Knorozov's argument for a syllabary (Thompson 1965 : 652–657).

In the years since Thompson's chapter was published, additional supporting evidence for Knorozov's syllabic interpretation has accumulated. Floyd G. Lounsbury (1973) led the way in challenging Thompson's position, and,

since then, a flood of new decipherments has made it possible to provide phonetic readings for a great many signs (e.g., Fox and Justeson 1980; 1984; Grube and Stuart 1987; Houston 1984; Kelley 1968; Lounsbury 1984; Mathews and Justeson 1984; Stuart 1985; 1987). The claim that the Maya script contains a mixture of logographic and syllabic signs is no longer controversial, and Maya epigraphers now concentrate their efforts on expanding the inventory of syllabic readings (e.g., Stuart 1987), rather than on debating the nature of the writing system.

One peculiarity of the history of the decipherment of Maya writing is that major progress in phonetic decipherment *preceded* efforts to reconstruct the grammar of the hieroglyphs. In the case of Linear B, for example, recognition of gender and case suffixes served as a necessary first step to understanding the phonetic basis of the script (Ventris and Chadwick 1956 : 91–97). Although two grammatical morphemes in the Maya script, the third-person possessive prefix *u-* and the verbal perfective suffix *-ah*, were identified a long time ago (Kelley 1976 : 190–

191, 196), it is only recently that anyone has tried to work out the grammatical *structure* of the language or languages represented by the hieroglyphs, and these efforts took place only *after* many of the phonetic signs had been deciphered.

The principal reason why the grammar of the Maya hieroglyphs has received so little attention is that the grammar of the relevant Mayan languages was only poorly understood until recently. The nominal and verbal systems of most of those languages (e.g., Classical and Modern Chontal, Chol, Classical Cholti, Mopan, and Itza) were virtually unknown before the 1970's. The situation was quite different in the case of Linear B. Once scholars realized that it recorded a dialect of Greek, they could use a structural approach based on grammatical relations to decipher that script.

Since 1979, considerable progress has been made in determining the principles of noun and verb inflection in the Maya script (Bricker 1986; MacLeod 1984; Schele 1982). These discoveries have further substantiated Knorozov's (1958a; 1958b; 1967) model for the Maya writing system. They have also revealed principles of writing not recognized by Knorozov or other epigraphers that are shared with several Old World logosyllabic scripts (Bricker 1958b; 1987; 1989). The nominal and verbal constructions that are cited in this chapter exemplify several spelling rules that are associated with logosyllabic writing in other parts of the world.

FORM CLASSES

The Precolumbian Maya hieroglyphic writing system contains evidence of the basic nominal and verbal form classes of the Cholan and Yucatecan languages: absolute and possessed nouns, root and derived transitives and intransitives, and positional and inchoative verbs. Recognition of these form classes was greatly facilitated by Bishop Diego de Landa's so-called hieroglyphic alphabet and associated examples, which contain the signs for the third-person pronominal prefix *u*- and the verbal suffix -*ah* (Fig. 6-1). Landa's "alphabet" is not really an alphabet at all; it is, rather, an inventory of syllabic and logographic signs corresponding to the Spanish names for the phonemes of Classical Yucatec (Durbin 1969). The patterning of the grammatical signs in Landa's alphabet with respect to other signs in the script makes it possible to distinguish nouns from verbs and transitives from intransitives (Bricker 1986).

NOMINAL INFLECTION

Noun stems appear in several morphological environments in the Cholan and Yucatecan languages: (1) they can be inflected for possession with a prefixed person marker; (2) they can be quantified; (3) they can be "framed" with deictic particles; and (4) they can occur in a so-called absolute form, which means that they are not possessed, quantified, or signaled by deixis. There are many examples of "absolute" nouns, possessed nouns, and quantified nouns in the script, but no firm evidence of the use of deictic particles has been found to date.

Possession and Quantification

The collocation for the noun 'cacao' occurs in all three environments (Fig. 6-2). We know how it was read because it is spelled syllabically as **ca-ca-w(a)**. The examples in Figure 6-2 illustrate the principle of vowel insertion, in which an extra vowel has been inserted at the end of the word so that it can be written with three CV syllables (C = consonant, V = vowel). The extra vowel (/a/) is not pronounced. The possessed form (*u-cacaw* 'his cacao') takes Landa's first grapheme for "u" (compare Figs. 6-1 and 6-2*a*). The "absolute" form (*cacaw* 'cacao') is consistent with the Yucatecan pattern, taking neither a prefix nor a suffix (Fig. 6-2*b*). It comes from the *Madrid Codex*, which is believed to have originated in the Yucatan peninsula (Thompson 1960: 26). The third example in Figure 6-2 deviates

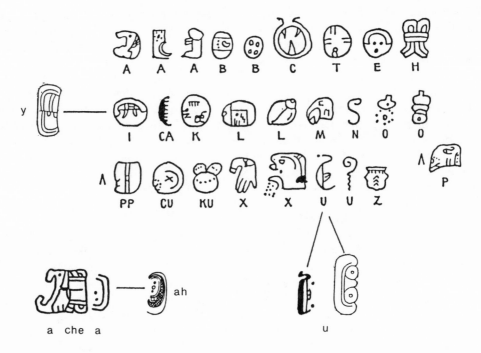

FIGURE 6-1. Grammatical affixes in Landa's "alphabet" and an associated example. After Tozzer 1941:170.

from both Cholan and Yucatecan rules of quantification: there should be a numerical classifier between the coefficient and the noun.

Numeral classifiers are also nouns. The noun *kin* 'day' functions as a temporal classifier in calendrical contexts, but it is sometimes treated as an ordinary noun. Figure 6-3*a* illustrates its use as a numeral classifier with a coefficient of 16 (three bars and one dot). The word is represented by a logogram rather than by two CV syllables. We know that it was read as *kin* because it appears with a phonetic complement, **ne,** which indicates that the final consonant of *kin* is /n/. In Figure 6-3*b, kin* is inflected for possession with a variant of the third-person pronominal prefix *u-* and the relational suffix *-el.* In this case, **ne** has two functions: it not only complements the final consonant of *kin,* but also provides

the vowel /e/ in a syllabic spelling of the relational suffix *-el.* This is an example of *consonant-insertion.* An extra consonant (/n/) has been inserted between *kin* and *-el* so that the grammatical suffix can be spelled syllabically as **ne-l(e).** The extra consonant is not pronounced. The collocation appears between the two parts of a Calendar Round permutation on Structure 1 at Kabah and refers to *u-kin-el* 'the day' 2 Chuen on the third of Muan (Fig. 6-4). Figure 6-5 shows that *kin* could also be inflected for possession without a relational suffix. The *kin* collocation is part of a parallel couplet, *u-kin y-akab* 'the day, the night'. The second part of the couplet is spelled syllabically as **ya-ka-b(a).** Both examples come from the northern part of the Yucatan peninsula, and the noun *kin* can be inflected for possession with or without a relational suffix in the Yucatecan languages.

72

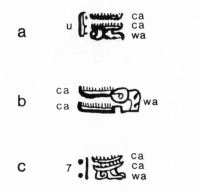

FIGURE 6-5. 'The day, the night' couplet on Lintel 2 of the Four Lintels at Chichen Itza, E5–F5 (Beyer 235, 347).

FIGURE 6-2. Absolute, possessed, and quantified 'cacao' collocations: *a*, D. 10b; *b*, M. 70a; *c*, M. 95a. After Villacorta C. and Villacorta 1976:30, 364, 414.

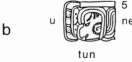

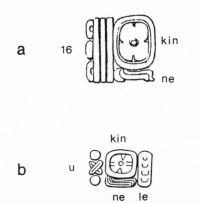

FIGURE 6-6. Cardinal and ordinal *tun* collocations: *a*, Chichen Itza, Monjas L. 4A, D1b; *b*, P.N. 12, A12. From *Maya Hieroglyphic Writing: An Introduction*, by J. Eric S. Thompson, figs. 32 39, 39 4. New edition copyright © 1960, 1971 by the University of Oklahoma Press.

FIGURE 6-3. Quantified and possessed 'day' collocations: *a*, Pal. Fol., D17; *b*, Kabah Str. 1. *a* from Maudslay 1889–1902:4:Pl. 82; *b* from Proskouriakoff and Thompson 1947:Fig. 1g.

2 Chuen   u-kin-el   ti 3 Muan

FIGURE 6-4. Inscription on Kabah Str. 1. After Proskouriakoff and Thompson 1947:Fig. 1g.

The numeral classifier for another time period, the 360-day *tun*, illustrates the use of the third-person pronoun in ordinal constructions (Fig. 6-6). Figure 6-6*a* provides an example of the *tun* glyph, complemented by **ne,** with a coefficient of 11 (two bars and one dot). The example comes from Chichen Itza in the heart of the Yucatec-speaking area, and it would have been read as *buluc tun* '11 *tuns*' in Classical Yucatec. In Figure 6-6*b*, a third-person pronoun is prefixed to the coefficient 5 (one bar). It represents an ordinal construction and would have been read as *u-ho-tun* 'the fifth *tun*' in Classical Yucatec or Classical Chontal. This method of forming ordinal constructions is identical to the one used in those

73

languages. The example comes from Piedras Negras, in the area where a language ancestral to Modern Chol was spoken at the time of the Spanish Conquest. It contrasts with the formation of ordinal numbers in Modern Chol, which does not employ a pronominal prefix and adds a *-lel* suffix to the classifier, for example, *ti chΛm-p' el-lel* 'in the fourth place'.

The second half of the couplet mentioned in the discussion of the possessed form of *kin* exemplifies another morphological parallel between the Cholan and Yucatecan languages and the hieroglyphic script (Fig. 6-5). The syllabic spelling of *y-akab* represents the possessed form of *akab,* the word for 'night' in Classical Yucatec. Until now I have considered only consonant-initial nouns (*cacaw, kin,* and *tun*), which take *u-* as a pronominal prefix. Vowel-initial nouns like *akab* require the insertion of epenthetic /y/ between the prefix and the noun. In many cases, the /u/ is dropped, leaving *y-* as the marker of the third-person possessor before vowel-initial roots; *y-akab* is an example of this morphophonemic rule.

The *y-*allomorph of the third-person pronoun appears frequently in possessed collocations based on the noun *ahaw* 'lord, ruler'. Figure 6-7 illustrates some alternative spellings of *y-ahaw kak* 'the lord of fire'. The first example contains a logogram for *ahaw* complemented by **ya** and **wa.** The pronominal prefix *y-* is embedded in the first phonetic complement, **ya.** The second and third examples provide syllabic spellings of *y-ahaw* as **ya-ha-w(a).** The full syllabic spelling of *kak* 'fire' in the third example consists of two instances of Landa's grapheme for "ka" (compare Figs. 6-1 and 6-7c). Abbreviated versions of *kak,* in each case followed by a semantic determinative, appear in Figures 6-7a and 6-7b. They represent the principle of *consonant-deletion,* in which the final consonant of *kak* has been deleted so that the word can be spelled with a single CV syllable.

There are also a few examples of the logogram for *ahaw* preceded by Landa's graph-

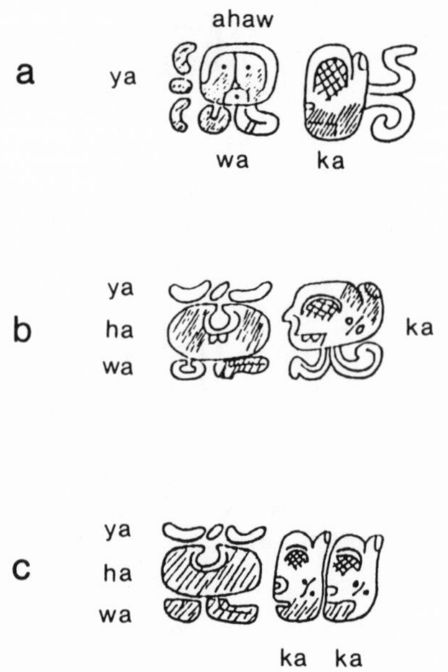

FIGURE 6-7. 'Lord of fire' collocations at Chichen Itza: *a,* Four Lintels II, H2–G3 (Beyer 176, 245); *b,* Four Lintels I, G3–H3 (Beyer 16), *c,* Four Lintels I, H5–G7 (Beyer 23).

FIGURE 6-8. 'His lord' collocation on page 64c of the *Madrid Codex.* After Villacorta C. and Villacorta 1976:352.

eme for "u" or its variants (e.g., Fig. 6-8). In those cases, the prefix must have had the value *uy-*, and the collocation in Figure 6-8 would have been read as *uy-ahaw* 'his lord'. But such examples are rare. The text frequency of the *y-*allomorph of the third-person pronoun is also greater than *uy-* in the Classical and Modern Cholan and Yucatecan languages (Bricker 1986:82).

Abstract Nouns

An abstract noun, *ahaulel* 'rulership, reign',

can be derived from *ahau* 'lord, ruler' in the Cholan languages (the Yucatecan cognate is *ahaulil*). Figure 6-9 illustrates one of the hieroglyphic spellings of *chum-wan ta ahaulel* 'he was seated in office' in the Maya inscriptions. It occurs frequently on monuments in the Cholan area and refers to the accession of rulers to office.

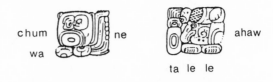

FIGURE 6-9. Accession compound on Dos Pilas Stela 8 (F14–G14). After a drawing by Ian Graham.

Agentive Nouns

The script contains numerous examples of the use of gender prefixes with nouns in agentive constructions. It shares with the Cholan and Yucatecan languages the masculine-gender prefix *ah-*, which is illustrated by the example of *ah-cacaw* 'cacao man' in Figure 6-10a. The inscriptional variant of the feminine-gender prefix *na-* has been attested only in Chontal (Knowles 1984:214). The more common form of that prefix is *ix-* in Chontal, as well as in the other Cholan and Yucatecan languages. An example of the use of the *na-*prefix in a woman's title, *na-ahaw-kin* 'Queen Day', appears in Figure 6-10b.

VERBAL INFLECTION

Root Transitives

ACTIVE VOICE. The verbs in the script also have parallels in the Cholan and Yucatecan languages. Active root transitives have two stems: an imperfective stem marked by a -*Vw* suffix and a perfective stem marked by an -*ah* suffix. Figure 6-11a illustrates the imperfective stem of *ak*, the Cholan verb meaning 'to offer'. The verb is *y-ak-aw* 'he was offering it', spelled syllabically as **ya-ka-w(a)**. The example comes from Palenque, in the Chol-speaking region. The perfective stem of *pak* 'to plant' appears in Figure 6-11b. The verb is *u-pak-ah* 'he planted it', spelled syllabically as **u-pa-ka-ah** in the *Dresden Codex*. Note that *u-* and *y-* mark the third-person subjects of verbs, as well as the third-person possessors of nouns, with the former prefixed to consonant-initial stems (*pak*) and the latter

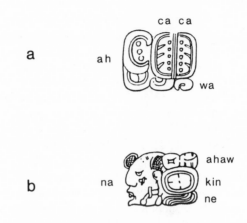

FIGURE 6-10. Agentive nouns: *a, ah-cacaw* (Tik. T. 1, L. 3, F10); *b, na-ahaw-kin* (P.N. 3, D7). *a* from Maudslay 1889–1902:3:Pl. 74; *b* from Marcus 1976c:Fig. 2.

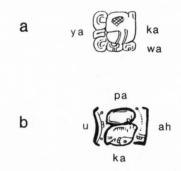

FIGURE 6-11. Active transitive verbs: *a, y-ak-aw* 'he was offering it' (Pal. Inscr. E, Q7); *b, u-pak-ah* 'he planted it' (D. 15b). *a* from Maudslay 1889–1902:4:Pl. 60; *b* from *Maya Hieroglyphic Writing: An Introduction*, by J. Eric S. Thompson, fig. 42 60. New edition copyright © 1960, 1971 by the University of Oklahoma Press.

to vowel-initial stems (*ak*). This is also the case in the Yucatecan languages, Chol, and Classical and Modern Chontal. The -*Vw* suffix has been attested only in Tojolabal, which is neither a Cholan nor a Yucatecan language, although it is today spoken in a region where hieroglyphic inscriptions have been found. The perfective suffix -*ah* occurs with active transitive roots in the Yucatecan languages, and it is likely that the *Dresden Codex*, which contains the *u-pak-ah* example mentioned above, came from the Yucatan peninsula (Thompson 1972:16).

PASSIVE VOICE. The imperfective stems of passives derived from root transitives were marked by -Ø (no suffix), as is shown in the example of *u-tup* 'it was being extinguished' in Figure 6-12*a*. Here, again, the verb is spelled syllabically, as **u-tu-p(a)**. The perfective stems of passives derived from root transitives were marked by an -*ah* suffix, which is illustrated by a syllabic spelling of *tup-ah* 'it was extinguished' in Figure 6-12*b*. These examples also come from Palenque.

Figure 6-12 also provides evidence that the language or languages represented by the Precolumbian script had a split ergative verb system. In Figure 6-12*a*, the imperfective passive verb takes an ergative prefix, *u-*, as its subject, whereas the subject of the perfective passive verb in Figure 6-12*b* is marked by an absolute suffix (in this case, there is *no* suffix because the third-person absolutive suffix is represented by a zero morpheme). All passive verbs in the script exemplify the ergative split, employing an ergative prefix with imperfective stems and an absolutive suffix with perfective stems, as is also the case in the Cholan and Yucatecan languages (Bricker 1986:165).

NOUN INCORPORATION. The ergative split also shows up in several examples of noun incorporation in the *Dresden Codex* (Bricker 1985a). The verb *pak* 'to plant' appears in two morphosyntactic environments in the almanac on pages 15b and 16b (Fig. 6-13). It is inflected as a perfective transitive, *u-pak-ah*, in the captions over the first three pictures. The

FIGURE 6-12. Imperfective and perfective inflection of a passive verb: *a, u-tup* 'it was being extinguished' (Pal. Inscr. M, K7); *b, tup-ah* 'it was extinguished' (Pal. Inscr. M, A9). *a* from Maudslay 1889–1902:4:Pl. 61; *b* from Robertson 1983: Fig. 96.

verb is followed by a syllabic spelling of *tzen* 'food', which serves as its direct object, and two collocations that refer to the anthropomorphic figures in the pictures, which represent the subject. The verb in the caption over the fourth picture is different. It must be read as *u-pak* because it lacks Landa's grapheme for "ah." In this case, the direct object *tzen* 'food' has been incorporated in the verb stem, yielding *u-pak-tzen* 'he was food-planting'. The structure of this stem is identical to that of imperfective transitives with an incorporated noun in Classical and Modern Yucatec.

The immediately preceding almanac in the *Dresden Codex* contains minimal-pair examples of the imperfective and perfective inflection of an incorporated stem based on *mak* 'to gulp' and *wah* 'tortilla' (Fig. 6-14). The captions over the first three pictures begin with a compound verb stem composed of the ergative person marker, *u-*, a syllabic spelling of *mak,* and the incorporated object, *wah,* which is represented by a main sign complemented by **wa** over the semantic determinative for food (Fig. 6-14*a*). The verbs in the captions over the last three pictures lack the ergative pronoun and take the peru-pak-ah tzen   u-pak-ah tzen   u-pak-ah tzen   u-pak   tzen

FIGURE 6-13. The planting almanac on pages 15b and 16b of the *Dresden Codex*. After Villacorta C. and Villacorta 1976:40, 42.

u-mak   wa u-mak   wa u-mak   wa

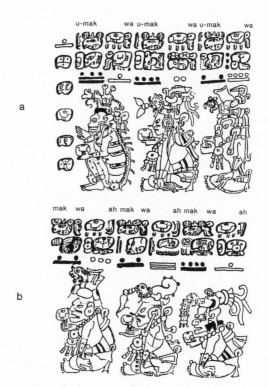

a

mak   wa   ah mak   wa   ah mak   wa   ah

b

FIGURE 6-14. The "tortilla-gulping" almanac on pages 13b and 14b of the *Dresden Codex: a*, D. 13b; *b*, D. 14b. After Villacorta C. and Villacorta 1976:36, 38.

fective suffix -*ah* (Fig. 14*b*). In these, as in the previous cases, the verb is *mak* (spelled syllabically with Landa's graphemes for "ma" and "ka" [Fig. 6-1]), and the incorporated object is *wah* (the phonetic complement *precedes* the logogram here).

The imperfective stem of *mak-wah* is *u-mak-wah* 'he was tortilla-gulping' (Fig. 6-15*a*). It has the same structure as the *u-pak-tzen* example described previously. The perfective stem of *mak-wah* is *mak-wah-ah* 'he tortilla-gulped' (Fig. 6-15*b*). It differs from the Yucatecan equivalent, *mak-wah-n-ah*, only in the absence of the derivational suffix -*n*. The ergative split is manifested in the use of the ergative pronoun (*u*-) with the imperfective stem and the absolute pronoun (-*Ø*) with the perfective stem.

77

a u 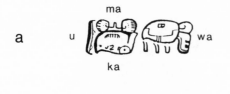 wa

b  ah

FIGURE 6-15. Imperfective and perfective in-flection of a transitive verb with an incorporated noun: *a, u-mak-wah* 'he was tortilla-gulping'; *b, mak-wah-ah* 'he tortilla-gulped'. From *Maya Hieroglyphic Writing: An Introduction*, by J. Eric S. Thompson, figs. 2 58, 2 59. New edition copy-right © 1960, 1971 by the University of Oklahoma Press.

a u  xaw an

b u 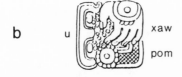 xaw pom

c  pom ma

FIGURE 6-16. Imperfective and perfective inflection of an active derived transitive verb: *a, u-xaw-an* 'he was sprinkling it' (Cop. B, B7); *b, u-xaw pom* 'he sprinkled incense' (Quir. A, D5); *c, pom* 'incense' (La Pasadita, L. 2, C2). *a* and *b* from Maudslay 1889–1902:1:Pl. 37; 2:Pl. 7; *c* from Simpson 1976:Fig. 4.

Derived Transitives

A derived transitive verb that appears with some frequency in period-ending contexts is the so-called hand-scattering glyph (Fig. 6-16). This glyph is clearly polyvalent. David Stuart (1984b) has demonstrated that it was read as *mal* 'to scatter, spill' in some environments, and I have presented evidence that it was read as *xaw* 'to sprinkle' in period-ending contexts (Bricker 1986:138–146). The verb *xaw* seems to follow the Cholan paradigm for derived transitives in the inscriptions of Qui-rigua. The imperfective stem is marked by the active imperfective suffix *-an* (Fig. 6-16a). Figure 6-16b illustrates what I take to be the active perfective stem of this verb, together with its direct object, which I read as *pom* 'in-cense' because it is complemented by **ma** in an example from La Pasadita (Fig. 6-16c). The verb stem is marked by no suffix (-∅), as is appropriate for perfectives based on derived transitives in the Cholan languages (Kaufman and Norman 1984:99–100). There is also an apparent example of the imperfec-tive antipassive stem *u-xaw-al* 'he was sprin-kling' at Quirigua (Fig. 6-17a). The perfective passive stem *xaw-ah* 'it was sprinkled' ap-pears on an unprovenienced limestone panel, followed by an abbreviation for *kak* 'fire', which functions as its subject (Fig. 6-17b).

Root Intransitives

Very few root intransitives have been posi-tively identified in the script. The glyph for 'to be born', which I read as *ay,* is probably a root intransitive (Fig. 6-18). Like passives, it exemplifies the ergative split in the Cho-lan and Yucatecan languages, employing the *y*-allomorph of the third-person ergative pre-fix (represented by Landa's grapheme for "i" [compare Figs. 6-1 and 6-18a]) as its subject in imperfective constructions and the third-person absolutive suffix (represented by -∅) in perfective constructions (Fig. 6-18b).

Positionals

The script contains numerous examples of

a   u   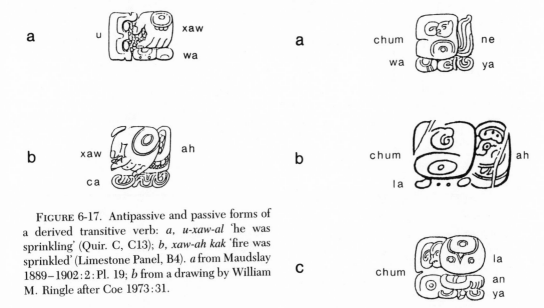   xaw

wa

a   chum   ne

wa   ya

b   xaw   ah

ca

b   chum   ah

la

FIGURE 6-17. Antipassive and passive forms of a derived transitive verb: *a, u-xaw-al* 'he was sprinkling' (Quir. C, C13); *b, xaw-ah kak* 'fire was sprinkled' (Limestone Panel, B4). *a* from Maudslay 1889–1902:2:Pl. 19; *b* from a drawing by William M. Ringle after Coe 1973:31.

c   chum   la

an

ya

FIGURE 6-19. Perfective and participial inflection of a positional verb: *a, chum-wan-ya* 'he was seated then' (Pal. Inscr. E, L10); *b, chum-lah* 'he was seated' (Pal. 96 Gl., D5); *c, chum-lan-ya* 'he was seated then' (Pal. Fol., N7). *a* and *c* from Maudslay 1889–1902:4:Pls. 60, 82; *b* from Palacios 1935:Fig. 16.

a   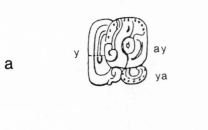   y   ay

ya

b   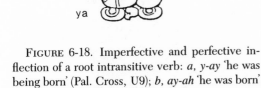   ay   ah

ya

FIGURE 6-18. Imperfective and perfective inflection of a root intransitive verb: *a, y-ay* 'he was being born' (Pal. Cross, U9); *b, ay-ah* 'he was born' (Pal. Fol. B16). From Maudslay 1889–1902:4:Pls. 75, 82.

the positional verb for 'to sit' (Fig. 6-19). The glyph was deciphered as Cholan *chum* (cognate with Yucatecan *cum*) by William Ringle (1985), and the positional suffixes were first recognized by Barbara MacLeod (1984). The perfective suffix of positional verbs is *-wan* in Classical and Modern Chontal, Classical Cholti, and Modern Chorti; it is formed syllabically by **wa** and **ne** in Figure 6-19*a*. The Yucatecan counterpart of this suffix is *-lah*, which is spelled syllabically by **la** and **ah** in Figure 6-19*b*. Modern Chol uses *-le*, a cognate of Yucatecan *-lah*, as its perfective positional suffix.

It is interesting that there are examples of both suffixes in the inscriptions of Palenque and Copan. No one monument at Palenque has both types of suffixes, whereas the Hiero-

79

glyphic Stairway at Copan contains examples of *chum* with both *-wan* and *-lah.* Because Palenque is situated near the present boundary between Chol and Chontal, the use of two perfective suffixes at that site could have resulted from contact between the two languages in Precolumbian times. Similarly, the co-occurrence of *-lah* and *-wan* on the same monument at Copan implies contact between languages ancestral to Chorti and Classical Cholti and either Chol or Classical Yucatec during the Classic period.

MacLeod (1984) has also identified the positional participial suffix *-lan,* which is spelled syllabically as **la-an** in Figure 6-19c. Imperfective positionals were inflected with an ergative prefix and no suffix (-Ø). Figure 6-20a contains an example of *chum* with imperfective inflection, followed by its subject, the *tun* glyph (complemented by **ne**). The *tun* glyph is conflated with *chum* in Figure 6-20b. Positionals represent a class of intransitive verbs. Figures 6-19 and 6-20 show that they observe the ergative split already described for passive intransitives, employing the ergative prefix with imperfective stems (Fig. 6-20) and the absolutive suffix with perfective and participial stems (Fig. 6-19).

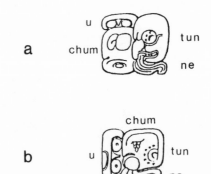

FIGURE 6-20. Imperfective inflection of a positional verb: *a, u-chum tun* 'the *tun* was being seated' (Pal. Inscr. M, B1); *b, u-chum tun* 'the *tun* was being seated' (Pal. Inscr. E, T9). From Maudslay 1889–1902:4: Pls. 60, 61.

Inchoatives

Finally, there is at least one example of an inchoative verb in the script. The middle picture on page 68a of the *Dresden Codex* contains a sky band with the so-called Mars beast hanging down from it (Fig. 6-21). The caption above it begins with a verb followed by the glyph for Mars. Mars was a morning star on the date associated with the text and the picture, rising about an hour and a half before sunrise (Bricker and Bricker 1988: Table 2). The main sign of the verbal collocation is a variant of the sky glyph (compare Fig. 6-22a and 6-22b). The word for 'sky' was *caan* in Classical Yucatec (Pío Pérez 1866–1877:37), the language of the *Dresden Codex,* and the sky glyphs in both collocations are complemented by **na,** indicating that the final conso-

FIGURE 6-21. *Dresden* 68a. After Villacorta C. and Villacorta 1976:146.

a   caan   
na

b   caan   ah
na

FIGURE 6-22. An inchoative verb derived from *caan* 'sky': *a*, D. 56a; *b*, D. 68a. After Villacorta C. and Villacorta 1976:122, 146.

nant of *caan* is /n/. Juan Pío Pérez (1866–1877:37) glosses *caan-ah,* an inchoative verb derived from *caan* 'sky, above', as 'to rise'. The collocation in question represents a logo-syllabic spelling of the perfective stem of this verb. The sense of the caption is "Mars rose," which is an accurate description of the movement of the planet on the morning of the given date.

CONCLUSIONS

In this brief presentation, I have shown that the noun and verb morphology of the Pre-columbian Maya writing system closely paralleled the system used by the Classical and Modern Cholan and Yucatecan languages. The script contains abundant evidence of an ergative split between the imperfective and perfective stems of intransitive verbs, and, in most cases, stems belonging to the major form classes employed the same inflectional and derivational affixes as their cognates in the later languages. Furthermore, Cholan and Yucatecan forms of writing can sometimes be distinguished, especially in the for-

mation of ordinals, positionals, and derived transitives. It is interesting that ordinal numbers seem always to follow Yucatecan rules of derivation, suggesting that the pattern attested in Modern Chol is probably of recent origin. The use of *na-* rather than *ix-* as the feminine-gender prefix in the monumental inscriptions also has implications for historical linguistics.

As was the case with Linear B, the analysis of the grammatical structure of the Maya hieroglyphs has increased our understanding of the phonetic basis of the script. Knorozov (1958a; 1958b; 1967) documented the use of vowel-insertion as a mechanism for spelling CVC roots with CV syllables (as CV-C[V]). However, this principle alone may not be sufficient when nouns and verbs represented by logograms, rather than syllables, take inflectional suffixes. It was sometimes necessary to invoke a principle of consonant-insertion to facilitate spelling a -VC suffix with two CV syllables (e.g., Figs. 6-3*b* and 6-22*b*). The Maya were not unique in adopting this solution to the problem of how best to represent grammatical suffixes in a mixed writing system composed of both logograms and syllables. Sumerian employed the same convention to solve a similar problem (Justeson and Stephens 1980:7). However, epigraphers did not recognize the use of consonant-insertion in Maya writing until they were ready to move beyond the word as the unit of analysis and consider the inflectional system in which it was embedded. There is little doubt that the more we learn about the grammar of Maya hieroglyphics, the more success we will have in deciphering the phonetic component of the script.

7. A New Look at the Dynastic History of Palenque

LINDA SCHELE

THE FORMAL STUDY of the dynastic history of Palenque began with Heinrich Berlin's (1968) identification of four rulers and their "seating" dates on the Tablet of the 96 Glyphs. Working independently, George Kubler (1969) also found Berlin's Ruler A, whom he called Sun-Shield, and later he recognized another king, whom he called Snake-Jaguar (Kubler 1972). These three studies were but the opening breakthroughs in two decades of intensive and highly productive studies of Palenque's history, the second phase of which began with the Primera Mesa Redonda de Palenque in 1973. From that important conference came the first systematic study of the full dynastic history (Mathews and Schele 1974; Lounsbury 1974). The important advancements made at the Mesa Redonda were nurtured by Elizabeth Benson, who sponsored a series of miniconferences at Dumbarton Oaks between 1973 and 1977. These critically important meetings provided the forum in which major methodological advances were pioneered and the details of Palenque's history were fleshed out. Floyd Lounsbury, Peter Mathews, David Kelley, Merle Greene Robertson, and I were

the long-term participants in the miniconferences. This chapter represents the cumulative effort of these and other contributors who have over the years reconstructed at Palenque the most complete dynastic history now known from the Classic period.[1]

Retrospective accounts of Palenque's Early Classic history were recorded in four texts: the tablets from the Temple of the Cross,[2] the east and middle panels of the Temple of Inscriptions,[3] the edge of the sarcophagus lid,[4] and the sides of the sarcophagus in the Temple of Inscriptions. Each of these texts records its historical information in a formula specific to the discourse structure of that text (Fig. 7-1). In the Temple of the Cross, the birth of each king is connected by a Distance Number to his date of accession. Since the Distance Numbers correspond to the age of each king when he acceded, the dates of birth can be reconstructed by subtracting the ages from the accession dates. The entire chronology of this text is fixed in place by two devices: The earliest births and accessions are linked to the Initial Series date, and the later history is anchored to the period ending 9.0.0.0.0.

While the Long Count positions of the Cal-

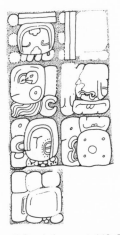

c. T. Inscriptions, east, A10–C1:
[It was] 13.10.3 after he had
been seated as *ahau*, Ah Chaacal, Ah Nab, Holy Palenque
Ahau.

a. Tablet of the Cross, R8–R12:
[It was] 1.16.7.17 after he had
been born on 5 Ahau 3 Zec,
Ah Chaacal, Ah Nab, and then
he acceded on 5 Caban Seating
of Zotz'.

d. Sarcophagus, 16–17:
On 5 Caban 5 Mac (9.4.10.4.17)
he died, Chaacal Ah Nab Uinic.

b. T. Inscriptions, east, A1–B9:
On 9.4.0.0.0 13 Ahau 18 Yax,
G9 ruled, they offered to the
cycle, the holy thing, GI, GII,
GIII.

FIGURE 7-1. The formulaic passages for Chaacal I from the three ancestor lists.

endar Round dates on the Temple of the Cross
can be disputed, those on the east panel of the
Temple of Inscriptions are indisputable. In
the discourse formula of that inscription (Fig.
7-1), each accession is linked by Distance
Number to the nearest major period ending.
Whenever possible, the scribes chose a *katun*
ending, but when more than one accession
had occurred within a *katun*, they used the

lahuntun or *oxlahuntun* for the anchor date
(Lounsbury 1975–1976). The chronological
span of the Temple of Inscriptions covers the
nine *katuns* between 9.4.0.0.0 and 9.13.0.0.0,
thus anchoring all accessions within this time
span firmly to the Long Count.

The same nine *katuns* provide the chronological framework of the sarcophagus lid,
where the deaths of the kings are recorded.

83

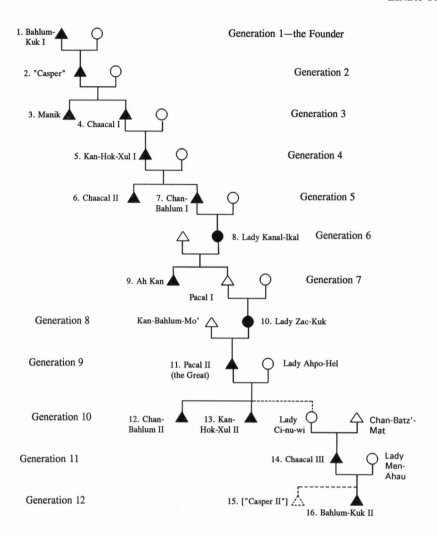

FIGURE 7-2. The dynasty of Palenque.

Lounsbury's (1974) analysis demonstrated that the sequence of these deaths is anchored by the *katun* endings 9.7.0.0.0 and 9.10.0.0.0, whereas Berlin (1977:136) observed that these two period endings divide the nine *katuns* registered in the *katun* history on the tablets above into three parts of three *katuns* each.

Since the histories of these three texts overlap and anchor into the Long Count in different ways, they provide one of the most detailed and complete dynastic histories now

known for the Early Classic period. Those rulers appearing in all three lists have their birth, accession, and death dates preserved. For those occurring in only one or two of the lists, we are missing either their birth or death dates, but some of these missing data can be deduced from other information. These historical data of the first half of Palenque's history are summarized in Figure 7-2 and Table 7-1.

One example from these overlapping histo-

TABLE 7-1. Vital Statistics of the Palenque Dynasty

No. of Reign	Name of Ruler	Year of Birth (A.D.)	Age at Birth of Next Ruler	Year of Accession (A.D.)	Age at Accession	Year of Death (A.D.)	Age at Death	Length of Reign	Interregnum
1	Bahlum-Kuk I	397	25.3	431	33.9		38.3–	4.4	
2	"Casper"	422	37.2	435	13.0		64.9–	51.9	
3	Manik	459	5.6	487	7.7		41.5–	3.9	
4	Chaacal I	465	24.8	501	35.9	524	59.1	23.5	4.2
5	Kan-Hok-Xul I	490	33.3	529	38.8	565	74.7	35.9	0.2 (85 days)
6	Chaacal II	523	0.9	565	41.6	570	46.8	5.2	1.7
7	Chan-Bahlum I	524		572	47.5	583	58.7	10.8	0.9 (323 days)
8	Lady Kanal-Ikal			583		604		20.8	0.1 (58 days)
	Pacal I					612 Mar 5			
9	Ah Kan			605		612 Aug 7		7.6	0.2 (72 days)
10	Lady Zac-Kuk			612		640			
	Kan-Bahlum-Mo'			642					
11	Pacal II	603	32.1	615	12.3	683	80.4	68.1	0.3 (132 days)
	Lady Ahpo-Hel			626*		672		46.6	
12	Chan-Bahlum II	635	9.4	684	48.6	702	66.7	18.1	0.1 (53 days)
13	Kan-Hok-Xul II	644	5.3	702	57.5	***	18.2		
	Xoc	650	20.9	720	70.4			1.4	
14	Chac-Zutz'	671	7.6	723	52.3		71.8–	8.2+	
	Chaacal III	678		721	42.3				
				Gap of 30 years					
15?	Bahlum-Kuk II			764				20+	
16?	6 Cimi-Ah Nab–Pacal			799					

*The east panel of the Temple of the Inscriptions (Q3–Q11) records the seating in office and death of Lady Ahpo-Hel, the mother of Pacal's children. The glyph recording the office, TV:126:757, is unique to the second half of this passage, but it may be related to a TV.757 variant of the T1001 title appearing in a woman's name on Yaxchilan Lintel 10 (C5). I suspect that this office-taking at Palenque corresponds to the marriage of Lady Ahpo-Hel to Pacal, and that the wife (or wives) of the ruler held offices specific to women. It seems likely, however, that the accessions recorded for Lady Kanal-Ikal and Lady Zac-Kuk were not of this type; the offices they take are the same as those of male rulers.

***Unknown.

+Minimum but probably longer.

ries will serve to illustrate the way in which they work. On the tablet from the Temple of the Cross, the fourth king, Chaacal I, appears in a passage typical of that discourse pattern. The text reads (Fig. 7-1*a*), "[It was] 17 [days], 7 *uinals*, 16 *tuns*, 1 *katun* after he had been born on 5 Ahau 3 Zec, Ah Chaacal, Ah Nab, and then he acceded on 5 Caban Seating of Zotz'." While the chronological sequence of the Temple of the Cross allows debate on where these Calendar Round dates fall in the Long Count, the east panel of the Temple of Inscriptions makes it absolutely clear. The opening passage anchors Chaacal's accession date to a *katun* ending written in an Initial Series form (Fig. 7-1*b–c*) as follows: "On 9.4.0.0.0 13 Ahau 18 Yax, G9 ruled, they offered it to the cycle, the holy thing, GI, GII, GIII. [It was] 3 days, 10 *uinals,* and 13 *tuns* [after] he had been seated as *ahau* Ah Chaacal, Ah Nab, Holy Palenque Ahau." By specifying that the accession took place 13.10.3 before 9.4.0.0.0, both the birth and the accession dates are firmly fixed. The matrix of period-ending dates and the way they anchor events before, during, and after Chaacal's reign also limit the Long Count placement of his death date on the sarcophagus side (Fig. 7-1*d*) to only one possibility. This combination of data yields a clear chronological pattern for Chaacal I's life (Table 7-2).

The Tablet of the Cross has the earliest segment of the dynastic history. Lounsbury (1975–1976; 1976; 1980) solved the chronological problems involved with the mythological portion of the tablet and provided the evidence of its function as the religious basis of legitimacy for Pacal and his descendants (Schele and Freidel 1984; 1990).[5] The mythological section bridges into historical time through a section featuring a legendary ruler named U-Kix-Chan who lived in the time of the Olmec (Fig. 7-3). Born on 5.7.11.8.4 1 Kan 2 Cumku (11 March 993 B.C.), U-Kix-Chan acceded on 5.8.17.15.17 11 Caban 0 Pop (28 March 967 B.C.) at age twenty-six. These dates fall precisely into Olmec times,

although, unlike the First Mother, who acceded at age 815, his age marks him as a human, if legendary, ruler. I believe that the intention here was analogous to the use of the Toltec as the legendary origin of dynasties in the Postclassic period. However, while the time of U-Kix-Chan marks him as legend, he is recorded as Ch'ul Bac Ahau, a "Holy Palenque Ahau."

The king who is represented as the founder, Bahlum-Kuk I, lived considerably later (Schele 1986b), although there are unsolved problems with his dates (Fig. 7-4*a*). His accession passage records that he was born on 5 Cimi 14 Kayab, and that 1.2.5.14 later he acceded, with 1 Kan 2 Kayab given as the date. Unfortunately, that Distance Number does not represent the interval between those two dates, and no one has proposed a reasonable explanation of the error. I have elected to place Bahlum-Kuk immediately before the second ruler's dates, which are anchored to 9.0.0.0.0.[6] This gives 8.18.0.13.6 (31 March A.D. 397) for his birth and 8.19.15.3.4 (11 March 431) for his accession.

An unusual Emblem Glyph appears in Bahlum-Kuk's name phrase. On the Temple of the Cross, its main sign is composed of T44 **to** superfixed to T606 **tan** (Fig. 7-4*a*). In his name phrase from the secondary text of the Temple of the Foliated Cross (Fig. 7-4*b*), this combination has T110 **ko,** prefixed to the main sign, giving a combination that appears in several other important contexts. On the Temple of the Sun, the heir designation of Kan-Xul I is recorded (Fig. 7-4*c*) as occurring in a place of the same name, Toc-tan, and Lady Ahpo-Hel, the mother of Chan-Bahlum I and Kan-Hok-Xul II, is recorded as a Toc-tan *uinic* (Fig. 7-4*d*). Finally the end of the ninth *baktun*, as it is recorded on the Temple of the Cross (Fig. 7-4*e*), occurs with this Toc-tan glyph.

David Stuart and Stephen D. Houston (n.d.) have shown that glyphs in similar contexts at other sites record geographical features within the larger polity. I propose ex-

TABLE 7-2. The Chronology for Chaacal I

Temple of the Cross	Temple of Inscriptions	
9.1.10.0. 0 5 Ahau 3 Zec		Birth
+1.16.7.17		
9.3. 6.7.17 5 Caban 0 Zotz'	9.3. 6. 7.17 5 Caban 0 Zotz'	Accession
	+ 13.10. 3	
	9.4. 0. 0. 0 13 Ahau 18 Yax	**Temporal anchor**
	9.4.10. 4.17 5 Caban 5 Mac	Death

a. [It was] 3.6.10.12.2 after it had happened 9 Ik (0 Yax, 2.1.0.14.2) and then he was born, U-Kix-Chan [on 5.7.11.8.4 1 Kan 2 Cumku].

b. [It was] 1.6.7.13 after he was born U-Kix-Chan, and then he acceded U-Kix-Chan, on 11 Caban 0 Pop [5.8.17.15.17]. Holy Palenque Ahau.

FIGURE 7-3. The birth and accession of U-Kix-Chan.

87

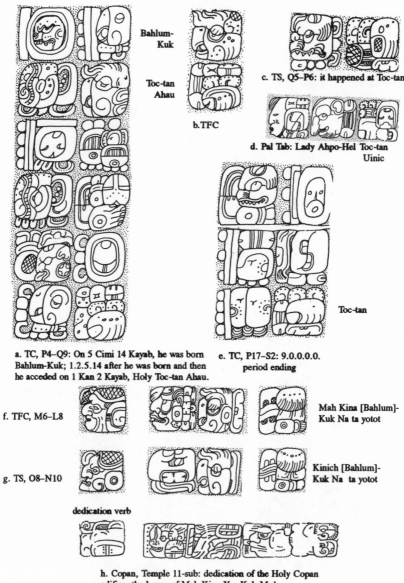

a. TC, P4–Q9: On 5 Cimi 14 Kayab, he was born Bahlum-Kuk; 1.2.5.14 after he was born and then he acceded on 1 Kan 2 Kayab, Holy Toc-tan Ahau.

b. TFC

c. TS, Q5–P6: it happened at Toc-tan

d. Pal Tab: Lady Ahpo-Hel Toc-tan Uinic

e. TC, P17–S2: 9.0.0.0.0. period ending

f. TFC, M6–L8   Mah Kina [Bahlum]-Kuk Na ta yotot

g. TS, O8–N10   Kinich [Bahlum]-Kuk Na ta yotot

dedication verb

h. Copan, Temple 11-sub: dedication of the Holy Copan edifice, the house of Mah Kina Yax-Kuk-Mo'.

FIGURE 7-4. Passages on the founder, Bahlum-Kuk I.

actly this function for the Toc-tan glyph at Palenque: it is the name of the section of Palenque from which Bahlum-Kuk and Lady Ahpo-Hel came, where Kan-Hok-Xul was made the heir. My suspicion is that this region is the Group of the Cross and the small valley to the south of it.[7]

This last supposition appears to be confirmed by Chan-Bahlum II's record of his dedication of the Group of the Cross on

TABLE 7-3. Arrangement of the Figures on the Sarcophagus Sides

Ruled	Depicted	Position
Chaacal I	Chaacal	East, south figure
Kan-Hok-Xul I	Kan-Hok-Xul	West, south figure
Chaacal II		
Chan-Bahlum I	Chan-Bahlum I	East, middle figure
Lady Kanal-Ikal	Lady Kanal-Ikal	West, middle figure
		East, north figure
Ah Kan		
	Pacal I	West, north figure
Lady Zac-Kuk	Lady Zac-Kuk	North, east figure
		South, east figure
	Kan-Bahlum-Mo'	North, west figure
		South, west figure

9.12.18.5.17 3 Caban 15 Mol. In these passages (Fig. 7-4f–g), he named the Group for the founder: the Mah Kina Bahlum-Kuk Na and the Kinich Bahlum-Kuk Na. This practice is analogous to the dedication stair of Temple 11-sub at Copan (Fig. 7-4h), where a later ruler (perhaps the seventh successor) named his new building after the founder of his dynasty, Yax-Kuk-Mo', and at Copan there is no doubt that the founder is the ruler intended (Stuart and Schele 1986; Schele 1986b; Grube 1988).

The kinship relationships between these early rulers of Palenque can be deduced from the ten portraits that were carved on the sides of Pacal's sarcophagus (Fig. 7-5). These figures are named by two-glyph phrases juxtaposed to their portraits (Berlin 1959; Schele 1976). However, two of the rulers named on the upper tablets were not included among the portraits, and one person who did not become ruler is depicted. A comparison between the depicted people and the list of rulers suggests an explanation (see Table 7-3).

There are a number of anomalies in this pattern: (1) there were two Chaacals who ruled, but only one is depicted; (2) Pacal I is depicted, but he never ruled; (3) Ah Kan ruled, but he is not depicted; (4) the woman Lady Kanal-Ikal is depicted twice; and (5)

Lady Zac-Kuk and Kan-Bahlum-Mo' are depicted twice. The doubled portraits on the north and south ends represent the people recorded as Pacal's parents in the final clause of the sarcophagus—Lady Zac-Kuk and Kan-Bahlum-Mo'. Lady Kanal-Ikal may have been doubled precisely because she was a woman and because the accession of her children transferred the throne to a different lineage.[8]

The other three anomalies are more difficult to explain. Why is only one Chaacal depicted? Why was Ah Kan eliminated? And finally, why was Pacal I given an honored place when he never ruled? The answer to these questions lies in the vital statistics of the early dynasty (Table 7-1). The fourth column lists how much time elapsed between the birth of one person and the next. I assume that a gap of fifteen years or more allows for a generational relationship, but a gap of less probably marks members of the same generation—in other words, siblings (if these kings were in the same family, as I believe they were). This span between births identifies Manik and Chaacal I as one pair of siblings (5.6 years between births), and Chaacal II and Chan-Bahlum I as a second pair (.9 year separation). Given that only one Chaacal is shown in portraiture, he must be either the grandfather or the grandson of the same

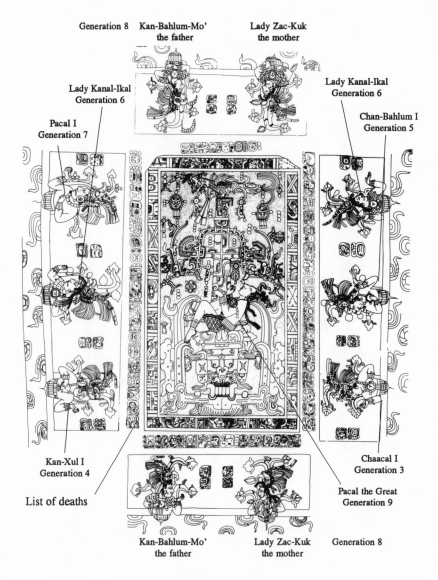

Generation 8 Kan-Bahlum-Mo'
the father

Lady Zac-Kuk
the mother

Lady Kanal-Ikal
Generation 6

Lady Kanal-Ikal
Generation 6

Pacal I
Generation 7

Chan-Bahlum I
Generation 5

Kan-Xul I
Generation 4

Chaacal I
Generation 3

List of deaths

Pacal the Great
Generation 9

Kan-Bahlum-Mo'
the father

Lady Zac-Kuk
the mother

Generation 8

drawing by M. G. Robertson

FIGURE 7-5. The sarcophagus and the line of direct descent.

name, and since Chan-Bahlum of the second pair is clearly depicted, the best solution is to assume that only one member of each sibling pair is shown. Chaacal I, whose accession opens the east panel in the temple above the tomb, is the Chaacal shown, while his grand-

son, Chan-Bahlum, the younger of the two brothers in his generation, sits next to him in the center of the east side.

I also believe Pacal I was depicted on the sarcophagus because he was in one of these sibling pairs. The sarcophagus text lists Ah

90

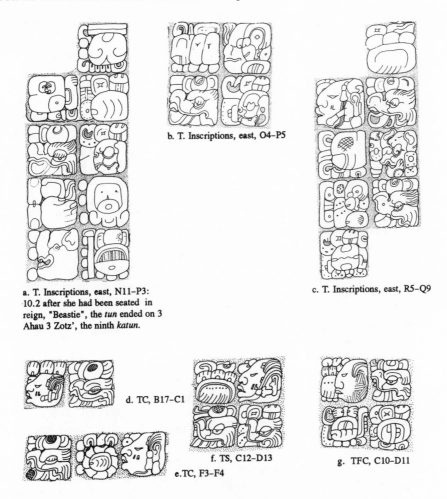

b. T. Inscriptions, east, O4–P5

a. T. Inscriptions, east, N11–P3:
·10.2 after she had been seated in
reign, "Beastie", the *tun* ended on 3
Ahau 3 Zotz', the ninth *katun*.

c. T. Inscriptions, east, R5–Q9

d. TC, B17–C1

f. TS, C12–D13

e. TC, F3–F4

g. TFC, C10–D11

FIGURE 7-6. The names of the First Mother from the Group of the Cross.

Kan's death first and then Pacal I's, although this order reverses their chronological order. Pacal I died in March; Ah Kan died five months later, in August. With brothers, each may reign in his turn, but the descendants of only one can inherit the throne in the next generation. The sarcophagus images, then, depict the brother in each pair whose children inherited the throne—in other words, these portraits document the direct line of descent rather than historical succession. I propose this as the explanation for why Pacal I was included, while Ah Kan was excluded.

These two were brothers, but Pacal I died before he could ascend to the throne. He was depicted because his child, Lady Zac-Kuk, inherited the throne in the next generation, for she apparently was the next to accede after Ah Kan. If this reconstruction is correct, then the genealogical history of the Early Classic segment of the dynasty can also be reconstructed (Fig. 7-2) by presuming that the people on the sarcophagus sides are ancestors.

One last problem in the early dynastic history remains to be resolved. In the history of Katun 9 on the east panel of the Temple of

Inscriptions, a woman is said to have acceded to the throne on 9.8.19.7.18 3 Etz'nab 6 Ceh. In all three passages recording the name of this woman (Fig. 7-6a–c), she is called by the same glyph sequence that names the mother of the gods in the Temple of the Cross (Fig. 7-6d, e). I have always taken this woman to be Pacal's mother, Lady Zac-Kuk, and presumed that this oblique way of naming her was Pacal's way of asserting his own status as her son. The birth date of the goddess was manipulated to be in a contrived relationship with Pacal's birth date. Lounsbury (1976), who first detected this numerological device, explained it as a way of asserting that Pacal and the First Mother were "like-in-kind." I believe that Pacal's use of the goddess' name for his mother in the east panel accession text is an example of the same strategy.

The pivotal king in Palenque's history was Pacal the Great. Mathews and I (1974) detailed the information from the corpus that relates to his life and dates. However, soon after the publication of our paper, Alberto Ruz Lhuillier (1977) reiterated his own reading (1973:119–122; 1976) of the sarcophagus text. I believe there is no question of the glyphic evidence concerning his man's life, but Ruz's challenge came because an age estimate of fifty was given soon after the tomb was opened. Ruz and others believe that the age estimate of the skeleton must take precedence over epigraphic interpretation. For my part, I am not qualified to evaluate age estimates from skeletal material,[9] but I can affirm that the epigraphic data are among the most firmly grounded chronologies known from the New World. Since colleagues and the public continue to question the discrepancy between the two age estimates, I perceive that the epigraphic evidence is not well understood by nonspecialists. This publication is an appropriate context to review the matrix of chronological data that lock the dates of Pacal's life in place.

Pacal's birth date is recorded in an Initial Series date on the Hieroglyphic Stairs of House C, where the birth is tied to his accession by a Distance Number (Fig. 7-7a). This Initial Series date firmly sets the birth at 9.8.9.13.0 with no possibility of moving forward or backward in time, but this is not the only anchor in his chronology. On the Temple of Inscriptions, east panel, his accession date is tied by a Distance Number to the end of the tenth katun on 1 Ahau 8 Kayab (Fig. 7-7b), and on the west panel, his birth and accession are locked into the end of the ninth katun on 3 Ahau 3 Zotz' (Fig. 7-7c). J. Eric S. Thompson (1950:184) explains what this means in terms of the simple arithmetic of the Maya calendar:

A statement, such as 6 Ahau 13 Muan, completion of count of 14 katuns, fixes the position of a date without equivocation, for such a date can not repeat for 949 baktuns, approximately 375,000 years. Even a simpler statement, in which the katun number is unspecified, places a date in the LC [Long Count] with sufficient precision for most purposes, for 6 Ahau 13 Muan will not again end a katun for 949 katuns, which is slightly less than 19,000 years. This is so because there are 73 month positions on which a katun can end and 13 possible coefficients of Ahau. Even the statement "count of tun completed" attached to a date is sufficient for most purposes, for any given tun ending can not recur until the lapse of 949 tuns (the same combination of 73 month positions and 13 coefficients of Ahau).

Given this arithmetic, the dates of Pacal's birth and his accession cannot be moved except in units of 375,000 years into the past or future because they are linked to katun endings which are named by date and number. His death is just as fixed in time. On the Palace Tablet, his younger son, Kan-Hok-Xul, tells us (Fig. 7-8b) that his father died 18.5.18 after the period-ending 12 Ahau 3 Ch'en 13 tuns (9.11.13.0.0)—thus giving an anchor that also falls within Thompson's cycle of 375,000 years.

But the scribes were not satisfied with simply anchoring the individual dates of Pacal's

a. Hieroglyphic Stairs, A1–A12: On 9.8.9.13.0 8 Ahau 13 Pop, he was born Mah Kina Nab Pacal, Holy Palenque Ahau. 12.9.8 later on 5 Lamat 1 Mol he acceded, Kina Pacal.

b. T. Inscriptions, east, R9–R3: 17.13.12 after he had been seated in reign, the tun ended on 1 Ahau 8 Kayab, it was the seating of the 10th *katun*, the half period of the *baktun*.

c. T. Inscriptions, west, E1–E9: 12.9*.8 after he had been born Kina Pacal on 8 Ahau 13 Pop and then he acceded Mah Kina Pacal on 5 Lamat 1 Mol, 2.4.8 after 3 Ahau 3 Zotz', the seating of the *tun*.

FIGURE 7-7. Passages recording Pacal's birth and accession.

life into the time stream; they also specified the time spans between these events. On the sarcophagus sides, they specified that four *katun* endings, *chan u chum tun*, passed between his birth and death (Fig. 7-8a). These were 9.9.0.0.0, 9.10.0.0.0, 9.11.0.0.0, and 9.12.0.0.0. In the closing passages of the west panel of the Temple of Inscriptions (Fig. 7-8c), his date of death is written with a Dis-

tance Number recording the length of his life (Mathews and Schele 1974: 65, Fig. 9; Schele 1978) as 4.1.10.18, or 80 years, 159 days. This life span is confirmed in the Group of the Cross on the Tablet of the 96 Glyphs, where Pacal is called a "5-*katun-ahau*." [10]

The final anchoring statements associated with Pacal's reign are perhaps the most extraordinary of all. On the west panel of the

a. Sarcophagus, south end

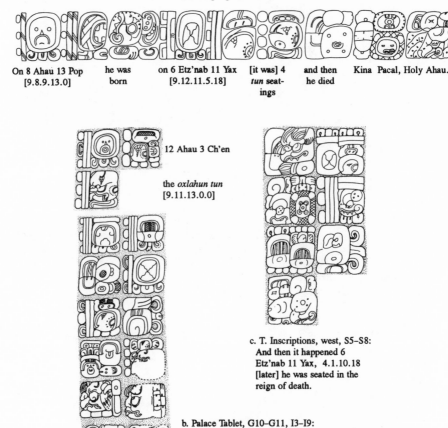

On 8 Ahau 13 Pop   he was   on 6 Etz'nab 11 Yax   [it was] 4   and then   Kina Pacal, Holy Ahau.
[9.8.9.13.0]   born   [9.12.11.5.18]   *tun* seat-   he died
             ings

12 Ahau 3 Ch'en

the *oxlahun tun*
[9.11.13.0.0]

c. T. Inscriptions, west, S5–S8:
And then it happened 6
Etz'nab 11 Yax, 4.1.10.18
[later] he was seated in the
reign of death.

b. Palace Tablet, G10–G11, I3–I9:
12 Ahau 3 Ch'en, the oxlahun tun [9.11.13.0.0].[It was]
18.5.18 and then it happened 6 Etz'nab 11 Yax. He died,
the 4-*katun* "batab" Mah Kina Ah Nab Pacal, He of Five
Pyramids.

FIGURE 7-8. Passages recording Pacal's death.

Temple of Inscriptions, his birth and accession dates are associated with mythological
events in the far distant past and future. The
first of these two passages (Fig. 7-9*a*) reads
"[It was] 1 day, 12 *uinals*, 2 *tuns*, 9 *katuns*, 2
baktuns, 18 *pictuns*, and 7 *calabtuns* [after] he
became *ahau* Zero-Square-nosed-Beastie, on
1 Manik 10 Zec, he became *ahau* Mah Kina
Pacal, Holy Palenque Ahau. "Of course, this
extraordinary passage does not help place

Pacal's accession in the Long Count, because
the interval of 1,246,826.82 years stands between the Calendar Round dates 1 Manik 10
Zec and 5 Lamat 1 Mol, no matter where
they fall in the Long Count. The second passage, however, is firmly locked into the Long
Count. It continues (Fig. 7-9*b*) by anchoring
the entire sequence to a period ending in the
distant future. The clause reads, "8 days, 5
uinals, 10 *tuns*, 11 *katuns*, and 10 *baktuns* un-

a. T. Inscriptions, west, F9–H3:
[It was] 7.18.2.9.2.12.1 [after] he
became *ahau*, Zero-Square-nosed-
Beastie on 1 Manik 10 Zec, he
became *ahau* Mah Kina Pacal, Holy
Palenque Ahau [on 9.9.2.4.8 5
Lamat 1 Mol].

b. T . Inscriptions, west, G4–H10:
[After 9.8.9.13.0 8 Ahau 13 Pop it
was] 10.11.10.5.8 until it will happen,
5 Lamat 1 Mol. After 1 *pictun* [it will
be] 8 days after the *tun*-seating 10 Ahau
13 Yaxkin [1.0.0.0.0.0] and then it will
happen, 5 Lamat 1 Mol [1.0.0.0.0.8].

FIGURE 7-9. The links to the distant past and future.

til it will happen[11] 5 Lamat 1 Mol. After 1 *pictun*, [it will be] 8 days after the *tun*-seating 10
Ahau 13 Yaxkin and then it will happen, 5
Lamat 1 Mol." The Distance Number in this
text counts from Pacal's birth on 9.8.9.13.0 to
the eightieth Calendar Round anniversary of
his accession. The critical information is that
this anniversary will happen eight days after
the end of the first *pictun*, a date corresponding to 23 October A.D. 4772. By tying Pacal's
birth, his accession, and the accession of a
god a million years in the past to this period
ending, the Maya established that the events
of his life happened in a cycle with its ex-
tremes anchored into our calendar at points

separated by 1,250,996.4 years. In other
words, they could have happened only once
in human history.

The last argument against the chronology
is that in some way the epigraphers do not
understand what the Maya intended to say—
that, for example, two people are being named
as one person, that the history is a fabrica-
tion, or that some special way of dealing with
time was being used. Concerning these possibilities, I can only say that each of those
propositions requires that all of the inscriptional data that use the same calendrics or
historical glyphs must be thrown out with the
Palenque data, including all knowledge about

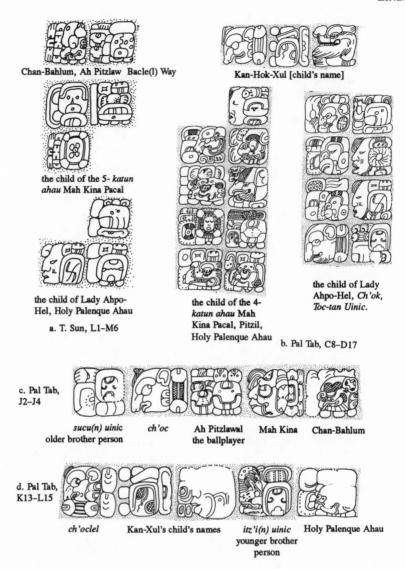

Chan-Bahlum, Ah Pitzlaw Bacle(l) Way

Kan-Hok-Xul [child's name]

the child of the 5- *katun ahau* Mah Kina Pacal

the child of Lady Ahpo-Hel, Holy Palenque Ahau

a. T. Sun, L1–M6

the child of the 4-*katun ahau* Mah Kina Pacal, Pitzil, Holy Palenque Ahau

the child of Lady Ahpo-Hel, *Ch'ok, Toc-tan Uinic.*

b. Pal Tab, C8–D17

c. Pal Tab, J2–J4

sucu(n) uinic older brother person

ch'oc

Ah Pitzlawal the ballplayer

Mah Kina

Chan-Bahlum

d. Pal Tab, K13–L15

ch'oclel

Kan-Xul's child's names

itz'i(n) uinic younger brother person

Holy Palenque Ahau

FIGURE 7-10. Kan-Hok-Xul's passages.

the Maya and the Mesoamerican calendar in Precolumbian, Colonial, and modern contexts. This includes the entirety of Tatiana Proskouriakoff's "historic hypothesis" and all of the histories that have been published for all Maya sites. Palenque's history and the readings of the inscriptions associated with Pacal, in fact, lie at the heart of a matrix of knowledge that involves all we think we know about the Maya calendar and history. We cannot selectively decide to disbelieve the inconvenient part of this matrix without tossing it all out the window.

Pacal was succeeded 132 days after his death by Chan-Bahlum and eighteen years later by Kan-Hok-Xul[12] (Mathews and Schele 1974). These two successors were, in fact, brothers (Schele 1979a:53; Schele, Mathews, and Lounsbury 1983), a relationship confirmed by the fact that their parentage statements both record Pacal and Lady Ahpo-Hel as their father and mother (Fig. 7-10a–b). Stuart (1989) has identified two other kinship terms in which Chan-Bahlum (Fig. 7-10c) is called **sucu(n) uinic** 'older brother' and Kan-Hok-Xul (Fig. 7-10d) is designated the **itz'i(n) uinic** 'younger brother'.

The older brother's life (Schele 1974; 1981; 1986a) was rich in accomplishments, including the Cross Group, the front piers of the Temple of Inscriptions, the temple at El Retiro (Blom and La Farge 1926:161–164), and a large tablet of which the Jonuta Panel was a part.[13] His younger brother, Kan-Hok-Xul, equaled his accomplishments by forging a heritage of equivalent power and refinement, including the north buildings of the Palace (Houses A, AD, and D), the Tower, Temple II of the North Group, and probably Temple 14, which was the apotheosis building for his older brother (Schele 1988; Schele and·Miller 1986:272–274). Kan-Hok-Xul's life did not end so easily as his older brother's. He had to wait until he was fifty-seven years old to inherit the throne after his long-lived father and brother died, and then he met his own death at the hands of the king of Tonina, the nearest kingdom to the south.

Mathews first brought to my attention a new panel at Tonina, carved in the style of Palenque (Fig. 7-11). In the scene, a rope-bound figure wearing the slit-cloth kilt of sacrifice (Schele 1984:18–21) leans back on an elbow as he looks backward over his shoulder. His Jester God headband marks his status as *ahau,* and the glyphic panel on his thigh affirms his identity as Kan-Hok-Xul. The verb in the main text is the Venus glyph over a phrase reading 'his place'.[14]

The date is unfortunately not decipherable because the month sign was never completed. The date has to be read as 11, 12, or 13 Akbal 16 Yax, Ceh, or Ch'en. The alternative readings falling within Kan-Hok-Xul's reign are:

9.13.11.10.3	11 Akbal	16 Ch'en
9.13.19.13.3	13 Akbal	16 Yax

FIGURE 7-11. Kan-Hok-Xul as captive at Tonina.

9.14.11.16.3	12 Akbal	16 Yax
9.14.12.0.3	13 Akbal	16 Ceh

The earliest of these dates is less than a year after Kan-Hok-Xul's accession, while the two latest ones fall after the next date of accession, 9.14.10.4.2. I am uncomfortable as well with the 9.13.19.13.3 placement, for it would give only nine years for Kan-Hok-Xul's great accomplishments to have been executed.[15]

Mathews (1983) examined the impact of Kan-Hok-Xul's unfortunate end on Palenque's political history and discovered that the period following it was one of disruption. The last two columns and the secondary texts of the Palace Tablet, for example, record a strange person Lounsbury (personal communication, 1976) first identified as another ruler of Palenque. I have discussed this person in detail (Schele 1979a:57–61), giving him the name Xoc, but recent discoveries have changed my mind about who and what he was.

First of all, the glyph we identified as a name is, in fact, *u kaba,* an expression meaning 'the name of'.[16] This character is then named by the glyph composed of the number 3, T117 **yo,** and the Jester God. The secondary text records that this fellow was born on 9.10.17.6.0, some six years after Kan-Hok-Xul, and that he went through a "mirror-in-hand" event (perhaps to get the 3-Jester-God

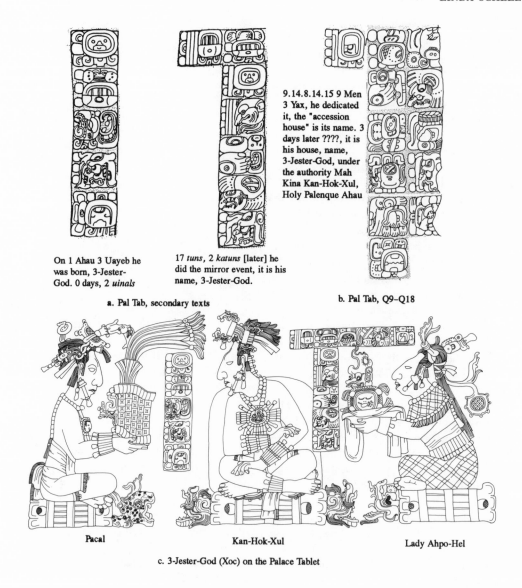

9.14.8.14.15 9 Men 3 Yax, he dedicated it, the "accession house" is its name. 3 days later ????, it is his house, name, 3-Jester-God, under the authority Mah Kina Kan-Hok-Xul, Holy Palenque Ahau

On 1 Ahau 3 Uayeb he was born, 3-Jester-God. 0 days, 2 *uinals*

17 *tuns*, 2 *katuns* [later] he did the mirror event, it is his name, 3-Jester-God.

a. Pal Tab, secondary texts

b. Pal Tab, Q9–Q18

Pacal

Kan-Hok-Xul

Lady Ahpo-Hel

c. 3-Jester-God (Xoc) on the Palace Tablet

FIGURE 7-12. 3-Jester-God and the dedication of House AD.

title as his name) on 9.13.14.8.0, five years before the best-guess date of Kan-Hok-Xul's capture (Fig. 7-12*a*–*b*). However, in the new readings of his passages, Xoc (or 3-Jester-God) never acceded to office. The last event in the main text of the Palace Tablet, which we had taken to be his accession, is, instead, the dedication ritual for House AD (Fig.

7-12*c*). The "knot-in-hand" glyph I previously interpreted as "accession" functions as the proper name of the house he dedicated.[17] The event is a variant of the "rattlesnake rattle-fire" dedication ritual, followed by the proper name Accession House, and then *u kaba* 'is its names'. The passage closes with *yotot* 'it is the house of', the name 3-Jester-God, an unknown glyph, and Kan-Hok-Xul's name.

The unknown glyph between the two names has been the subject of study since Mathews (1975) pointed out that it stands between the names of Yaxchilan kings and visitors from other sites. David Stuart (personal communication, 1985) identified the same glyph on Hieroglyphic Stairs 1 at Yaxchilan, where it records the ritual action done by those visitors. Stuart (personal communication, 1988) identified the hand sign as phonetic *ye*, while Stuart, Grube, and I have independently recognized that the second sign is simply the fully expanded version of the phonetic sign *te* conflated with T69 *he*. *Yeteh* is the possessed form of *eteh*, a term derived from *et*, which is glossed by John J. Attanasi (1973:264) as 'work, authority' with the following derived forms: *e'tal* 'religious cargo, position of responsibility, authority, public office', *e'tel* 'work[ed]', *et'ihibäl* 'office', *ehtihil* 'office', and *etihib* 'mayordomo's sceptre of authority'. 3-Jester-God (Xoc) is then identified by this *yeteh* glyph as the 'officeholder' of Kan-Hok-Xul. He is therefore identified as a subordinate even though his liege lord very probably was a captive of Tonina at the time of the dedication.

Several pieces of new information emerge from these new interpretations. First of all, Kan-Hok-Xul was very likely not present at the dedication, but his role was taken by a surrogate, named 3-Jester-God (Xoc). This character never became king, but he may have served as the de facto head of government, since he placed his birth and mirror events flanking the main figure in the scene as if to claim the same status. Since the flanking figures in the scene are clearly Pacal and Lady Ahpo-Hel (Schele 1979a:52–57), we can deduce that the central figure was originally intended to be the king and their child, Kan-Hok-Xul. Since we have no reason to suggest that the 3-Jester-God person was their child or that he held the throne at all, he clearly was not intended to be there in the original composition. He was, instead, a very high ranking *ahau* who apparently kept Pal-

enque going while the king was held captive—I suspect for at least ten years—by the Tonina king.

Precedents for holding captives in custody for long periods before dispatching them are found in the inscriptions of Dos Pilas and Seibal, as well as at Naranjo. Stephen Houston (personal communication, 1986) pointed out to me that the Seibal captive Ich'ak Balam was taken captive by one Dos Pilas king and killed by his successor many years later. Two other captives, Kinichil Cab and Shield-Jaguar of Ucanal, were kept alive and used in sacrificial rituals by Smoking-Squirrel for almost seventeen years. By keeping the aged Kan-Hok-Xul alive (he was 66.81 at the capture date and 75.77 at the house dedication), the Tonina king apparently prevented the ruling house from installing a new ruler at Palenque. Presumably, Kan-Hok-Xul died or was killed sometime between the house dedication and the next accession, about a year and a half later.

The next king, Chaacal III, acceded to the throne on 9.14.10.4.2 9 Ik 5 Kayab, a date contrived to be like-in-kind to the accession of the First Mother as it was recorded on the Tablet of the Cross (Lounsbury 1976:220) by Chan-Bahlum II. This appeal to the mythology of the Temple of the Cross was required, apparently, because the new king based his claim on descent from his mother, just as Pacal had done two generations earlier. His father is recorded on the Temple 18 jambs (Fig. 7-13c), and he was clearly neither Chan-Bahlum nor Kan-Hok-Xul. On the right jamb of the same building, a woman is likened to the First Mother by being declared a *yitah* 'sibling'[18] (Fig. 7-14b). Mathews and I have taken this reference to be to Chaacal III's mother, although there is no surviving text where this woman's name shows up following a 'child of mother' glyph.

Chaacal's buildings include Temple 18, which had the door jamb panels and a huge, now-destroyed stucco text and scene on the rear wall of the temple. Various components of this inscription have been recovered over

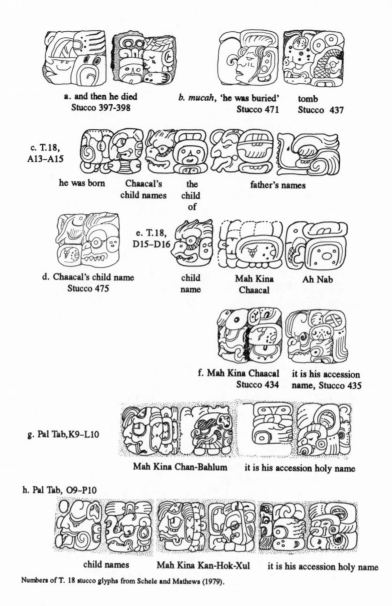

a. and then he died
Stucco 397-398

b. *mucah*, 'he was buried'
Stucco 471

tomb
Stucco 437

c. T.18,
A13–A15

he was born   Chaacal's
child names

the
child
of

father's names

e. T.18,
D15–D16

d. Chaacal's child name
Stucco 475

child
name

Mah Kina
Chaacal

Ah Nab

f. Mah Kina Chaacal
Stucco 434

it is his accession
name, Stucco 435

g. Pal Tab, K9–L10

Mah Kina Chan-Bahlum

it is his accession holy name

h. Pal Tab, O9–P10

child names   Mah Kina Kan-Hok-Xul   it is his accession holy name

Numbers of T. 18 stucco glyphs from Schele and Mathews (1979).

FIGURE 7-13. Passages from Temple 18 and formal naming patterns.

the years (Blom and La Farge 1926:175–176; Fernández 1954; Ruz 1956:147–168; Schele and Mathews 1979:Nos. 391–548), but no one has been able to reconstruct it. Among the glyphs, however, are a death (Fig. 7-13a) and a burial (Fig. 7-13b)—perhaps of Kan-Hok-Xul, or, more likely, of Chaacal's father, whose name appears repeatedly in the stucco glyphs. I suspect this burial refers to the man in Tomb 2, who went to the afterlife with a jade Jester God, a royal belt, and an incised spondylus shell pectoral among his accoutrements. Since Kan-Hok-Xul was probably not buried at Palenque, this man should have been a highly placed noble of *ahau* rank, such as his father.

Chan-Bahlum, Kan-Hok-Xul, and Chaacal have one other thing in common. They acquired names from the ancestral list of Palenque's dynasty when they became king. On the Palace Tablet, Kan-Hok-Xul is named by a three-glyph phrase consisting of "rodent-bone" (**ch'oc**), "three axe over earth" or its head variant, and **mat(a)**, a title of some sort (Schele 1979a:63). The ancestral name, Mah Kina Kan-Hok-Xul,[19] is added to these three names only in the passage recording his accession. This dynastic name (Fig. 7-13*h*) is followed by a two-glyph phrase reading "his accession holy name" (*u* "accession" *ch'ul kaba*). Chan-Bahlum's name on the Palace Tablet (Fig. 7-13*g*) is followed by the same phrase identifying his "accession" name, although we do not have a clear distinction in his inscriptions between a pre- and a post-accession name phrase. Chaacal III, however, does have a name, apparently an iguana head (*huh*), which appears in his name both before and after accession (Fig. 7-13*c−e*). Although no longer in its original position, there is a stucco glyph from Temple 18 recording "his accession name," *u* ("accession") *kaba*. I suggest it originally identified Chaacal's special name from the ancestral list.

In our original examination of Palenque's history (Mathews and Schele 1974), I had trouble separating Chaacal III from another important person of his times—Chac-Zutz', who commissioned the Tablet of the Slaves and who is mentioned on the Tablet of the Scribe from the Southwest Court of the Palace. Soon afterward, I accepted Mathews' contention that these were two individuals, but for many years, we presumed, because of the iconography of the Tablet of the Slaves, that Chac-Zutz' was a ruler. The identification of a subordinate rank called *cahal* (Mathews and Justeson 1984:211–212), however, suggests that Chac-Zutz' was never a king at all. In the last passage on the Tablet of the Slaves (Fig. 7-14*a*), he has this *cahal* title in his name (Schele 1991), thus identifying him

as a high-ranked *ahau* subordinate to the high king, Chaacal III. According to Stuart's (1984a) distributional study of this title, it was carried by subordinates who governed subsidiary sites or served as functionaries for the high kings. *Cahal* lineages often provided wives for kings, and they played important roles in the internal politics of their polities.

The Tablet of the Slaves was set inside a building in Group IV to the west of the sacred precinct of Palenque. The two-hundred-year-old cemetery found under the floor of the central plaza of this group (Rands and Rands 1961) identifies it as a residential group of long use. Chac-Zutz', its patriarch during the reign of Chaacal III, was very probably a high-level functionary, perhaps a war chief, for the king. It is also possible, however, that he was Chaacal's half-brother by the same mother. On the Tablet of the Slaves, Chac-Zutz' represented his parents with their names in small panels near their heads. While the name of his father (Fig. 7-14*c*) is clearly different from Chaacal's, his mother's name (Fig. 7-14*c*) is the same as that of the woman named with Chaacal on the Temple 18 doorjambs (Fig. 7-14*b*) and in the stucco glyphs (Fig. 7-14*d*).

Although this identification of kinship with the king must remain tentative for the present, the prominence of Chac-Zutz' in the inscriptional record bespeaks the growing importance of the secondary ranks of Maya nobility during the eighth century. This importance is reinforced by the Tablets of the Scribe and the Orator, which were mounted as balustrades on either side of the stairway on the south side of the Tower. Showing two people dressed in the costume of sacrifice as they kneel in the midst of a bloodletting ritual,[20] these figures flanked a large stucco scene that was once mounted on the south side of the Tower.

The Southwest Court where these objects were found was the place where many of Palenque's kings took office and the most sacred spot within the confines of the Palace. Pacal's accession tablet is mounted inside the west

101

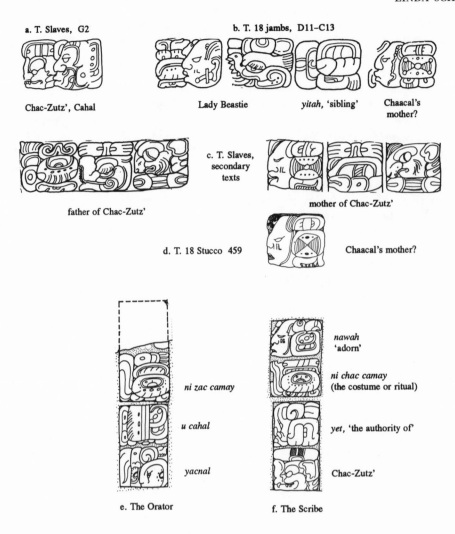

a. T. Slaves, G2

Chac-Zutz', Cahal

b. T. 18 jambs, D11–C13

Lady Beastie   *yitah,* 'sibling'   Chaacal's mother?

c. T. Slaves, secondary texts

father of Chac-Zutz'

mother of Chac-Zutz'

d. T. 18 Stucco 459

Chaacal's mother?

ni zac camay

u cahal

yacnal

e. The Orator

nawah 'adorn'

ni chac camay (the costume or ritual)

yet, 'the authority of'

Chac-Zutz'

f. The Scribe

FIGURE 7-14. Passages recording Chac Zutz'.

corridor of House E. Kan-Hok-Xul showed himself seated in front of Pacal's tablet in his own accession scene, and Chaacal repainted the corridor with a scene of his accession, including an inscription along the eaves recording the contrived relationship between his accession and the First Mother's. The Tablet of the 96 Glyphs was mounted on the lower step between the Scribe and the Orator and the Tablet of the Creation, and several other small but exquisite panels were found in this court, which also had steam baths for cleansing rituals.

In this most sacred of spots, Chac-Zutz' and perhaps another *cahal* (Fig. 7-14*f*) kneel in a *nawah* rite, adorned (Bricker 1986:157–158) in the accoutrements of the sacrificial ritual they are performing. The kind of adornment they wear is apparently recorded as **ni.zac:ca:ma:y(a)** for the Orator and **ni.chac.ca:ma:y(a)** for Chac-Zutz'. I have found no meaning that makes sense in this

102

context, but I suspect that these phrases describe the slit-cloth costume and the banner each man carries. The important thing for my argument is that both men are *cahals:* they are highly ranked, but their positioning in this court among the portraits and inscriptions of kings in their accession rites is an act of extraordinary honor. I suspect that this sharing of royal prestige with subordinates resulted from Chaacal's need to hold his throne through alliance. His interactions with *cahal* lineages included marrying a *cahal* woman as his principal wife and designating her child as his heir (Fig. 7-15*a*).

His son, Bahlum-Kuk II, took the throne on 9.16.13.0.7 (8 March A.D. 764). Although Palenque's reduced circumstances limited the scale of Bahlum-Kuk's monuments,[21] he managed to leave as his heritage the tablet I consider the most beautiful ever carved by the Maya—the Tablet of the 96 Glyphs. This small panel was mounted in a niche in the center of the upper step on the south side of the tower. Its inscription begins with the period ending on 9.11.0.0.0 and the dedication of a house on 9.11.2.1.11 (4 November A.D. 654). The text continues with the accessions of Kan-Hok-Xul, Chaacal, and then Bahlum-Kuk himself. Each of these seatings took place in the building Pacal had dedicated shortly after the *katun* ending. Called the Zac Nuc Na, the White Big House, this must have been House E. The location of the 96 Glyphs points to this house; it was here that those accessions took place. The Palace Tablet shows Kan-Hok-Xul in front of the Oval Palace Tablet; the painted inscription in the House E corridor records Chaacal's accession; and, finally, House E was painted white during its entire history. I had originally taken the absence of Chan-Bahlum's name from this accession list as evidence that he was not in Chaacal's descent line and that Kan-Hok-Xul was Chaacal's father. Now I think his name is absent simply because he acceded to office in some other location. The Tablet of the 96 Glyphs lists only those seatings that took place on Pacal's throne—the

del Río throne that once sat below the Oval Palace Tablet.

The last ruler to be named in the Palenque inscriptions was a step down indeed from the glories of the past. This tiny inscription was found on a blackware vase deposited in a cache offering in Room 2 of Group 3 (Zavala 1951) (Fig. 7-16). The date, 9.18.9.4.4 7 Kan 17 Muan, corresponds to the accession of a king, who was presumably the last ruler of Palenque. The name, 6 Cimi Ah Nab Pacal,[22] refers to the earlier Pacal and to the way his name was written in the Palace inscriptions. Perhaps more important, the name of this final ruler includes a rare, if not unique, example of a calendrical name in the Classic inscriptions. I find it interesting that Robert L. Rands (personal communication, 1975) says the clay comes from the alluvial plain to the north of Palenque, which is the region where Thompson (1970:3–47) placed the Putun Maya. Thompson noted that personal names among the Putun of the Postconquest period evidence a strong intermingling with Nahuatl-speakers, including the use of day names as personal names. This very early occurrence at Palenque may foreshadow the calendar names of later usage.

With 6 Cimi Ah Nab Pacal, the written history of Palenque ends, but his use of the great Pacal's name points to the custom of re-using royal names from the past. In the Early Classic history, Chaacal II was apparently named for his grandfather, Chaacal I, but with Pacal the Great, this practice took on a different scale and function. From his reign onward, the Late Classic historical succession is a mirror foldout of the Early Classic list of ancestors on the sarcophagus sides—if the women are eliminated. Bahlum-Kuk II replicated the founder, Bahlum-Kuk. Chaacal III reflected Chaacal I, while his son, Kan-Hok-Xul I, had his replication in Kan-Hok-Xul II, the younger of Pacal's sons. The older son took Chan-Bahlum I's name, while Pacal himself took the name of his grandfather, who did not live long enough to take the throne. The only Early Classic progenitor who does

a. Bahlum-Kuk's parentage

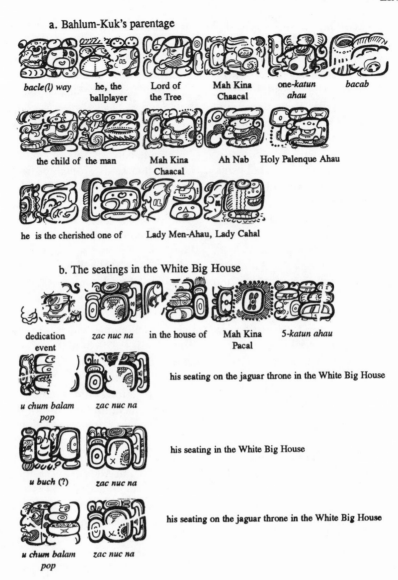

bacle(l) way he, the Lord of Mah Kina one-*katun* *bacab*
  ballplayer the Tree Chaacal *ahau*

the child of the man Mah Kina Ah Nab Holy Palenque Ahau
  Chaacal

he is the cherished one of Lady Men-Ahau, Lady Cahal

b. The seatings in the White Big House

dedication *zac nuc na* in the house of Mah Kina 5-*katun ahau*
event Pacal

u chum balam *zac nuc na* his seating on the jaguar throne in the White Big House
pop

u buch (?) *zac nuc na* his seating in the White Big House

u chum balam *zac nuc na* his seating on the jaguar throne in the White Big House
pop

FIGURE 7-15. Passages from the Tablet of the 96 Glyphs.

FIGURE 7-16. The Initial Series Pot.

not have a replication is "Casper," the second successor in the line. I think that perhaps this missing replication ruled during part of the thirty years between the last date on the Tablet of the Slaves and the accession of Bahlum-Kuk II. And since Bahlum-Kuk is recorded as the son of Chaacal II, I anticipate that the missing ruler, if he is ever found, will turn out to have used "Casper" as his accession name and that he will be Bahlum-Kuk's older brother.[23]

NOTES

1. The Dumbarton Oaks miniconferences and the role they played in the decipherment of the Maya writing system have never been adequately described. Held once or twice a year, these meetings allowed the five of us to come together and debate the problems of decipherment in Palenque's inscriptions. During these debates and in the subsequent correspondence and preliminary manuscripts relating the results of our stud-ies, we worked out many of the critical decipherments and pioneered the use of syntactical paraphrases as the method of study. By 1975, Lounsbury had prepared paraphrased translations from many Palenque texts for use in his seminars at Yale, and I had completed and circulated my own by 1978. By 1977, full paraphrased translations of unprecedented completeness were in existence and began to be presented in a public forum at the University of Texas Workshops on Maya Hieroglyphic Writing. The methods and clause structures identified in those early papers and the Texas workbooks laid the foundation for more recent discourse studies of the same texts. Our techniques of breaking the larger texts into their constituent clauses resulted in the forging of an approach based on syntactical analysis and the identification of many of the discourse conventions. The ongoing results include not only dynastic history and breakthroughs into mythology and calendrics, but also many of the literary conventions, such as couplets, deletion and gapping, and the function of the Anterior and Posterior Event Indicators as critical discourse features. The present analysis represents a distillation of the work of the miniconferences and the Texas Workshops. I also wish to acknowledge the insights contributed over the years by David Stuart, Stephen Houston, Barbara MacLeod, Martha Macri, Victoria Bricker, Kathryn Josserand, Nicholas Hopkins, and all of the others who have corresponded and debated these issues with me. Palenque has played a vital role in the study of Maya hieroglyphic writing from the viewpoints of the historical hypothesis, mythology of kingship and the political institutions, linguistic reconstruction of the grammatical and phonological system of the Classic period, phoneticism, discourse analysis, and many other areas involving written information.

2. The chronological problems that long plagued epigraphers were finally solved by the miniconference team in 1975. See Lounsbury 1976 and the 1978, 1981, 1984, and 1987 workbooks for the Workshop on Maya Hieroglyphic Writing, University of Texas.

3. In his 1975–1976 seminar on Maya hieroglyphic writing at Yale University, Floyd Lounsbury first presented the formula used in the east panel of the Temple of Inscriptions. My 1980, 1983, and 1986 workbooks for the Texas workshops were expansions of Lounsbury's original analysis. Berlin's (Ruz 1973:113–114) chronology was substantially the same as Lounsbury's.

4. Lounsbury (1974) first published the paraphrases and chronological solution to the history on the sarcophagus lid. However, Heinrich Berlin worked out exactly the same chronology and came to many of the same conclusions concerning the history recorded on the sarcophagus in a 1975 paper that he declined to publish after the appearance of Lounsbury's work in 1974. Berlin (1977:129–147) published an overall analysis of Palenque's early history in his large study of Maya glyphs published in Guatemala. Although some details are different, the overall chronology and historical reconstruction are essentially the same as mine.

5. Berlin (1963) first used these mythological passages and related sections of the middle panel of the Temple of Inscriptions to identify the gods he named the Palenque Triad. Following Berlin's work, Kelley (1965) identified the births of these three gods in the mythological portions of the Group of the Cross. Lounsbury (1980) corrected several chronological misunderstandings and added the mother and father of the gods to the list of deities. His analysis of "contrived" numbers demonstrated how events in the lives of historical rulers, like Pacal and Chaacal III, were linked numerologically to dates special to these gods. The rulers of Palenque declared themselves to be "like-in-kind" to the gods by means of these devices.

6. See Lounsbury (1985:45, 57) for his analysis of the dates associated with U-Kix-Chan and Bahlum-Kuk.

7. *Toc* is glossed in Chol (Aulie and Aulie 1978:112; Kaufman and Norman 1984:132) as 'cloud' and 'fog' as well as 'to burn underbrush'. The same two glosses occur in Colonial Tzeltal and Tzotzil (de Ara 1986:384; Laughlin 1988:317). The 'burn' meaning seems less appropriate than the 'cloud' or 'fog' glosses, for ground mist regularly accumulates and hangs over the valley south of the Group of the Cross well into the morning hours, during both summer and winter. I think Toc-tan may refer to this valley as the 'cloud place'.

8. I believe that the inheritance pattern at Palenque and most Classic Maya sites was patrilineal. In this system, Lady Kanal-Ikal would have been a member of the royal lineage and the child of a ruler, but her children would have belonged to her husband's lineage. Their accession would have transferred the throne to that lineage from Bahlum-Kuk's descent line.

9. The discussion appended to Schele 1981:116–117 is the only public debate in which Lounsbury and I have commented on the data. My own understanding of the problem comes from discussions with Rebecca Storey, a respected physical anthropologist and paleodemographer with extensive experience at Teotihuacan and Copan. I understand that it is fairly easy to estimate ages of children, young adults, and even adults, but that after age fifty, it is extremely difficult to distinguish individual ages. The photographs published by Ruz (1973:189–191) show that bones of the skull above the nose and the pelvis were badly disintegrated before the tomb was opened, thus making estimates even more difficult. Furthermore, since only portions of the skull were removed from the tomb and taken to Mexico City, only these would have been available for additional studies in the 1970's. These fragments have since been returned to Palenque and put back in the tomb, but no cross sections of the long bones or any other recent techniques for estimating age have been conducted on the skeleton.

Important new information on the aging of skeletons was presented recently in "The Skeletons of Spitalfields," a film in A&E's *Footsteps of Man* series. The film documents an experiment conducted with over a thousand skeletons disinterred from the crypt under Christ Church, Spitalfields, London, England. Laid to rest during the eighteenth and early nineteenth centuries, these skeletons belonged to a wide cross section of Spitalfields society, but unlike most archaeological contexts, very precise biographical data were preserved in church, public, and family records. As part of the experiment, the skeletons' identities and vital statistics were concealed from the researchers, and both physical anthropologists and dental surgeons were asked to age the skeletons. The standard techniques used by archaeologists regularly underestimated the age of very old skeletons by twenty to thirty years. In the example shown in the film, a seventy-seven-year-old woman was judged to be forty-three by anthropological techniques; surface examination of the teeth yielded forty-five; and examination of the amount of transparency in a tooth root yielded seventy-one. The estimate from the standard archaeological techniques was thirty-four years short.

Having participated in film projects myself and seen the problems involved in them, I was suspicious that the results had been exaggerated or misrepresented in some way. I asked Rebecca Storey, who happened to have seen the same broadcast, if the film could be trusted. Having had her own curiosity aroused, she had contacted the researchers in England and determined that the research and its results were accurately represented and that the research is still ongoing.

The Spitalfields research bears on the problem of Pacal. Because of the very wide variability in the aging processes of human beings, the Spitalfields researchers found it very difficult, if not impossible, to get accurate age estimates of the very old, especially using standard anthropological techniques. Their estimate fell from twenty to thirty years short of the actual age—and curiously enough, this is just about the gap between the fifty-five-year estimate from the bones and the eighty-year record from the inscriptions. Ages recorded in written history throughout the

ancient world are often at variance with the estimates made by the science of physical anthropology. When faced with a discrepancy between history as the ancients wrote it and science as we apply it, we almost always choose the science and dismiss the history as flawed or exceptional. Spitalfields suggests that written history is a far more accurate source than we have been willing to admit, and it challenges the certainty we assigned to the results of our own research techniques.

10. Tatiana Proskouriakoff (1963:153) first suggested that the "ben-ich *katuns*" referred to the latest *katun* in which a person had lived. Lounsbury (1973) demonstrated that the "ben-ich" sign is a title reading *ahau* or *ahpo* in the Classic period. At Palenque, Pacal's *katun* titles referred to his long life, except for those in texts from the Palace. There, on the Tableritos and the bench in the south corridor of the subterranean chambers, Pacal is noted at 9.11.0.0.0 as a 2-*katun* lord, a notation that does not correspond to his age (2.10.5.0), but rather to his *katuns* in office as king. These *katuns* of reign apparently became the convention in the Palace, for Kan-Hok-Xul referred to his father as a 4-*katun* lord on the Palace Tablet. His length of reign was 3.9.1.10.

11. Terrence Kaufman (personal communication, 1988) and Benton Leaf (personal communication, 1988) independently recognized this collocation, **u.to:ma,** the future participial of the verb *ut* 'to happen or occur'. This particular version of *ut* (Stuart 1984c), the verb of the Anterior and Posterior Event Indicator, usually occurs with period endings that were yet to happen at the time the inscription was carved.

12. In our original naming of the Palenque kings, Mathews and I used the name Hok for this king based on Wolfgang Cordan's (1963) reading. In my own later work (Schele and Miller 1983), I came to doubt this reading and thus changed his name to reflect the other three components of his name (Schele 1979a). However, new evidence has confirmed the original reading. Recent decipherments by Stuart, Houston, and Nikolai Grube

(personal communication, 1988–1989) have shown that T607 has the phonetic value **ho,** confirmed in the 'fire-drilling' (**hoch'**) and 'his characters' (**u wohil**) contexts in Yucatecan texts. Since T607 is frequently infixed into the T684 bundle, it can be taken as a phonetic complement specifying the initial consonant of **hok.** On Stela 9 at Copan, T41 **ku** is likewise infixed in the bundle, but to confirm its final consonant as a glottalized *k*. I now accept **hok** as the reading of T684, and as a result I will refer to this ruler by all three names that have been used for him—Kan-Hok-Xul.

13. I first recognized that a fragment in the Houston Museum of Fine Arts and another in a private collection were from the same tablet as the Jonuta Panel. Donald Hales (personal communication, 1985) has since searched for other pieces of this tablet and found a central standing figure that went between the two seated figures of the Jonuta and Houston sections. Subsequently, Peter Mathews pointed out that a glyphic panel in a European collection went on top of the Houston section. Chan-Bahlum's name is on the Jonuta Panel and on the European fragment. Franz Blom (Blom and La Farge 1926:161) says that a panel was in the rear sanctuary of the El Retiro building, but that a tree crushed the center of the temple a few days before he got there. Alfonso Morales (personal communication, 1984) found newspaper accounts of a plane carrying the Jonuta Panel, which crashed at Jonuta in the 1940's. From this report, we know the panel came from elsewhere, and I suspect it may have been from Blom's ruined temple at El Retiro.

14. The glyph under the Venus sign consists of T1 **u** prefixed to the "impinged bone," a glyph that consistently appears in locational phrases. Both Nikolai Grube and I have considered the reading of **pan,** a locative still used today in Chol terms such as *panlumil* 'earth' and *panchan* 'sky'. Here it may record the concept of "star over his place," rather than the "star over Emblem Glyph" form found at other sites.

15. The third possibility, 9.14.11.16.3, is the only one that has any astronomical associations, and "star-war" events were often timed by stations of Venus and Jupiter. That day, 27 August A.D. 723, was only four days before the maximum elongation of the evening star (separation of 46.41°; the maximum was 46.46°), and Jupiter was frozen at its first stationary point. However, this Long Count position is even later than the last date on the Dumbarton Oaks Panel, 9.14.11.2.7, which I have taken to be the apotheosis date for Kan-Hok-Xul. Whether my interpretation of the Dumbarton Oaks tablet is correct or not, the fact that this alternative is 1.12.1 after Chaacal's accession makes it unlikely that Kan-Hok-Xul would have been involved in a war event.

16. Judie Maxwell first suggested this reading for the "Glyph B elbow" to me, although David Stuart and Nikolai Grube came to the same conclusion independently. The phonetic value is confirmed on the Casa Colorado, where a phonetic substitution T1.669.501, **u ka:ba,** replaces the "elbow."

17. David Stuart (personal communication, 1987) first suggested this alternative interpretation to me.

18. This is a reading of David Kelley's (1962a) relationship glyph, T17.565:88, tentatively proposed to me by David Stuart (personal communication, 1988). I have tested the reading and the interpretation throughout the corpus and find it to be extremely productive. *Ihtan* is 'sibling' in Chorti. Although the term is restricted to females in modern Chol, it clearly stands between two males and between males and females of the same generation in the Classic inscriptions. Furthermore, at Site Q and Nah Tunich, people in this relationship are called *yitah itzin uinic* and *yitah sucun uinic*—'sibling younger brother person' and 'sibling older brother person' (Stuart 1989). I accept the reading and interpret its presence on the Temple 18 jambs to declare that the historical woman is the "sibling" of the First Mother as a way of asserting her divinity. Pacal used ex-

actly the same strategy with his own mother.

19. See Schele 1988 for a discussion of the Dumbarton Oaks Tablet and the linkage between this Kan-Hok-Xul and his ancestor of the same name.

20. Claude Baudez and Mathews (1979) argued that these two figures are captives, but I still find their argument less convincing than that they are nobles shown in the act of sacrifice. They are bound, for example, by cloth rather than a rope (Schele 1979a:64–66).

21. Robert L. Rands (personal communication, 1975) sees Bahlum-Kuk's reign (the Balunte period) as a time when the region controlled by Palenque was greatly reduced when compared to the Otolum and Murciélagos periods. Presumably, a shrinking of the hegemony also reduced the available labor pool and the resources Bahlum-Kuk could tap to create monuments to his reign.

22. David Stuart and Nikolai Grube have convinced me that the signs in the *ah nab* (T181.23:585) title should be read *hanab* and that this collocation substitutes for the T583 part of his name. Floyd Lounsbury (personal communication, 1975) long ago suggested that the double shield in his name should be read *chimal pacal,* with the propeller shield being the *chimal* and the flayed-face shield the *pacal.* His observation that there are two components in the name seems to be correct, but David Stuart sees the substitution pattern differently. Both he and Grube have noted that the *hanab* syllabic collocation always substitutes for the propeller shield, while the *pacal* spelling replaces the flayed-face shield. Stuart further suggested that T583 represents some sort of flower. I am not yet convinced of the iconic identification, but Mathews, Lounsbury, and I have checked the distribution pattern of this name at Palenque and affirmed that Stuart and Grube are completely correct. I now accept their reading of the name as Hanab Pacal.

23. In the first half of Palenque's history, a child of the younger brother inherited the throne. Although this pattern of inheritance was violated in Kan-Hok-Xul's successor, it seems to have been the preferred pattern at Palenque. If it is true and if the missing ruler had been Chaacal's younger brother, Bahlum-Kuk should have recorded him as his father. Given that he named Chaacal as his father, I think it more likely that Bahlum-Kuk was the younger of two brothers, who were both the children of Chaacal III.

8. Classic Maya History and Politics at Dos Pilas, Guatemala

STEPHEN D. HOUSTON

IN THE AREA outlined by the Pasion and Salinas rivers are no fewer than seventeen sites with Maya hieroglyphic inscriptions (Fig. 8-1). If we include the entire Pasion drainage, the total becomes even greater: twenty-two sites with 225 carved monuments (Houston 1987:13; cf. Mathews and Willey 1986:Fig. 2). This number compares favorably with most other regions in the southern lowlands of the Yucatan peninsula, where sites with monuments tend not to concentrate in such dense clusters, and with such epigraphic riches.

The true importance of the region, however, lies not in the quantity of texts, but in the quality. Unusually full inscriptions occur in many competing centers, particularly those near Lake Petexbatun, allowing scholars to examine relationships between autonomous and semiautonomous elites of the Late Classic period (ca. A.D. 550–900). This is not to say, however, that such detail is easily interpreted, for no one article can do justice to the historical complexity of the region (Houston and Mathews 1985; Johnston 1985; Mathews and Willey 1986). Accordingly, I focus here not on the full range of Pasion history, but on the works and lives of a single dynasty—that of Dos Pilas, Guatemala. I do so because the epigraphic record of the family is relatively manageable (consisting of sixteen stelae, nineteen altars, nineteen panels, fifteen miscellaneous stones, four hieroglyphic stairways, one hieroglyphic and one iconographic bench), and because the rulers of Dos Pilas were important actors in the dynastic politics of the Pasion drainage. In this chapter, I explore the historical significance of the dynasty by discussing, first, the identifying title, or Emblem Glyph, of the family; second, the overall dynastic sequence; and third, the broader implications of Dos Pilas history.

IMPLICATIONS OF THE DOS PILAS EMBLEM GLYPH

Three decades ago Heinrich Berlin (1960:16–27; 1977:90) identified an Emblem Glyph, which he attributed not so much to Dos Pilas as to the Lake Petexbatun region to the east of the escarpment on which Dos Pilas lies. Berlin had noticed that the Emblem enjoyed an unusually broad distribution: it served as

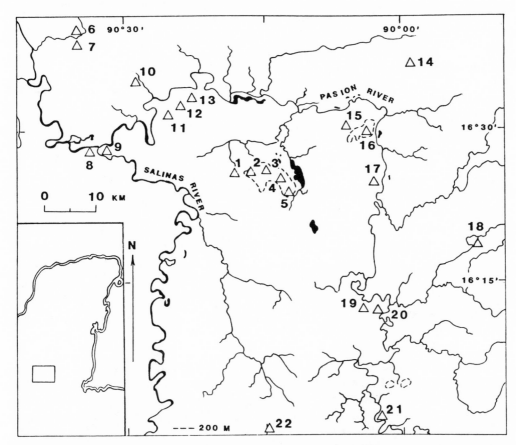

FIGURE 8-1. Map of the Pasion River region, showing archaeological sites: *1*, Dos Pilas; *2*, Arroyo de Piedra; *3*, Tamarindito; *4*, El Excavado; *5*, Aguateca; *6*, El Pato; *7*, El Chorro; *8*, El Pabellon; *9*, Altar de Sacrificios; *10*, Itzan; *11*, La Amelia; *12*, El Caribe; *13*, Aguas Calientes; *14*, El Chapayal; *15*, Anonal; *16*, Seibal; *17*, El Cedral; *18*, Machaquila; *19*, La Reforma III; *20*, Tres Islas; *21*, Cancuen; *22*, Chinaha.

the principal Emblem of Dos Pilas, Aguateca, and La Amelia, and also appeared at Seibal. Other researchers, among them Joyce Marcus (1976a:63–68; 1983b:Fig. 8; 1984:Fig. 6), suggested that Berlin's discovery pointed to a "Petexbatun confederacy": a political association of "lower-order" centers rather than the more typical grouping of subordinate towns serving a "primate" city. Berlin also noticed the appearance of the Tikal Emblem at Dos Pilas, raising the possibility that Dos Pilas and its neighbors recorded part of Tikal's "missing history," an epoch between 9.8.0.0.0 and 9.12.9.17.16 (Coggins 1975; Jones and Satterthwaite 1982:Table 5). According to this interpretation, Dos Pilas harbored an expatriate branch of the Tikal dynasty, which later reverted to its site of origin.

These views were reasonable for the time, but additional research points to other conclusions. In the first place, a "Petexbatun confederacy" is tenable only in the sense that the Dos Pilas dynasty seems to have controlled more than one center. Other sites near Lake Petexbatun, such as Arroyo de

111

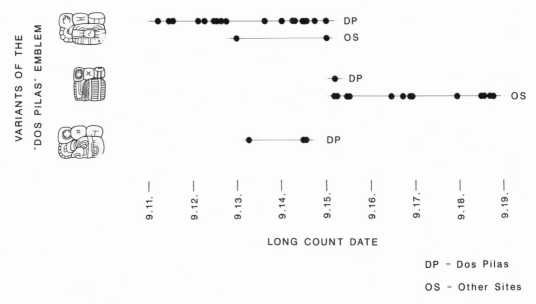

FIGURE 8-2. Examples of the Dos Pilas Emblem Glyph.

Piedra, apparently fell only briefly under the hegemony of Dos Pilas (Houston 1987:295). To describe them as components of a confederacy misrepresents a complex pattern of autonomy and subordination. Further, the very term "confederacy" connotes equality of partnership in a collective political enterprise, a concept that finds little support in Petexbatun epigraphy. In the main, local texts document dynastic competition and ephemeral alliance rather than sustained "confederation," a description perhaps more appropriate to the politics of northern Yucatan (Freidel and Schele 1989).

In the second place, the Emblem of Dos Pilas and Aguateca is, for all intents and purposes, identical to that of Tikal (Fig. 8-2). The glyph conforms to the range of variation of the Tikal Emblem (T569ms), albeit with an increasing preference through time for a particular form of the sign (i.e., T716ms, Houston and Mathews 1985:Fig. 3). Thus, Berlin was in error when he distinguished between a Tikal and a local, "Petexbatun," Emblem. They are simply variants of the same sign.

What are we to make of this? At the very least, it presents a problem of nomenclature. Michael Closs argues that the Pasion version of the Emblem should be described as a "Tikal Emblem glyph" (Closs 1985), an opinion which, as will be seen below, is more or less correct. Nonetheless, I very much favor the term "Dos Pilas Emblem," for the reason that the history of Dos Pilas is, on the whole, distinct from that of Tikal.

Until recently, many scholars believed that Dos Pilas inscriptions filled the lacunae in Tikal's monumental record, a view best labeled the "missing history hypothesis" (e.g., Coggins 1975). Yet the Dos Pilas dynasty existed independently of Tikal's (Houston 1987: 275–286). Early members of the dynasty perhaps occupied the Petexbatun region during the time of the hiatus or later, and their descendants form a continuous succession of rulers before, during, and after the enthronement of Ruler A of Tikal, at which time Tikal begins again to record its history in hieroglyphs. If there was contact between the areas (and evidence suggests that there was), it occurred between different lines of rulers.

But the problem remains of determining

112

the relationship between sites using the Dos Pilas/Tikal Emblem and of discerning the ultimate connection with Tikal. At this juncture, we must define three concepts. The first is "polity," a unit over which Classic rulers exercised real or imagined dominion. Peter Mathews and John Justeson have argued that Emblem Glyphs refer indirectly to such polities, although within the context of royal appellatives (1984); more recent decipherments, by David Stuart and others, suggest that the entire glyph is to be read, in paraphrase, "holy or divine lord (of) X" (Stuart, personal communication, 1988). The second concept is "dynasty," an elite descent group ruling over a polity. The third is "toponym," the place name of a particular site controlled by the dynasty, or even of sectors within a site (e.g., "El Duende" at Dos Pilas; see Byland and Pohl 1987:11, for comparable evidence from the Mixteca). Stuart and I have proposed the existence of such toponyms, which frequently appear at the end of texts, following an expression meaning "it happened (within)" (Stuart and Houston n.d.). Toponyms not only enable the epigrapher to establish where certain events took place, but often form the "main signs" of Emblem Glyphs (the "X" in the paraphrase above).

Thus, a dynasty may rule several centers, each identified by its respective toponym. A polity (to which an Emblem alludes) in turn encompasses these centers. In more concrete terms, the Dos Pilas dynasty evidently controlled a polity that embraced more than one site. The toponyms of three of these centers, Dos Pilas, Aguateca, and Seibal, are known (Aguateca Stelae 1:D10a, 2:G6b, 7:F2, Graham 1967:Figs. 3, 5, 17): T?:556 for Dos Pilas, T176:200:173 for Seibal, and T74:184:299:529 for Aguateca, with some slight variation in affixation and configuration of signs. The implications of these toponyms are discussed more fully elsewhere (Stuart and Houston n.d.), but for the moment one thing is clear: the Dos Pilas dynasty inscribed monuments at several sites, each of which contributed importantly to the history of the

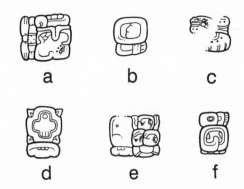

FIGURE 8-3. Probable toponyms of the Pasion area: *a*, Aguateca; *b*, Altar de Sacrificios; *c*, Dos Pilas; *d*, Machaquila; *e*, Seibal; *f*, Tamarindito.

family (Fig. 8-3).

The notion of a toponym and its relation to Emblem Glyphs also helps clarify the connection between the Dos Pilas and the Tikal dynasties, which appear to have used the same Emblem. Mounting evidence suggests that the use of toponyms precedes Emblem usage; that is, only toward the end of the Early Classic period, when dynasties spread over several distinct centers, did Emblems begin to convey a meaning beyond "holy lord of such-and-such a place" (Houston and Johnston 1987). At this point, Emblem Glyphs became more generalized, to include a conception of dominion over multiple centers. Consequently, the Dos Pilas Emblem, which clearly originated as a toponym at Tikal, must ultimately have derived from that center. And, more pertinent here, it must have been adopted in the Pasion region *after* its meaning became generalized at Tikal. This internal evidence suggests, first, that the Dos Pilas dynasty either came from Tikal or at least claimed derivation from it and, second, that the dynasty laid claim to the title sometime after the middle of the Early Classic period.

Nonetheless, available data suggest that Dos Pilas' relationship to Tikal was complex. It has been established that the Dos Pilas dynasty was distinct from Tikal's, although almost certainly the former stemmed from the latter. We also know that the families were in contact with one another during the middle of the Late Classic period: the name of Tikal Ruler A's father, the so-called Shield Skull, appears both on Dos Pilas Hieroglyphic Stairway 2 (David Stuart, personal communication, 1989) and on the newly discovered Hieroglyphic Stairway 4, and an incised text from Tikal Burial 116 commemorates the death of Dos Pilas Ruler 2 (who, incidentally, is identified by the *toponym* of his site, the one feature to distinguish him from a Tikal lord [Proskouriakoff 1973:173]).[1]

But there is also evidence of turbulence in the relationship. Hieroglyphic Stairway 2 at Dos Pilas records a battle at the site of Tikal during the first years of Dos Pilas' history. And a later record on the same monument refers to war against the site of Dos Pilas, apparently in connection with Ruler A's father. Hieroglyphic Stairway 4, a recent find by Stacey Symonds of the Vanderbilt Petexbatun Project, provides much firmer evidence for warfare between Tikal and Dos Pilas: after an initial reverse, Ruler 1 of Dos Pilas apparently captured Shield Skull and may even have interred his remains at the site. This dynastic upset may have led to a short interregnum at Tikal, since Shield Skull's successor, Ruler A, did not inherit the throne until at least three years later.

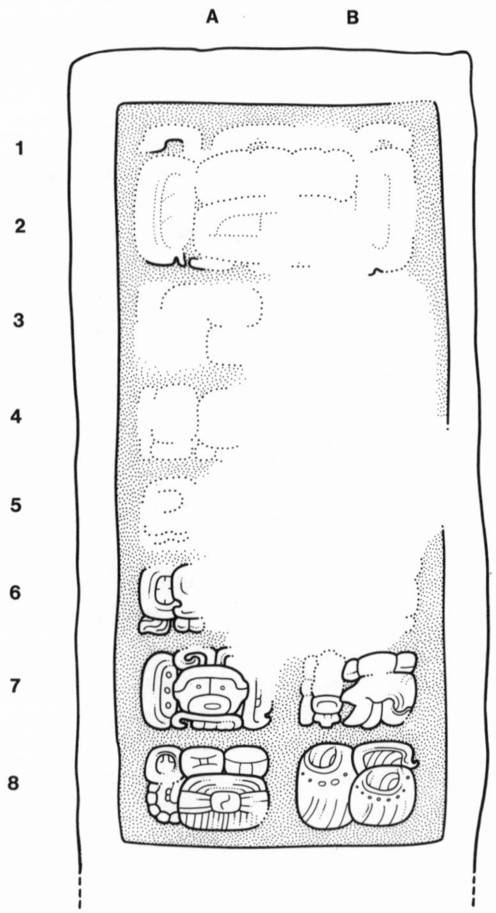

The Origins of the Dos Pilas Dynasty

There exist only two hints of lords before Ruler 1, the first well-documented lord at Dos Pilas. One piece of evidence comes from Panel 6, which refers in a parentage statement to an individual who is otherwise unattested at Dos Pilas. This individual may well be the father of Ruler 1. The other evidence is more tentative. On Tamarindito Stela 4 (dating to 9.6.0.0.0) occurs a name apparently belonging to a foreign lord. The appellative differs from that of Tamarindito Ruler 2, who erected the stela, but resembles

FIGURE 8-4. Dos Pilas Panel 6, with name of possible early ruler of the Dos Pilas dynasty at B7.

greatly the name on Dos Pilas Panel 6 (Fig. 8-4). Conceivably, Stela 4 and Panel 6 record the same individual, who perhaps lived an extraordinarily long time. Another possibility—that these men come from different generations of the same family—is perhaps more reasonable, if only because Stela 4 and Panel 6 have widely divergent dates.[2] Thus, Tamarindito Stela 4 may document a member of the Dos Pilas dynasty who has no other record.

The evidence from Tamarindito is tenuous but important. It suggests that the Dos Pilas dynasty resided near Lake Petexbatun during

114

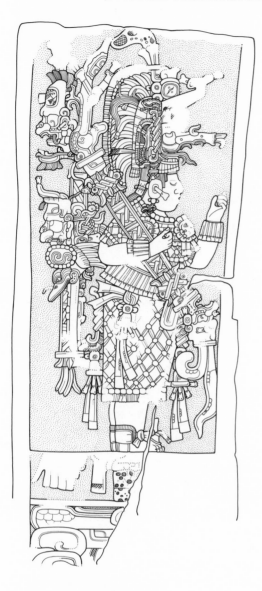

FIGURE 8-5. Dos Pilas Panel 10.

less than a regional power during this period. In addition, many of Dos Pilas' marriage "alliances" probably took place during the reigns of Ruler 1 and, less likely, Ruler 2. An intrusive dynasty might be expected to use such a device to consolidate its position (note that this stratagem was used by some Postclassic polities of Central Mexico [Calnek 1982:59]).

Recent excavations by the Vanderbilt project have also revealed a new panel from the central structure on the summit of Structure L5-49. Although the panel dates to the Late Classic period, it nonetheless refers to an individual who celebrated the beginning of the era at 13.0.0.0.0. In an eroded passage, the text also records the names of this figure's parents, as well as a possible reference to the so-called Woman of Tikal (see below; David Stuart, personal communication, 1990). Nikolai Grube points out that the protagonist of the panel is the same as an individual mentioned on Tikal Stela 5 (personal communication, 1990). Presumably, then, Tikal and Dos Pilas shared not only the same Emblem, but also a connection to a poorly understood figure in mythological time.

DOS PILAS RULERS: WORKS AND LIVES

Ruler 1

With Ruler 1, Dos Pilas moves into an era of more complete historical documentation (see Fig. 8-6 for the Dos Pilas dynastic sequence, and Table 8-1 for a complete set of dates). Ruler 1 is unique at the site for having two variant names, which glyphic passages confirm to be equivalent (Houston and Mathews 1985:9–10, Figs. 5–6). His dates are less secure. Peter Mathews and I argue elsewhere that Ruler 1 acceded at 9.10.12.11.2 (Houston and Mathews 1985:11). We support this argument with a supposed parallelism between anniversary phrases involving *hel* signs (ibid.: Fig. 7). The phrases purportedly read, in loose paraphrase, "the completion of the change of Ruler X's *n*th *katun* in office."

Additional evidence now indicates that the

the hiatus. (Indeed, the bottom register of Panel 10 may represent a carving from this early phase of Dos Pilas history; Fig. 8-5.) But it should also be noted that, despite its proximity to Dos Pilas (less than four kilometers), Arroyo de Piedra fails to mention its neighbor during this time. This omission suggests, perhaps, that Dos Pilas was something

TABLE 8-1. Dates of Dos Pilas Rulers

Long Count	Calendar Round	Julian Date	Monument
Earlier Dates			
13.0.0.0.0	4 Ahau 8 Cumku	−3113 Sep 11	Pan 18
Ruler 1			
(9.9.2.11.2	8 Ik 5 Ceh)	625 Oct 15*	HS. 2
(9.9.12.11.2	8 Ik 5 Ceh)	625 Oct 15*	HS. 4
(9.)10.15.0.0	6 Ahau 13 Mac	647 Nov 7	HS. 4
(9.10.15.4.9)	4 Muluc 2 Cumku	648 Feb 4	HS. 4
(9.)11.0.0.0	(12 Ahau 8 Ceh)	652 Oct 11	HS. 2
(9.11.4.5.14)	6 *Ix 2 Kayab	657 Jan 12	HS. 2
(9.11.9.15.19)	9 Cauac 17 Yaxkin	662 Jul 10	HS. 2
(9.11.)10.0.0	11 Ahau *18 Ch'en	662 Aug 20	HS. 2
(9.11.)10.0.0	11 Ahau *18 Ch'en	662 Aug 20	HS. 2
(9.11.11.9.17)	9 Caban 5 Pop	664 Feb 20	HS. 2
(9.12.0.0.0)	10 Ahau 8 Yaxkin	672 Jun 28	HS. 2
(9.12.0.8.3	4 Akbal 11 Muan)	672 Dec 8	HS. 2
(9.12.0.8.3)	4 Akbal 11 Muan	672 Dec 8	HS. 4
9.12.*0.*10.11	13 Chuen 19 Kayab	673 Jan 25	St. 8
(9.12.4.16.2	4 Ik) *5 Zotz'?	677 Apr 25	HS. 2
(9.12.5.9.14)	*2 Ix *17 Muan	677 Dec 13	HS. 2
(9.12.5.10.1)	9 Imix 4 Pax	677 Dec 20	HS. 2
(9.12.5.10.1)	9 Imix 4 Pax	677 Dec 20	HS. 4
(9.12.6.16.17)	11 Caban 10 Zotz'	679 Apr 30	HS. 2
(9.12.6.16.17)	11 Caban 10 Zotz'	679 Apr 30	HS. 4
(9.12.)7.0.0	8 Ahau 13 Tzec	679 May 26	HS. 2
(9.12.)7.0.0	8 Ahau 13 Tzec	679 May 26	HS. 2
(9.12.10.0.0)	9 Ahau (18 Zotz')	682 May 10	St. 9
(9.12.)10.0.0	9 Ahau 18 Zotz'	682 May 10	HS. 2
9.12.10.0.0	9 Ahau 18 Zotz'	682 May 10	HS. 4
(9.12.12.11.2)	2 Ik 10 Muan	684 Dec 4	HS. 2
9.12.12.11.2	2 Ik 10 Muan	684 Dec 4	HS. 4
(9.12.13.17.7)	6 Manik 5 Zip	686 Apr 3	Pan. 7
(9.)13.0.0.0	8 Ahau 8 Uo	692 Mar 15	AGT St. 5
Ruler 2			
9.12.*0.*10.11	13 Chuen 19 Kayab	673 Jan 25	St. 8
(9.13.6.2.0)	11 Ahau 18 Uo	698 Mar 24	St. 8
(9.13.10.11.12	5 Eb 10 Zac)	702 Sep 11	St. 8
(9.13.13.8.2)	1 Ik 5 Yaxkin	705 Jun 17	St. 1
(9.13.)15.0.0	13 Ahau 18 Pax	706 Dec 31	St. 1
9.14.0.0.0	6 Ahau 13 Muan	711 Dec 1	St. 14
(9.14.0.0.0)	6 Ahau 13 Muan	711 Dec 1	St. 8
(9.14.0.0.0	6 Ahau 13 Muan)?	711 Dec 1	ARP St. 7
(9.14.)5.0.0	*12 Ahau *8 Kankin	716 Nov 4	St. 11
(9.14.)5.0.0	12 Ahau 8 Kankin	716 Nov 4	HS. 1
(9.14.5.3.14)	8 Ix 2 Cumku	717 Jan 17	St. 14
(9.14.6.2.0)	*9 Ahau *3 Pax?	717 Dec 9	HS. 1
(9.14.6.6.0)	11 Ahau 18 Pop?	718 Feb 27	St. 16
(9.14.6.10.2)	2 Ik 0 Xul	718 Feb 24	St. 16
(9.14.9.16.15)	6 Men 18 Zac	721 Sep 14	HS. 1
(9.14.)10.0.0	5 Ahau 3 Mac	721 Oct 9	St. 15

TABLE 8-1. (*continued*)

Long Count	Calendar Round	Julian Date	Monument
(9.14.10.4.0)	7 Ahau 3 Kayab	721 Dec 28	St. 15
(9.14.11.4.14)	*4 Ix 12 Kayab?	723 Jan 6	HS. 1
(9.14.11.4.15)	5 Men 13 Kayab	723 Jan 7	HS. 1
(9.14.)13.0.0	6 Ahau 8 Ceh	724 Sep 23	HS. 1
(9.14.15.1.19)	11 Cauac 17 Mac	726 Oct 22	St. 8
(9.14.15.2.3)	3 Kan *2 Kankin	726 Oct 26	St. 8
Ruler 3			
(9.14.15.5.15)	9 Men 13 Kayab	727 Jan 6	St. 8
9.15.0.0.0	4 Ahau 13 Yax	731 Aug 18	St. 5
9.15.0.0.0	4 Ahau 13 Yax	731 Aug 18	St. 5
9.15.0.0.0	4 Ahau 13 Yax	731 Aug 18	St. 5
9.15.4.6.4	8 Kan 17 Muan	735 Nov 29	St. 2
(9.15.4.6.4)	8 Kan 17 Muan	735 Nov 29	AGT St. 2
(9.15.4.6.5)	9 Chicchan 18 Muan	735 Nov 30	St. 2
(9.15.4.6.5)	9 Chicchan 18 Muan	735 Nov 30	AGT St. 2
(9.15.4.6.11)	2 Chuen 4 Pax	735 Dec 6	St. 2
(9.15.4.6.11)	2 Chuen 4 Pax	735 Dec 6	AGT St. 2
(9.15.)5.0.0	10 Ahau 8 Ch'en	736 Jul 22	AGT St. 2
(9.15.9.)9.0	5 Ahau 8 Kayab	740 Dec 28	HB. 1
(9.15.9.)9.0	5 Ahau 8 Kayab	740 Dec 28	AGT St. 2
(9.15.9.16.11)	13 Chuen 14 Xul	741 May 28	AGT St. 1
(9.15.9.16.12)	1 Eb 15 Xul	741 May 29	HB. 1
Ruler 4			
(9.14.9.16.15)	6 Men *18 Zac	721 Sep 14	HS. 1
(9.15.9.16.15)	4 Men 18 Xul	741 Jun 1	AGT St. 1
(9.15.9.17.17)	13 Caban 20 Yaxkin	741 Jun 23	AGT St. 1
(9.15.)10.0.0	3 Ahau 3 Mol	741 Jun 26	AGT St. 1
(9.15.10.13.0)	3 Ahau 18 Uo?	742 Mar 13	St. 4
(9.15.10.17.15)	7 Men 13 Yaxkin	742 Jun 16	HB. 1
(9.15.)11.0.0	(12 Ahau 18 Yaxkin)?	742 Jun 21	St. 4
9.15.13.13.0	4 Ahau (3 Uo)	744 Aug 9	SBL HS. 1
(9.15).15.0.0	9 Ahau 18 Xul	746 May 31	SBL HS. 1
(9.15.16.7.17)	6 Caban 10 Kankin	747 Oct 30	SBL HS. 1
(9.15.16.7.17)	6 Caban 10 Kankin	747 Oct 30	SBL HS. 1
9.15.16.12.1	12 *Imix 14 Cumku	748 Jan 22	AGT St. 6
(9.16.9.4.19)	13 *Cauac 7 Mol	760 Jun 25	AML HS. 1
(9.16.9.15.3)	9 Akbal 11 Cumku	761 Jan 15	TAM HS. 2
Later Rulers			
9.15.16.12.1	12 *Imix 14 Cumku	748 Jan 22	AGT St. 6
(9.16.9.4.19)	13 *Cauac 7 Mol	760 Jun 25	AML HS. 1
(9.16.18.15.11)	1 *Chuen 14 Kayab?	769 Dec 7	AGT St. 6
(9.16.19.0.14)	*5 Ix 12 *Pop?	770 Feb 8	AGT St. 6
(9.16.19.0.17)	8 *Caban (15 Pop)?	770 Feb 11	AGT St. 6
(9.16.19.10.11)	7 Chuen 9 Zac	770 Aug 24	AGT St. 6
(9.)17.0.0.0	13 *Ahau 18 Cumku	771 Jan 20	AGT St. 6
(9.17.0.0.0)	13 Ahau 18 Cumku	771 Jan 20	SBL St. 6
(9.17.0.0.0)	13 Ahau 18 Cumku	771 Jan 20	SBL St. 7
(9.17.)10.0.0	12 Ahau 8 Pax?	780 Nov 28	SBL St. 5
(9.)18.0.0.0	11 Ahau 18 Mac	790 Oct 11	AGT St. 7

TABLE 8-1. (*continued*)

Long Count	Calendar Round	Julian Date	Monument
(9.)18.0.0.0	11 Ahau 18 Mac	790 Oct 11	AGT St. 14
(9.18.)10.0.0	10 Ahau 8 Zac	800 Aug 15	SBL St. 7
(9.18.11.12.0)	12 Ahau 18 Zotz'	802 Apr 7	AML HS. 1
(9.18.11.13.4)	10 Kan *2 Xul	802 May 1	AML HS. 1
(9.18.13.17.1)	1 *Imix 9 Ch'en	804 Jul 6	AML Pan. 2
(9.18.13.17.1)	1˙ Imix 9 Ch'en	804 Jul 6	AML HS. 1
(9.18.17.1.13)	2 Ben 6 Zac	807 Aug 12	AML Pan. 1
(9.18.17.1.13)	2 Ben 6 Zac	807 Aug 12	AML Pan. 1

NOTE: Julian equivalents accord with the 584,285 correlation advocated by Lounsbury (1982:166).

ABBREVIATIONS: AGT, Aguateca; AML, La Amelia; ARP, Arroyo de Piedra; SBL, Seibal; TAM, Tamarindito. Monuments without site designations are from Dos Pilas.

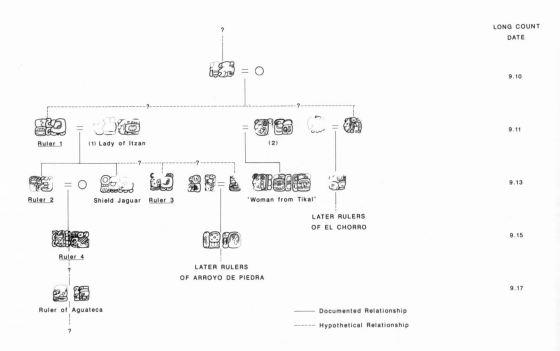

FIGURE 8-6. The dynastic sequence of Dos Pilas. (Note that birth sequence of siblings is not always secure.)

argument is in error. To begin with, there appears to be a genuine distinction between T573, which occurs in an explicit anniversary expression on Hieroglyphic Stairway 1 (Houston and Mathews 1985: Fig. 7c), and T676, which marks the supposed anniversary of Ruler 1's accession (ibid.: Fig. 7b). Many epigraphers believe the signs to be equivalent (Riese 1984b: 266), but David Stuart suggests that T676 may simply express an ordinal construction, such as "second" in place of "two" (personal communication, 1987). A growing body of evidence supports this view. For one, the signs use different subfixes: T676 usually takes T178, perhaps as a phonetic complement to the Chol ordinal suffix -ñumel (Schumann 1973: 31) or possibly as an ordinal construction at Palenque, -tal (Schele 1982: Fig. 31). For another, the signs consistently appear in distinct glyphic contexts (pace Riese 1984b). Scribes at Seibal uniformly employ T676 to indicate the first katun of cycle 10 (e.g., Stelae 10 and 11), and a similar practice with respect to rulers occurs at Yaxchilan (e.g., Yaxchilan Lintel 37, Graham 1979: 83).

To return to Dos Pilas, the anniversary expression on Hieroglyphic Stairway 2 may now be read, "completion, third his katun, Ruler 1," or in less awkward paraphrase, "completion of Ruler 1's third katun" (note the corrected ordinal), an anniversary that appears in much clearer form on Dos Pilas Hieroglyphic Stairway 4. Since there are no explicit references to royal titles, the allusion may well be to Ruler 1's birth rather than to his accession. This placement accords well with data from Aguateca Stela 5, which shows that Ruler 1 was in his fourth katun at 9.13. 0.0.0, thereby placing his birth sometime before 9.10.0.0.0. But there is one major problem: Ruler 1's other katun notations, particularly those at the site of Naranjo, would seem to be consistent with a later date of birth. The inscriptions of Palenque have a similar set of discrepancies in their record of royal katuns (Linda Schele, personal communication, 1983).

Parentage statements (Houston and Ma-

thews 1985: 11, 14, Fig. 8; Jones 1977: 41; Schele, Mathews, and Lounsbury 1977) help identify Ruler 1's wives and children. One of his wives came from the site of Itzan, which has a slightly earlier historical record than Dos Pilas. Ruler 1 had two sons by this woman: Ruler 2 and Shield Jaguar, who ruled either very briefly or not at all. There is a more distant possibility that Shield Jaguar is simply a preaccession name of Ruler 2. Another consort gave birth to a third child, the so-called Woman from Tikal, whom Joyce Marcus cites as an example of Tikal's widespread influence (1976a: 58–60).[3] Parentage statements at Naranjo and a recently discovered fragment from Dos Pilas Hieroglyphic Bench 1 leave little doubt that this child came from the area of Dos Pilas. The woman is important because she contributed to the revitalization of the Naranjo dynasty, which had been seriously affected by war with Caracol (Sosa and Reents 1980). Her impact on Naranjo did not stop there: at least one later ruler of Naranjo used the name employed by her half-brother, Ruler 2. That she enjoyed such influence must speak in part for the prestige and influence of her home site. Recently discovered fragments from Hieroglyphic Bench 1 show that she died at about the time of Ruler 3's death.

Ruler 1's relations with foreign sites extended beyond the transfer of one of his children to Naranjo. During his reign, or perhaps slightly before, a woman from Dos Pilas married into the dynasty of El Chorro, producing an heir for that family (Houston and Mathews 1985: 14).[4] Hieroglyphic Stairway 4 explicitly refers to Ruler 1 as the ahau—possibly "ally" in this connection—of a lord of Site Q, probably Calakmul. In contrast to Tikal, which had poor relations with Site Q, Dos Pilas seems to have had amicable ties with the site.

There is also much evidence of warfare. Hieroglyphic Stairways 2 and 4 record not only a battle against Tikal and the capture of its ruler, probably under the auspices of Site Q (Mathews 1979b), but also the capture of

Torch Macaw (most likely a title accorded to captives) and, as mentioned previously, a war against the *site* (not the dynasty) of Dos Pilas. This last reference is enigmatic, since a war against the home site would seem to be extraordinary.

Before leaving Ruler 1, it is necessary to discuss Aguateca Stela 5, which poses several historical problems. The stela is now in a myriad of fragments, many undocumented and some still buried (Houston and Mathews 1985: Fig. 19). Nonetheless, at least one date on the monument is fairly clear. This date is 9.13.0.0.0, at which time Ruler 1 celebrated a period ending. The other dates on the monument are less easily deciphered. Specifically, the dedicatory date should fall in the reign of Ruler 4, whose names and titles appear on the stela; yet the date seems instead to fit squarely in the time of Ruler 1 (Houston and Mathews 1985:24). Mathews and I were perplexed by this matter, although we overlooked one possible solution: if one presumes that some of the text on Stela 5 is missing (a reasonable proposal, given the fragmentary state of the monument), the dedicatory date may simply be 9.16.5.0.0, from which is counted the only Distance Number remaining on the stela.[5] This Distance Number duly arrives at the accession date of Ruler 4; indeed, a portion of an accession verb appears just before the end of the clause. A second, hypothetical, Distance Number may then have linked the accession date to 9.13.0.0.0. Obviously, Stela 5 will continue to be a problem until its fragments are assembled and the gaps in its text filled. But the solution proposed here suggests that Aguateca Stela 5 may be the final monument, not of Ruler 1's reign, but rather of Ruler 4's.

Ruler 2

As mentioned above, Ruler 2 was the child of Ruler 1 and a woman from Itzan. His key dates are well documented, thanks to a superb study by Peter Mathews of Dos Pilas Stela 8, which supplies much of this informa-

tion (Mathews 1979a). Of particular note is the reference to his death and probably his burial date on a bone text from Tikal, in the grave of Tikal Ruler A, a possible distant relative (Proskouriakoff 1973:170). The inscription of Stela 8 specifies that his burial took place at Dos Pilas, perhaps in Structure L5-1 or in Structure P5-7, near which many of his stelae occur.

Ruler 2 has an unusually complete historical record. He is responsible for many of the monuments at the site and seems to have been more inclined than other rulers to erect stelae at *hotun* endings (at least insofar as this can be judged from extant sculptures). A good example of his monuments is Stela 15, which makes extensive use of couplet constructions, including the first known references to the sites of Seibal and Aguateca.[6]

The longest inscription of Ruler 2's reign is Hieroglyphic Stairway 1, which records his parentage and suggests, in an eroded section, that he fathered Ruler 4, whose birth date may be inscribed on the monument. Another expression on the stairway commemorates Ruler 2's accession (Houston and Mathews 1985:11, Fig. 7). In the bottom central riser, a subsidiary text contains an elite (but nonroyal) title that involves the stewardship of secondary sites under the aegis of a royal dynasty (Mathews and Justeson 1984:212–213). The title is also documented in association with a captive on Tamarindito Hieroglyphic Stairway 1, indicating that this status is not restricted to the Usumacinta River drainage, although, to be sure, it is most common there.[7]

References to Ruler 2 are widespread. Tamarindito Hieroglyphic Stairway 3 mentions him sometime around 9.14.0.0.0, at which time he performed an event (now eroded in the text) under the auspices of a local ruler, most likely the twenty-sixth ruler of the Tamarindito dynasty (Fig. 8-7). Another reference to Ruler 2 appears in a posthumous citation on Arroyo de Piedra Stela 2 (E3b–F3; Houston and Mathews 1984:15, 17). On this monument Ruler 2 is mentioned as an "overlord," whose name is recorded before the parents of the local ruler (Houston and Mathews 1985:27); the mother of this ruler also comes from Dos Pilas, although the father is of the Tamarindito/Arroyo de Piedra dynasty. Finally, Ruler 2's name may appear on the shattered Stela 7 at Arroyo de Piedra, which probably dates to 9.14.0.0.0.[8]

Ruler 3

Two of the longest stelae texts at Dos Pilas date to the reign of Ruler 3. Stela 8, for example, recounts events that occurred, for the most part, during the life of Ruler 2; yet it also mentions the accession of Ruler 3, who came to rule within days of Ruler 2's burial. Unfortunately, the text fails to explain the relationship between the dynasts. There are no surviving parentage statements in the Petexbatun region after 9.14.11.4.15, a date slightly before the reign of Ruler 3 (Houston and Mathews 1985:17). The only clue is one on Stela 11, which suggests that Ruler 3 may have been the brother of Ruler 2.

It is from the time of Ruler 3 that we have the best glyphic evidence of subordinate lords residing at Dos Pilas. This evidence comes from Hieroglyphic Bench 1 and Panel 19, excavated in 1990 by Joel Palka of Vanderbilt University. Both are found in groups that may have been occupied by people other than the ruler, including perhaps the spouse of a king (cf. Webster 1989). Panel 19 is of special interest for its explicit depictions of three members of the nobility, one of whom may have been the guardian of a son of the ruler.

Much like his predecessors, Ruler 3 continued to interact aggressively with other sites in the Pasion drainage. Among his most important achievements was the capture of a Seibal lord, Yich'ak Balam. As a result of this action, the Dos Pilas dynasty controlled Seibal for ten years (Lounsbury 1982:154, 165), enough time, it seems, to supervise the construction of a tomb by a local lord. A branch of the dynasty perhaps controlled Seibal for another fifty years (Houston and Mathews

1985:17).

Ruler 3 is not the first Dos Pilas lord to erect monuments at Aguateca; that honor apparently must go to Ruler 2 or even Ruler 1 (cf. comments on Aguateca Stela 5). But his monuments are the first surviving records from the site. One stela (Stela 2) duplicates information on Dos Pilas Stela 2, and the other (Stela 3) celebrates a *hotun* ending.

This pattern of stela erection has other implications: it is extremely unusual for a dynasty to erect coeval monuments at two sites, particularly when there does not seem to be any evidence of a local, subordinate dynasty. Aguateca and Dos Pilas are an example, then, of a phenomenon best described as "twin capital" settlement, which may be a response to the logistical difficulties of political administration. Tamarindito and Arroyo de Piedra may be another instance of "twin capitals" in the Pasion.

Ruler 3's death is recorded on Aguateca Stela 1, and it is to that site that excavators may have to turn in search of the lord's burial. Aguateca Structure 6 at Aguateca is perhaps the most likely sepulcher for the ruler, since Stela 1 once stood in front of it.

Ruler 4

Ruler 4 is the last member of his family to be documented at Dos Pilas. Nonetheless, most of his dates come from other sites. Aguateca Stela 1 indicates that Ruler 4 acceded to rule only days after the demise of his predecessor, Ruler 3; Tamarindito Hieroglyphic Stairway 2 has his last date, 9.16.9.15.3, after which he disappears from the epigraphic record. Between these dates are references from Seibal (Hieroglyphic Stairway 1) and Cancuen (Hieroglyphic Stairway 1). The former commemorates Ruler 4's last attested Period Ending rites and perhaps the carving of the monument (see Stuart 1987). The stairway is also a tangible expression of Dos Pilas' continued influence over Seibal.[9]

The Cancuen monument, of which some

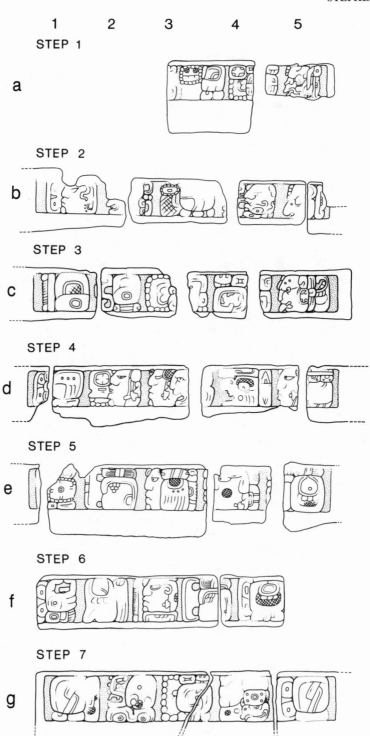

FIGURE 8-7. Tamarindito Hieroglyphic Stairway 3.

fragments were formerly attributed to a site near Cancuen (Rafael Morales, verbal communication, 1983; Houston and Mathews 1985:18; Reents and Bishop 1985:Fig. 5), contains a reference to Ruler 4, who evidently presided over an event by a local lord.[10] Peter Mathews has suggested that Ruler 4 captured a member of the Cancuen dynasty (Houston and Mathews 1985:18). We now know that the supposed Emblem is in fact a reference to a place known as *acul*, which differs wholly from the true Cancuen Emblem. Dos Pilas Panel 19 provides ambiguous evidence that Ruler 4 (or one of his siblings or first cousins) was a child of a royal woman from Cancuen; conceivably, his status as overlord derived from this marriage into the ruling family of Cancuen.

Ruler 4 seems also to have captured a lord from the site of El Chorro, with which Dos Pilas formerly enjoyed amicable relations (Houston and Mathews 1985:18). Another captive is from Yaxchilan; this lord may have been taken during or perhaps slightly before the interregnum between Shield Jaguar I's death and the accession of Bird Jaguar IV (Mathews and Willey 1986). Possibly the capture occasioned the interregnum.

Ruler 4 apparently died as he lived: violently. The Tamarindito/Arroyo de Piedra dynasty, which once gloried in its connections with Dos Pilas, may eventually have warred against Ruler 4 and perhaps killed him; at least, there are no later references to the lord (Peter Mathews, verbal communication, 1983; Houston and Mathews 1985:18). At this time, Dos Pilas' textual record falls silent, and within a few years a squatter settlement would appear in the Dos Pilas plaza (Houston 1987).

Ruler 4 is remarkable for the number of sites at which his name appears, although whether this stems from his achievements or, more likely, from those of his predecessors, is less than clear. Certainly his reign is marked by dramatic changes in foreign relations, with the dissolution of some of Dos Pilas' old alliances and the apparent weakening of Dos Pilas as a dynastic seat. In administrative terms, the important question is whether Ruler 4's successes in some manner presaged his failure. Did the long reach of the dynasty outstrip the administrative ability of this Late Classic polity (Johnston 1985:56)? Or did its initial success stem from administrative and tactical innovations?

Later Rulers

Rulers at other sites in the Pasion drainage continue to use the Dos Pilas Emblem after the apparent demise of Ruler 4, although Dos Pilas itself lacks any certain records from this period. The dominant site seems now to be Aguateca, which begins to erect stelae that are considerably more massive than earlier monuments at the center.

The first record of note is Aguateca Stela 6, which displays a weathered Initial Series date (9.15.16.12.1—Graham 1967:Fig. 15). This is the birth date of a ruler of the Dos Pilas dynasty, who apparently acceded to the throne at 9.16.19.0.14. In a striking parallel, the span between this date and the final date of Ruler 4 corresponds closely to an unusually long interregnum at Yaxchilan (see above). Nevertheless, an intervening ruler may yet be found between Ruler 4 and the Aguateca lord, who perhaps descends from a different branch of the family.

The Stela 6 ruler very likely appears on Aguateca Stela 7, dating to 9.18.0.0.0 (Graham 1967:Fig. 17), although the poor condition of Stela 6 makes comparisons difficult. The most persuasive evidence that the lords are the same is the 3-*katun ahau* title on Stela 7; this notation, which establishes limits on the age of the ruler, is congruent with the birth date on Stela 6.

Earlier rulers at Dos Pilas seldom recorded the names of sculptors (Stuart 1986), the first examples perhaps being on Aguateca Stela 5 and Seibal Hieroglyphic Stairway 1. The clearest instance, however, exists on Aguateca Stela 7, which was probably the last stela to be erected by the Dos Pilas dynasty at its "core" sites of Dos Pilas and Aguateca (Graham 1967:Fig. 18). One sculptor apparently came from Tamarindito, where he enjoyed high status (note the *ahau* title, Lounsbury 1973); the other originated at an unknown site, the Emblem of which occurs in full form on Seibal Stela 8. This sculptor was of lower rank than the other: the reference on Aguateca Stela 7 is merely "he of X" rather than "*ahau* of X." The sculptor of the Seibal stairway probably came from this site, where he occupied similar status.[11]

The Dos Pilas dynasty occupied other sites during the last one hundred years of Cycle 9 (Houston and Mathews 1985:18–19, 23–24). One branch of the family was responsible for the panel and staircase ensemble that constitutes La Amelia Hieroglyphic Stairway 1. The stairway dates, which Mathews has reconstructed, reveal the birth and accession dates of a La Amelia lord. He was born on 9.16.9. 4.19 (just before the terminal date of Ruler 4's reign), underwent a preaccession rite some forty-two years later (cf. Houston and Mathews 1985:15), and then acceded to rule within days of this rite. Later events on the stairway refer to ballgames in which figures on the side panels participate.

The stairway at La Amelia demonstrates that La Amelia was in contact with Aguateca. At positions H1–G3 occur the name and titles of the ruler on Aguateca Stela 7, who possibly presided over an "heir-designation" rite involving the lord of La Amelia (Fig. 8-8). The implications of this reference are the following: first, that the Dos Pilas Emblem, here in late form with appended T115 affix, was in simultaneous use in at least two sites; second, that both lords, who evidently participated in the same polity, employed the *ahau* title; and third, that the Aguateca lord may have been the more important of the two. In short, the Dos Pilas polity still embraced a large area, although perhaps with diminished political centralization.

One of the titles of the ruler of La Amelia, T12.168:44:519, is also found at the sites of Seibal and Chapayal (Houston and Mathews 1985:19, 23–24). Mathews and I propose

that this title is a personal name, probably referring to one individual (ibid.:23). But the disparity in dates and, most important, in times of accession suggests that they were different people (Peter Mathews, verbal communication, 1986; cf. Houston and Mathews 1985:Fig. 18). An important topic for future research is the subject of relations between La Amelia, Aguateca, Seibal, and Chapayal. Were they constituents of the same polity, as prior history would suggest, or did they rule independently?

Dos Pilas and Its Neighbors

Dos Pilas is not the only site in the Pasion drainage with a rich monumental record. At least twenty-four other sites possess monuments, ranging from eighty-five sculptures at Seibal to one carving at El Cedral. Twelve of these sites use Emblem Glyphs.[12] As Mathews and Justeson show (1984), Emblems refer not to sites, but rather to lordship over polities, which were largely autonomous in the conduct of foreign relations.[13] Toponyms specify sites within the polities. A review of the distance between autonomous sites, some the centers of long-lived dynasties and polities, indicates that Pasion polities may have fluctuated in size (depending on relative political success), but that most were relatively small, and nothing like the vast hierarchies proposed by Joyce Marcus (1976a:46). Itzan, for example, lies fourteen kilometers from Altar de Sacrificios and approximately ten kilometers from El Chorro. In an extraordinary case of political packing, Dos Pilas lies within four kilometers of Arroyo de Piedra.[14] This is not to say, however, that such sites were always free of foreign influence; the evidence from Arroyo de Piedra suggests intermittent loss of political autonomy.

It can be appreciated from various compilations that the Pasion region has a long written history, beginning before, and continuing long after, the dates of the Dos Pilas dynasty (Mathews and Willey 1986; Houston 1987: Table 8). What distinguishes the dynasty,

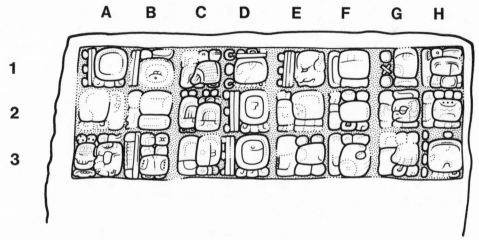

FIGURE 8-8. Hieroglyphic riser of La Amelia Hieroglyphic Stairway 1.

however, is not the length of its written record, which is unusually brief for such an important family, but, rather, the extension of its influence. For example, Dos Pilas evidently engaged in sustained contact with the northern Peten, where its dynasty probably originated (see above). The dynasty also captured lords from sites some fifty kilometers distant, including individuals from Yaxchilan. And, most important, the dynasty waged wars resulting in what appears to be direct control of vanquished centers. Dos Pilas lords either presided over or enacted rites at conquered sites, perhaps with the collusion of puppet rulers from local dynasties (Houston 1987: 294). How such control was maintained and enforced is still a mystery.

Yet part of Dos Pilas' success may be attributed to diplomacy. During or perhaps slightly before the reigns of Ruler 1 and Ruler 2, the dynasty intermarried with foreign royalty. Women from Dos Pilas figure in inscriptions at El Chorro and Arroyo de Piedra; and Ruler 1, in turn, married a lady of Itzan. In the case of Arroyo de Piedra, the marriage coincides with a time in which Ruler 2 of Dos Pilas was the overlord of Arroyo de Piedra (Houston and Mathews 1985: Fig. 12). Indeed, the marriage may express this relation, since such

ties help preserve the loyalty of subordinates (see Calnek 1982:59 and Carrasco 1984:45 for comparative evidence on hypogamous unions from the Postclassic Valley of Mexico).

The relationship with Arroyo de Piedra was apparently short-lived, as were many such alliances (Houston and Mathews 1985: 18). Nevertheless, it set a pattern that runs through much of Dos Pilas' history. Smaller sites under the control of Dos Pilas seem to have been ruled by separate families, some perhaps the junior branches of the Dos Pilas dynasty. This pattern became particularly pronounced after the probable capture and execution of Ruler 4. The principal seat of the dynasty then moved to Aguateca, and several smaller sites began to erect their own dynastic memorials. Presumably the events were related: a signal disruption in the dynasty may have led to more autonomy for subordinate families.

Of greater interest is the impact of Ruler 4's defeat, which resulted, it seems, in the decline of Dos Pilas. The nature of this dynastic crisis is problematical, since it may involve a number of events, including struggles over the succession and the occupation or desolation of Dos Pilas by Tamarindito. But whatever the result, the aftermath of Ruler

4's defeat apparently led to a restructuring of dynastic control, with the devolution of some power to smaller sites. This process may reflect the importance of Classic rulers and the political centrality of their person: a strong ruler may have ensured a strong polity, an ineffectual or defeated ruler, a weak one (Demarest 1986:185; 1989).

Political Geography in the Pasion

Several conclusions may be drawn from Pasion history. The first is that the region constitutes a well-defined political zone, since interactions occurred largely between sites in the drainage. (Similar interaction zones, also embracing distinct watersheds or contiguous sites, occur around Yaxchilan, Lake Peten Itza, and Tikal.) The second is that the polities fluctuated in influence, but that most were relatively small in size, with few being more than an approximate day's walk in radius (Brush and Bracey 1955; Adams 1978: 27); conceivably, this pattern resulted from fundamental constraints imposed by the inefficient transportation of goods (Sanders and Webster 1988:541). A third conclusion is that the polities included smaller sites ruled by dependent lords, whose autonomy seemed to grow through time. The Dos Pilas polity exemplifies this pattern. Fourth, some polities embraced several major centers. The "twin capitals" of Dos Pilas/Aguateca and Arroyo de Piedra/Tamarindito are especially good examples of coeval occupation by a single dynasty. Fifth, relations between polities alternated between war, a policy endorsed enthusiastically by Dos Pilas, and diplomacy, which took the form of marriage and attendance at important functions. One relation did not necessarily preclude the other. Sixth, the recorded history of Dos Pilas is comparatively brief, and certainly far shorter than the span of occupation implied by material remains at the site (Houston 1987: Fig. 72). Seventh and last, Pasion history may now be seen as immensely complicated, with rapid shifts in the political fortunes of key players. Each site has its own story, which must be evaluated in full

before writing in broad stroke the dynastic history of the Pasion.

ACKNOWLEDGMENTS

This chapter is based on my dissertation research, which was funded by the National Science Foundation, the Doherty Foundation, Dumbarton Oaks, and Sigma Xi. I also wish to thank Peter Mathews and David Stuart for their comments on Dos Pilas epigraphy, and William Fowler and John Monaghan for their comments on the style and substance of this paper. Readers wishing to learn more about the primary sources on Pasion epigraphy and archaeology should consult the bibliography of my dissertation (Houston 1987). Finally, Professor Arthur Demarest kindly allowed me to refer to recent discoveries made by the Vanderbilt Petexbatun Project, of which he is general director.

NOTES

1. Dos Pilas Hieroglyphic Stairway 4 follows an analogous pattern in regard to Tikal rulers: Shield Skull is simply referred to as a "native" of the "Tikal place," rather than as a holy lord. Evidently, the rulers of Dos Pilas and Tikal did not acknowledge the rights of their antagonists to use the Emblem Glyph.

2. The repeated use of royal names is attested in the inscriptions of Tamarindito, Yaxchilan, and Palenque.

3. Note that the existence of a second wife does not necessarily signal polygamy, although such surely existed among the Classic Maya. The second wife may simply have replaced the first.

4. Of course, the woman could also have come from Tikal, but I think the "proximity principle"—the closer the site to Dos Pilas, the more likely a connection with it—argues against such an interpretation. The same might also be said of the famous reference to "Tikal" (Dos Pilas?) on Seibal Stela 10 (Marcus 1976a:17).

5. I thank David Stuart for urging me to reevaluate the implications of the Distance Number on Stela 5.

6. Seibal Hieroglyphic Stairway has dates going back to 8.18.19.8.7, but these do not represent contemporary references.

7. Of course, it is also possible that the captive was taken from a site in the Usumacinta drainage.

8. Another interpretation is that this name belongs to a sculptor, since it occurs within a subsidiary text rather than in the main body of the inscription.

9. Some scholars assert that Dos Pilas' victory and continued influence over Seibal were of negligible significance, since Seibal was little more than a village through most of the Late Classic period (Norman Hammond, personal communication, 1989). In my judgment, this assertion is premature; published reports of investigations at Seibal make it clear that relatively little of the site has been excavated (Smith 1982). Accordingly, we can hardly be certain of Seibal's status at the time of the war with Dos Pilas.

10. In 1990, I visited Cancuen in the company of Stacey Symonds of Vanderbilt University. The site had been looted recently, and we documented gaping holes in the following structures (see Tourtellot et al. 1978: Fig. 5, for reference map): C-6c, C-15, C-22, as well as several trenches in mounds outside the Peabody Museum map. A number of the mounds went unreported by the Peabody team, and at least one structure still has standing architecture. Aside from glyphic fragments on sawn blocks of Hieroglyphic Stairway 1, there are at present no carved monuments visible at the site. Nonetheless, looting at Cancuen was not as serious as we had feared, and the site would well repay further study, particularly in areas to the south and north of the "acropolis" and ballcourt.

11. There is another possible interpretation of this compound (T12.854). A similar compound occurs with scribal titles at Xcalumkin (Glyph 20–22, Glyphic Group, North Building, inner doorway; David Stuart, personal communication, 1986). Perhaps the title is simply another belonging to scribes.

12. For the identification of particular Emblems, see Berlin (1958), Graham (1967: 51–99), Riese (1975:55–56), Houston and Mathews (1985: Fig. 3), and Houston (1987: Figs. 54, 55). The putative Emblem of Anonal may simply be a title.

13. I assume the existence of political autonomy when the following conditions are met: (1) that a site contain its own dynasty; (2) that a site not mention "overlords"; (3) that a site not record the performance or supervision of rites by foreign lords in an independent manner. Nonetheless, "autonomy" is a term used advisedly. A site may have an "overlord" who is little more than a nominal suzerain. Conversely, a site may be nominally autonomous, yet operate under the political or economic supervision of a foreign dynasty. The conclusions drawn here are based solely on explicit glyphic evidence.

14. Dos Pilas Structure P5-7 occurs about three kilometers from Arroyo de Piedra and may have been constructed at the time of Dos Pilas' superordinate relation to its neighbor. Thus, packing between centers may have been encouraged by unusually close political ties.

9. The Copan Dynasty

BERTHOLD RIESE

INTRODUCTION

T HE FIRST SECTION OF this overview of the Copan dynastic sequence begins with a discussion of two monuments, CPN 30 and CPN 158, and one textual pattern, the Hel Count (Riese 1982; 1984b). All three are crucial to understanding the sequence. The second section is devoted to biographies of Copan rulers and associated persons in chronological order and according to their presumed kinship relations. The third section summarizes and evaluates accomplishments of the Copan dynasty. For references to monuments, the nomenclature established by the Proyecto Arqueológico Copán (PAC) will be used throughout (Table 9-1).

Glyphic transcriptions are in the Thompson-Zimmermann system (Thompson 1962), and translations and citations from Mayan languages are in modern Chol if not otherwise stated. My theory of Maya writing and the methods I use to analyze and present it may be briefly outlined. Maya script is considered a two-tiered, mixed logosyllabic writing system. On the surface level, signs represent semantic concepts (i.e., logograms, which might be equated with lexemes when there is only one lexemic interpretation of a logographically expressed concept) or syllables. The concatenation of logograms and syllabic signs has to be transformed on a syntactic level (clauses, phrases, sentences) by applying specific rules (e.g., deletion of the final vowel of a syllabic sign when it is in word-final position). This transformation results in the final reading in Mayan languages, which enables the critical reader to verify and criticize the methods and results proposed, since they must conform with the rules of Mayan languages (preferably Chol in a reconstructed form of approximately A.D. 600) and cultural semantics. Therefore, I present the results of these procedures in tagmemic schemes. Problems of decipherment, reading order, and morphological interpretation are only lightly touched upon, and the analytical steps are not presented in detail here, since the scope of my overview is to present the content of Copan hieroglyphic texts with a focus on dynastic information and not the problems of ongoing linguistic analysis.

TABLE 9-1. Concordance of Copán Monumental Nomenclature

PAC Nomenclature	Traditional Nomenclature
CPN 1	Stela A
CPN 3	Stela B
CPN 7	Stela D
CPN 13	Altar G_1
CPN 16	Stela H
CPN 18	Stela I
CPN 22	Altar K
CPN 23	Altar L
CPN 26	Stela N
CPN 26bis	Stela N, Cribbing Frame
CPN 29	Stela P
CPN 30	Altar Q
CPN 31	Altar R
CPN 33	Altar T
CPN 34	Altar U
CPN 38	Stela 1
CPN 44	Altar Y
CPN 47	Stela 5
CPN 52	Stela 6
CPN 54	Stela 7
CPN 55	Stela 8
CPN 56	Stela 9
CPN 57	Stela 10
CPN 60	Stela 11
CPN 61	Stela 12
CPN 62	Stela 13
CPN 65	Stela 15
CPN 69	Stela 19
CPN 75	Stela 23
CPN 86	Altar H'
CPN 87	Altar I'
CPN 101	Altar W'
CPN 141	Structure 12, Reviewing Stand
CPN 145	Temple 11, North Door, West Panel
CPN 158	Hieroglyphic Stairway of Structure 2
CPN 190	Stela 49
CPN 2824	Stela 34
CPN 3033	Structure 11-Sub, Sculpted Step

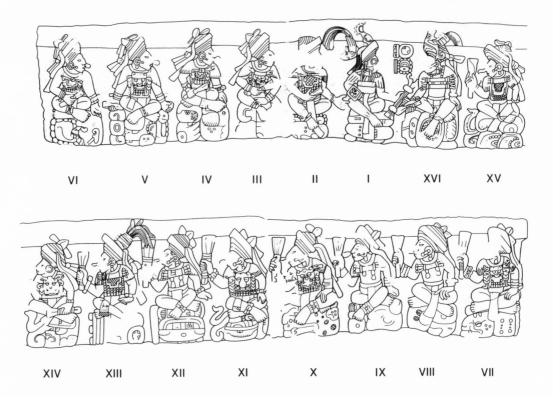

FIGURE 9-1. CPN 30, sides. Drawing by Anke Blanck, PAC.

DYNASTIC SYNTHESES IN COPAN SCULPTURES

The Dynastic Gallery of CPN 30

Sixteen persons are depicted on the periphery of CPN 30 (Fig. 9-1), each one sitting cross-legged on a hieroglyph. On the west side, two persons face each other. Between them is the Calendar Round date, 6 Caban 10 Mol, the accession date of the Copan ruler Rising-Sun. Its Long Count position is 9.16.12.5.17 (see below).

Following Herbert J. Spinden (1924:140–141), this sculpture has been interpreted as an astronomical congress held to determine the length of the tropical year; however, no one has been able to demonstrate that the text or the figural representation contain any related astronomical information (Carlson

1977). Internal evidence makes a dynastic gallery a more plausible explanation of CPN 30 (Davoust 1976). The sixteen figures depicted on the altar concur with the number and sequence of Copan rulers according to the Hel Count at the time of the carving of CPN 30 (see below).

The Dynastic Hel Count

In several important Maya cities, the Hel glyph with a numerical coefficient was used to count successive local rulers (Riese 1982). I proposed the reading *hal* (Chol) for T573a in these dynastic contexts for the following reasons. The internal design of T573a represents two intertwined bands and thus might pictographically represent the concept of "twining" or "weaving"; indeed, one of the major

130

TABLE 9-2. Repetitive Dates on CPN 158, Including at Least One
Initial Series

Step	Date No.		Maya Date	Ruler	Position
—			. . . 3 Mol	HE?	VIII
	1/NN	9.5.19.3.0	8 Ahaw 3 Zodz	LJ	IX
8/9	2/3	9.7.5.0.8	8 Lamat 6 Mac	SH	XI
7	4/5	9.9.14.17.5	6 Chicchan 18 Kayab	SJIM	XII
2/4	8/8a/10	9.13.18.17.9	12 Muluc 7 Muwan	ER	XIII
60/43	23b/26/28	9.15.6.16.5	6 Chicchan 3 Yaxk'in	3D	XIV
39/40	11/11a	9.15.17.13.10	11 Oc 13 Pop	SS	XV

meanings of *hal* is 'weaving' (Aulie and Aulie 1978:62). Its second major meaning, 'to last' or 'to pass' (referring to time), would be an appropriate reading for T573a in most contexts where this glyph is used. The hieroglyph for the *haab-* month Pop reads *k'anha-law* (corrected and phonemicized from the corrupt *kanhalam* of the only extant source), and this hieroglyph contains signs for all constituent morphemes or syllables: T281 for *k'an,* T573a for *hal,* and T130 (*wa*) for *aw.* Hel glyphs in dynastic counts at Early Classic Yaxchilan invariably bear the suffix T178 (*la*), which might indicate the concluding consonant /l/ of the main morpheme (*hal*). The initial *u*-morpheme (third-person singular possessive pronoun) of the dynastic Hel glyph, the following variable number, and the T573a Hel sign proper make it virtually certain that we are dealing with a numerical classifier. *Hal* is attested as such in Highland Mayan languages only. However, the root *hal* in Chol has a time-related meaning, as indicated above. For Lowland Mayan languages, the closest we can get to our preliminary reading of T573a in this context is the numerical classifier *yal,* which is attested in Yucatec only. The suffix T178 found in Yaxchilan can, of course, be a phonemic indicator of the concluding consonant of *yal* as well as of *hal.* Thus both readings, *hal* and *yal,* are possible.

At Copan, twenty-five such Hel Counts are known, covering coefficients from 3 to 16, and the overall picture is clear: Hel coeffi-cients increase with the progression of time. No single coefficient is associated with more than one nominal phrase, and there is no overlap of counting.

The Hieroglyphic Stairway (CPN 158) as a Dynastic Text

A pattern of date repetition is apparent for CPN 158 (Riese 1971:131–132). These dates, each written two or three times, always have one occurrence expressed as an Initial Series, while the others can be Calendar Round dates (Table 9-2).

Date groups 4/5 and 23b/26/28 have been identified as the accession dates of the Copan rulers, Smoke-Jaguar Imix-Monster (dates 4/5) and Three-Death (Dates 23b/26/28). As such, they appear in other texts. Date-pair 11/11a is followed on CPN 158 by the accession hieroglyph and the name of the Copan ruler Smoking-Squirrel. A loose fragment containing an accession glyph and the name of the ruler Eighteen-Rabbit (Gordon 1902: Pl. XII:M) should be joined to date group 8/8a/10, which, in its truncated state, has room for such additions. Another fragment (Gordon 1902:Pl. XII:L6) contains the calendrical information 3 Mol A9, and an accession glyph immediately follows on the same stone. As none of the complete accession dates contains a *haab* day 3 Mol, this must be part of an additional accession statement and date. It has been entered as such in

FIGURE 9-2. Yax K'uk' Mo's name phrase on CPN 30 (A5–B5). Drawing by Elisabeth Wagner.

Table 9-2. A further detached accession glyph (Step 56 : A), preceded by a 2-*k'atun* Distance Number, is not an independent statement, but a repetition that must originally have been linked to one of the existing accession statements.

Elements of this pattern are used for non-accession dates also. Three further date repetitions on CPN 158 (Dates 13/14, 23/23a, and 37/38), for example, do not include an Initial Series. The accession pattern as a whole, therefore, is established as having been used exclusively for accession dates. According to the chronology of the dates and the rulers associated with them, CPN 158 contains a complete list of the six immediate predecessors of Smoking-Squirrel, as shown in Table 9-2.

THE RULERS OF COPAN

Because of the lack of contemporaneous texts, the earliest rulers or mythical ancestors of the Copan dynasty are not well established. The following discussion thus should not lead the reader to assume firmly established identifications and chronological placements. However, Nikolai Grube (1988) has detected a pattern that might help reveal founding rulers or mythical ancestors with more certainty.

Yax K'uk' Mo', Ancestor of the Copan Dynasty?

A person Macaw or New Macaw (now called Yax K'uk' Mo'—with slight variations in spelling—by most investigators) was first tentatively identified by David H. Kelley (1976:

240; Fig. 9-2). This name appears in two different forms, A and B (Table 9-3). The basic equivalence of these two forms is plausible, since T744b of Form A seems to be an iconic merging of a quetzal (*k'uk'*) and a macaw (*mo'*) head, and signs found in Form B are known from other contexts (especially the *Dresden Codex*) to be nominal glyphs for the quetzal and the macaw. Furthermore, both clauses are complementarily distributed in an unstructured way in texts from 9.16.0.0.0 onward, which suggests that they are equivalent in meaning.

From its syntactical position and association with name-related expressions (e.g., *mahk'ina* or the Copan Emblem Glyph), it is clear that *yax k'uk' mo'* is a name or a title. That we are dealing with two or three individuals who share the same or similar name would reflect the great temporal distribution of this nominal phrase. Concurrently, the hypothesis that the name designates an important forebear of the dynasty to whom constant back references are made for reasons of legitimization is equally plausible, and it is currently favored by most researchers.

Decorated-Ahaw

A person who could be either an ancestor or a founder of the Copan dynasty according to his association with dates around 8.6.0.0.0 is Decorated-Ahaw (Fig. 9-3). He is mentioned but twice at Copan, on CPN 18 (at C5 left) and on the Peccary Skull from Tomb 1 (at B2). His nominal phrase is T74:184:126:535:23. The first part, T74:184, is the royal

TABLE 9-3. The Structure of Yax K'uk' Mo' 's Name Phrase

Form A

Constituent signs[a]	74	184	168		16	744b	279 280 106 130
		(671) (713)	544	116			142
Decipherment	mah	k'ina	ahaw		yax	k'uk' mo'	'o'
		WEST	k'in	ne			

Form B

| Constituent signs[a] | 604 | 60 61 | 168 | 533 | 102 103 335 | 582 627 | 279 |
| Decipherment | k'uk' | ? | ahaw | ahaw | al | mo | 'o' |

[a]Constituent signs here and in subsequent tables are from Thompson (1962).

title *mahk'ina*. The second part, T126:535: 23, is his presumed personal name. This name, though, does not completely agree with the glyph below the presumed founder of the Copan dynasty on CPN 30, although both share its *ahaw* part (T535 and T168, respectively). This poses a problem that may be resolved only when more texts are available. If Yax K'uk' Mo' and Decorated-Ahaw are tentatively placed at the beginning of the Copan dynastic sequence, a coordination of their role and interrelationship must be sought in the future.

Tok'

A male sitting on T13.518c:59 + 44:245 faces the Copan ruler Rising-Sun on the north side of CPN 23 (Fig. 9-4). Since the second glyph of his seat is similar to the glyph below the second ruler of the dynastic gallery on CPN 30, T44:761b, I tentatively identify the two persons sitting on those glyphs as the same individual. His name glyph might be tenta-

FIGURE 9-3. Decorated-Ahaw's name phrase on CPN 18 (C5). Drawing by Elisabeth Wagner.

tively deciphered as *tok'* 'flint knife'. If we accept the identification of Tok' as the second Copan ruler, the Calendar Round date associated with a "seating" glyph on CPN 23 would be Tok's accession date. Its placement in the Long Count would be one of the following four alternatives, presupposing a mean duration of 1.4.0.0 for the reign of each Copan ruler: 8.15.17.5.5 3 Chicchan 3 Uo, 8.16.9.8.5 2 Chicchan 3 Uo, 8.18.10.0.5 3 Chicchan 3 Uo, or 8.19.2.3.5 2 Chicchan 3 Uo. A concurring interpretation is to con-

133

FIGURE 9-4. Tok's name phrase on CPN 23 (B–C). Drawing by Elisabeth Wagner.

FIGURE 9-5. The 4-Hel Ruler's name phrase on CPN 2824. Drawing by Elisabeth Wagner.

sider Tok' a successor to Rising-Sun. Several facts support this interpretation. CPN 23 seems to be an unfinished monument, since its south side is only partly carved, and as such it should be a very late monument. Rising-Sun wears a beard on this monument. Beards worn by Maya rulers symbolize old age (or death?). The Calendar Round date followed by an accession glyph written between the two figures is so similar to CPN 30, albeit simpler in execution and details, that CPN 30 might have inspired the design of this altar. Under this hypothesis, the accession of Tok' took place either on 9.19.11.14.5 3 Chicchan 3 Uo or on 10.0.3.17.5 2 Chicchan 3 Uo, depending on the reconstruction of the *tzolkin* date.

The 3-Hel Ruler

No specific monuments that refer to Ruler III are known, except CPN 30, discussed above, where he sits on an almost completely eroded glyph.

The 4-Hel Ruler

The fourth person in the dynastic gallery of CPN 30 sits on T528:713a.672°556or610 (Fig. 9-5). This is presumably his name or a title. A similar glyph appears on CPN 2824. It is preceded there by T148.743var:23. Both glyphs reappear in the same sequence on CPN NN 22, a monument discovered in 1988 that was dysfunctionally reused as a step or a bench in Structure 26-Sub. Thus, the

name phrase of Ruler IV seems fairly well established, and his considerable antiquity is also established through the archaeological context of one monument that mentions him.

The 5-Hel Ruler

The fifth person in the dynastic gallery of CPN 30 sits on T61.1046°528.87?, which presumably represents his name or a title. A further record of Ruler V might have been written on CPN 158, where Step 15 (N) contains a 5-Hel glyph.

The 6-Hel Ruler

The sixth person in the dynastic gallery of CPN 30 sits on T632.1040, which is either his name or a title. No other records of this ruler are known.

Jaguar-Sun-God

Jaguar-Sun-God (Fig. 9-6) is mentioned on CPN 65 (C4) with the names T751+?.1010. He is the seventh or eighth ruler, according to the Hel Count that immediately follows his name. The name Jaguar-Sun-God corresponds fairly closely to the glyph below the seventh ruler in the dynastic gallery of CPN 30; this is borne out if we accept Head-on-Earth as the eighth ruler (see below). An alternative assumption—that Head-on-Earth is the same person as the CPN 65 ruler—is not very plausible, since the respective name glyphs are completely different. The positive

134

FIGURE 9-6. Jaguar-Sun-God's name phrase on CPN 65 (C4). Drawing by Elisabeth Wagner.

FIGURE 9-7. Head-on-Earth's name phrase on CPN 56 (F7). Drawing by Elisabeth Wagner.

evidence of CPN 30, the Hel Count, and the negative evidence just discussed all suggest that Jaguar-Sun-God was the seventh ruler of the dynastic sequence of Copan.

Head-on-Earth

Copan texts refer only twice to Head-on-Earth (Fig. 9-7). CPN 56 (F7) names him as T1000:526:142. He is stated to be the father of Cleft-Moon Leaf-Jaguar in that text (see below). Title glyphs, but no personal name, are written on CPN 3033 (at H1–?). Nevertheless, his identification in that text is possible because he is again called the father of Cleft-Moon Leaf-Jaguar.

Since Cleft-Moon Leaf-Jaguar is probably the ninth or tenth ruler, according to the Hel Count, Head-on-Earth should be the eighth or ninth, assuming direct patrilineal inheritance of the kingship in Copan, and also assuming that he was a ruler. Unfortunately, no Hel Count is associated with his name, which leaves us without direct evidence of his position in the sequence. No glyph similar to any part of Head-on-Earth's name is written on the vertical sides of CPN 30, certainly not in the appropriate position under the eighth or ninth person there. This poses a serious problem for the reconstruction of the Copan dynasty.

If Head-on-Earth was a ruler of Copan, his reign must be placed before 9.6.10.0.0, the dedicatory date of CPN 56, which is associ-

ated with his son and presumed successor. His accession originally may have been mentioned on CPN 158 in connection with the date . . . 3 Mol A9. This date, however, is incomplete and out of context, and its original association with Head-on-Earth remains speculative (Table 9-2). Two possible *k'atun*-age statements, both without numerical coefficients, are associated with Head-on-Earth on CPN 56 and CPN 3033. From these it might be deduced that he did not reach an age exceeding one *k'atun,* or approximately twenty years. *K'atun*-age statements shown without numerical coefficients (not discussed in Riese 1980) are interpreted as referring to a first *k'atun* on the analogy of such a practice in the count of lunar months in the Lunar Series.

The 9-Hel Ruler

If we disregard the 9-Hel reference on CPN 56 because it probably refers to the tenth ruler, as will be argued below, then we are left with two references to a 9-Hel ruler on CPN 190. The first reference gives name and title glyphs at Ap3–Ap5; the second, at Cp3–Cp5, contains titles only. The name glyphs here do not match the eroded name glyph under the ninth (or any other) person on the vertical sides of CPN 30. The identification of the CPN 190 person with the ninth official ruler of the Copan dynasty remains doubtful.

135

TABLE 9-4. The Structure of Cleft-Moon Leaf-Jaguar's Name Phrase

Constituent signs	213	751b	24 130 178	81
Decipherment		*bahlum*		?

Cleft-Moon Leaf-Jaguar

In its common variant, the name of Cleft-Moon Leaf-Jaguar (Fig. 9-8) partly repeats the name of Jaguar-Sun-God, the seventh ruler of Copan, and this kind of repetition might reflect a general naming pattern of the Classic Maya (see Table 9-4).

BIRTH AND KINSHIP RELATIONS. Since neither the birth of Cleft-Moon Leaf-Jaguar nor a *k'atun*-age statement for him is recorded in any preserved text, his birth date cannot be calculated. There are possibly two parentage statements for Cleft-Moon Leaf-Jaguar. The one on CPN 56 (E7) names his father as Head-on-Earth (F7). A similar statement on CPN 3033 identifies him as the 'child of NN (male)'. It is not clear whether these two statements actually involve the same parent, as has been assumed above, because in the latter, the name of his father is not given, and he is referred to only through general titles. On CPN 57, a jaguar name is linked with the name of the twelfth ruler in a way typical of intergenerational connections. If the jaguar referred to here is Cleft-Moon Leaf-Jaguar, he would be the father or uncle of the twelfth ruler.

ACCESSION AND POSITION IN THE DYNASTIC SEQUENCE. A fairly clear accession statement of Cleft-Moon Leaf-Jaguar is loosely associated with the Initial Series date 9.6.10.0.0 on CPN 56 (at F3), as first pointed out by Kelley (1976: Fig. 82). According to

the structure of the dates on CPN 158, Cleft-Moon Leaf-Jaguar's accession should be recorded there with Date 1 (Step 9) at 9.5.19.3.0 8 Ahaw 3 Zodz (Davoust 1978:93); but the accession glyph and his name glyphs are not recognizable in the expected position (at J–?) following the date and again after the Distance Number at Q–R, although a jaguar head is recognizable at R. These parts of the text are severely eroded, and even in old photographs, details are not clear. There is also a discrepancy between this statement and the accession statement on CPN 56. This discrepancy, though, poses no real problem, because the Initial Series of the stela is not directly followed by the accession statement, and a few intervening glyphs are destroyed. This time lag might explain why the accession statement on CPN 56 does not immediately follow the Initial Series date. Whatever the eventual solution of this discrepancy might be, the accession must fall into the time span between the two dates.

Cleft-Moon Leaf-Jaguar's name on CPN 56 is associated with a 9-Hel statement (at F5); he would therefore be the ninth official ruler of the Copan dynasty. This, however, poses a serious problem. On CPN 190, two 9-Hel statements are associated with nominal and title glyphs, at Bp2–Bp5 and Dp3–Dp5, respectively. Neither of these shows any similarity to the name of Cleft-Moon Leaf-Jaguar. On CPN 30, the ninth ruler is not represented by either a cleft-moon or a leaf-jaguar glyph. A cleft-moon glyph is found nowhere on that monument, and jaguar glyphs appear only with the seventh and tenth rulers.

TABLE 9-5. The Structure of Smoking-Heavens' Name Phrase

Constituent signs	122	1 128	(130) Head	561 764 Head	23
Decipherment	SMOKE	*u*	*wa*	*chan*	*na*

FIGURE 9-9. Smoking-Heavens' name phrase on CPN 29 (A11–B11). Drawing by Elisabeth Wagner.

Weighing the evidence, there seems to be a slight inclination toward regarding Cleft-Moon Leaf-Jaguar as the tenth instead of the ninth ruler; however, the contradicting evidence is such that I consider it premature to decide between these alternatives.

LIFE-SPAN AND DEATH. The death date of Cleft-Moon Leaf-Jaguar is not known, although Linda Schele (1986c) proposes 9.7.4.17.4 10 Kan 2 Ceh, found on Step 9 of CPN 158. This identification is extremely doubtful, though. It relies on an incomplete Distance Number and adduces a pattern of "accession-death" statements that is not found in Copan until much later. Thus, the death date remains unknown. It should be pre-9.7.5.0.8, which is the accession date of the next well-documented ruler, Smoking-Heavens. If Cleft-Moon Leaf-Jaguar actually was the tenth ruler and if the accession date of Smoking-Heavens is taken as Cleft-Moon Leaf-Jaguar's approximate death date, then he would have reached an age of thirty-four to forty-four years, which is not unreason-

able. If, however, we assume that he was the ninth ruler, no such calculation is possible.

Smoking-Heavens

Based on individual constituents, a linguistic reading of Smoking-Heavens' name phrase (Fig. 9-9; Table 9-5) is at hand, but the morphological synthesis is not yet achieved.

BIRTH. A record of Smoking-Heavens' birth is preserved on CPN 54 without an associated Calendar Round date. It seems out of place there, however, because the stela was not erected by his predecessor, but by Smoking-Heavens himself, and at a much later date. A further birth statement on CPN 44 is followed by a name which contains a head with a smoke prefix and which might refer to Smoking-Heavens. According to this text, his birth date is 9.7.1.7.6. Finally, a 4-*k'atun*-age statement on CPN 29 furnishes the time span 9.5.10.0.0–9.6.10.0.0 for his birth. The lack of agreement between these two birth dates might be explained by the CPN 44 dates, referring to a different person, perhaps the later ruler Smoke-Jaguar Imix-Monster or a nonruling person.

ACCESSION AND POSITION IN THE DYNASTIC SEQUENCE. The date pair 2/3 on Steps 8 and 9 of CPN 158 gives the date 9.7.5.0.8 8 Lamat 6 Mac. This pair has already been identified as a typical accession pattern record. And, as noted by Linda Schele and David Stuart (1986), it is followed by an accession glyph and by the name phrase of Smoking-Heavens. Thus, Smoking-Heavens acceded to the throne of Copan on 9.7.5.0.8 8 Lamat 6 Mac, at the improbably young age of four years, if his birth date, as previously identified, is correct.

CPN 30 furnishes the only direct evidence of the position of Smoking-Heavens in the dynastic sequence of Copan. The eleventh person represented on that monument sits on the name glyph T122.128?:561f.

LIFE SPAN AND DEATH. Although no death statement is preserved for Smoking-Heavens, Schele and Stuart (1986:14) assume that Date 4 of CPN 158 is his death date. This is reached by a Distance Number, which they reconstruct as 2.9.16.1. However, this is at variance with my identification of this date as the accession date of Smoke-Jaguar Imix-Monster, based on a slightly different reconstruction of the connecting Distance Number. Whatever the ultimate solution may be, it is clear that Smoking-Heavens must have died shortly before the accession of Smoke-Jaguar Imix-Monster at 9.9.14.17.5. His reign was of considerable length, calculated at fifty years.

Smoke-Jaguar Imix-Monster

The first and second parts of Smoke-Jaguar Imix-Monster's name phrase (Fig. 9-10; Table 9-6) contain the expressions Smoke-Jaguar and Imix-Monster, his proper names. The third part contains a God K expression and is clearly a title. The fourth part, if present, contains a k'atun-age statement. The fifth and final part contains the Copan Emblem Glyph. This is also a standard part of the name phrases of earlier and later Copan rulers and identifies them as such.

BIRTH AND ASCENDANCY. The birth date of Smoke-Jaguar Imix-Monster is not known from any direct chronological record; it must therefore be calculated by the k'atun-age method (Riese 1980). According to this calculation, he was born on 9.9.0.0.0, with a possible deviation of one day in either direction. Compared with the Initial Series date of CPN 54, which is 9.9.0.0.0, it does not seem coincidental that on this same stela a birth statement followed by possible nominal glyphs of

Smoke-Jaguar Imix-Monster and the Copan Emblem are found at B12–B13. It must be cautioned, however, that this birth reference does not immediately follow the Initial Series. It is preceded by unanalyzed glyphs, which probably refer to a predecessor of Smoke-Jaguar Imix-Monster, possibly Smoking-Heavens. No explicit parentage statements are given for Smoke-Jaguar Imix-Monster; however, his birth record on CPN 54, a monument dedicated by his immediate predecessor, Smoking-Heavens, strongly hints at a father-son relationship between these two rulers.

ACCESSION AND POSITION IN THE DYNASTIC SEQUENCE. Smoke-Jaguar Imix-Monster's accession at 9.9.14.17.5 6 Chicchan 18 Kayab is well documented in several Copan texts. Two of these, CPN 86 and 87, were probably written during his lifetime. On CPN 47, his accession is associated with the Initial Series date, and its two faces clearly form an iconographic accession program (Baudez and Riese 1990: Chap. 5). The office to which he acceded on that date is given as ahaw. According to the dates of his reign, especially his accession date, Smoke-Jaguar Imix-Monster must be the twelfth ruler.

The valley stelae, which are all dated around 9.11.0.0.0, lie well within the reign of Smoke-Jaguar Imix-Monster. They bear Hel glyphs with numerical coefficients of 10 to 13, although sometimes the exact numerical value is in doubt because of weathering. Two of these coefficients are associated with the name or title Yax K'uk' Mo', and none has an identifiable Smoke-Jaguar Imix-Monster clause associated with it. Therefore, a corroboration of his position in the sequence as twelfth ruler is not possible on the basis of the valley group of stelae. No Smoke-Jaguar or Imix-Monster glyphs are present on CPN 30. In place of the twelfth ruler, a 5-k'atun glyph is found; this could be an age statement used as a descriptive title. However, Smoke-Jaguar Imix-Monster did not quite reach this age. He is recorded on CPN 22 as attaining

TABLE 9-6. The Structure of Smoke-Jaguar Imix-Monster's Name Phrase

Position	I				II	III		
Constituent signs	122	(563a)	204 128	(609b) (751) (Animal Head)	1031	122	1030	118 125
Decipherment	SMOKE	ts'i?		JAGUAR	?		toh?	

FIGURE 9-10. Smoke-Jaguar Imix-Monster's name phrase on CPN 22 (O2–Q1). Drawing by Elisabeth Wagner.

an age of sixty to eighty years, and I calculate that he lived seventy years, plus or minus two or three years. In no way do we attribute to him an age of over eighty years, which the 5-*k'atun* statement on CPN 30 implies.

DEEDS AND EVENTS DURING HIS REIGN. The most notable accomplishment of Smoke-Jaguar Imix-Monster's reign is the erection of the valley stelae: CPN 75, Stela A13 at Quebrada Seca, CPN 62, Stela A14 at Petapilla, CPN 61, CPN 57, and CPN 69, listed here in a general east-to-west sequence. This is remarkable not only as an engineering and sculpting feat, but also as a spatial design of six major landmarks (stelae with occasional altars added, and platforms constructed to accommodate them), where each (with one exception) is in direct visual contact with at least one other of the group, although at a considerable distance. This system covers approximately twenty kilometers of sightlines from Santa Rita to Hacienda Grande. It thus encompasses the entire valley of Copan and its piedmont, but its purpose is unknown, contrary to the eclectic explanation given by

many authors since Sylvanus Morley (1920: 133–134) discussed the meaning of the sight-line between CPN 61 and CPN 57 in terms of astronomical observations. The uniqueness of these stelae is reflected also in the reference of Yax K'uk' Mo', found prominently on several of them.

DEATH AND BURIAL. Tomb 1 at Copan contained a peccary skull carved with hieroglyphs and pictorial designs. It includes an opening Calendar Round Date of 1 Ahaw 8 Ch'en (Riese 1971:135). If this date is contemporaneous with the carving of the skull, only two Long Count positions are feasible for this date: 9.10.3.11.0 and 9.12.16.6.0. Of these, the latter is preferable for the following reasons. CPN 38, which mentions the same person (Decorated-Ahaw) as does the Peccary Skull, has its contemporary dates in *k'atun* 12 and has 9.13.0.0.0 as its last date (on the accompanying altar). The scene contained in the carved medallion of the Peccary Skull shows two persons sitting next to a stela-altar ensemble. The altar is shown as the head of a Cauac-Monster. According to

139

the Copan sculptural tradition, zoomorphic altars of this form and design came into use only about 9.14.0.0.0. Therefore, a date as close as possible to 9.13.0.0.0 and 9.14.0.0.0 should be preferred for the Peccary Skull text. For these two reasons, I feel fairly certain in placing the Peccary Skull Calendar Round date at 9.12.16.6.0 1 Ahaw 8 Ch'en. This date is followed by an anniversary expression pertaining to Decorated-Ahaw. The same person is mentioned on CPN 18 in connection with the dates 8.6.0.0.0 and 8.6.0.10.8, and I have tentatively identified him as the founder of the Copan dynasty, or at least a very early and important member of it (see above).

The date of the Peccary Skull is very close to the possibly last known date of the reign of Smoke-Jaguar Imix-Monster recorded on CPN 22 (9.12.16.7.8). It might therefore well be true that CPN 18 was the last monument erected to the aging king Smoke-Jaguar Imix-Monster, and that in its reference to Decorated-Ahaw, it alluded to a genealogical theme. The Peccary Skull was perhaps carved at the same time as grave furniture for Smoke-Jaguar Imix-Monster, and therefore makes the same allusion to genealogy as does the stela. The date of the Peccary Skull, thus, might be his death date, perhaps slightly contrived to correspond to an anniversary of an important date in his life. The slightly later Date A on CPN 22 might be the date of his burial, or a death-related ritual. Perhaps CPN 22 was commissioned after Smoke-Jaguar Imix-Monster's death by an otherwise undocumented Leaf-Jaguar the Younger. Admittedly, these suggestions are very speculative.

As previously discussed, the calculated birth date of Smoke-Jaguar Imix-Monster falls at about 9.9.0.0.0. This gives us his age at death as roughly seventy years (depending on which date we accept as the death date). He ruled Copan for about fifty-five years.

Eighteen-Rabbit

Eighteen-Rabbit (Fig. 9-11) was first pro-

FIGURE 9-11. Eighteen-Rabbit's name phrase on CPN 1 (B10–C11). Drawing by Elisabeth Wagner.

posed as a Copan ruler by Kelley (1962a:333, Fig. 7). The name Eighteen Kan-Dog assigned to him by Kelley has been used but rarely; instead, Eighteen-Jog and, from 1974 on, Eighteen-Rabbit are the names used in the current literature.

Table 9-7 gives a summary analysis of Eighteen-Rabbit's name phrase. It excludes the intimate incorporation of elements (e.g., T122) from the following title glyphs into the proper name. Some rare exceptions to the prevailing pattern and all doubtful identifications have also been disregarded.

Schele (1979b) proposed that the name glyph of Eighteen-Rabbit be read *umul,* signifying 'rabbit' in Quiche. In Copan inscriptions we find the pertinent substitution pattern. On CPN 158 (Step C: A), T758°281 is employed as a substitute for T511 to represent the day Muluc; this occurs also in the context of Glyph B of the Lunar Series. T511 and T513 are probably mere graphic variants. T287 is a reduplication of T511 or T513; so we can transcribe its variants as 511.511 and 513.513. The reduplication probably results from a lack of space; only an elongated space that does not accommodate these basically round signs is available, making it necessary to duplicate and put them next to each other. If this is the reason for the reduplication, it would not have any effect on the meaning and reading of the glyphs. In spite of this substitution pattern, the reading *umul* remains problematic; the association of the seventh day (here: Muluc) with the day that means 'rabbit' in other Mesoamerican calendars is

TABLE 9-7. The Structure of Eighteen-Rabbit's Name Phrase

Constituent signs	XVIII		4	1		287	110
	VIII	Head	23	204	758	281	
Decipherment	18		na	u	RODENT	mul	
	waklahun			umul			

weak, since 'rabbit' is the eighth day in the Aztec and Mixtec calendars. Apparently using the word *muluc* to designate the seventh day is an innovation of the Yucatec Maya. The seventh day is called *toh* in the calendar of other Maya Indians. The reading *umul* is, however, supported in part by the prefixes T1 and T204, which have an independently derived reading of *u*. Its actual position allows us to take it as a phonemic indicator of the morpheme, which we have read as *umul*. This phonemic redundancy might be necessary because several very similar or even identical heads, all represented by T758, are read as *bah* or *ch'o* (see Bricker 1986:135–138; Coggins, personal communication). The proper name of Eighteen-Rabbit, TXVIII.1.758°281, would thus be read completely as *wac lahuh umul* (Quiche) 'Eighteen Rabbit'.

BIRTH. No text gives direct information about Eighteen-Rabbit's birth. To reconstruct his birth date, in a previous study (Riese 1980), I used the *k'atun*-age statements, giving 9.12.0.0.1–9.12.14.17.19 as the range of time in which his birth could have occurred.

RELATIONSHIP WITH LADY TURTLE (?). The stelae designated as CPN 1 and CPN 16 face each other across the northern part of the Main Plaza in Copan and form a pair in terms of iconography and inscriptions (Proskouriakoff 1965:483–484). The most obvious interpretation of this pairing is that CPN 1 represents the ruler Eighteen-Rabbit and CPN 16, his wife. The naming of Eighteen-Rabbit's wife would accord with the pattern known from stela pairs and rows at Naranjo, Piedras Negras, and elsewhere. Unfortu-

nately, neither CPN 1 nor CPN 16 refers to kinship relations in their respective texts, nor has it been possible to classify definitely the supposed name phrase of the lady as such. An interpretation somewhat at variance with the one proposed here assumes the referent of this name to be CPN 16, the stela itself. Both interpretations could coincide, if the stela had been given the name of the person portrayed on it.

ACCESSION AND POSITION IN THE DYNASTIC SEQUENCE. The date triplet 8/8a/10—9.13.18.17.9 12 Muluc 7 Muwan—on CPN 158 bears the characteristics of an accession date (see Table 9-2). For chronological reasons, it can refer only to the accession of Eighteen-Rabbit. And, indeed, two (or three?) now-disconnected fragments of CPN 158 give his name. One of these has an additional accession glyph preceding Eighteen-Rabbit's name. These fragments very probably are part of the accession records originally connected with Dates 8, 8a, and 10. This accession date is in good accord with the calculated birth date of Eighteen-Rabbit, and he would have been twenty-four to thirty-eight years old at his accession. The earlier discussion of CPN 30 shows that Eighteen-Rabbit is Copan's thirteenth officially recognized ruler. Additional corroboration comes from the text of CPN 3, where he is associated with a 13-Hel glyph.

LIFE SPAN AND DEATH. Kelley (1962a) demonstrated that Two-Legged-Sky, ruler of neighboring Quirigua, captured Eighteen-Rabbit on 9.15.6.14.6 6 Cimi 4 Zec. Reports of this event are abundant at Quirigua. This event is also mentioned once at Copan, where it is associated with Dates 23 and 23a of CPN 158. We do not know whether Eighteen-Rabbit's capture concluded with his sacrifice at Quirigua; however, according to Lowland Maya cultural patterns, with their predilection for sacrifice, this seems plausible. The fact that only thirty-nine days after his capture, the next ruler, Three-Death, was inaugurated in Copan might support this hypothesis. Eighteen-Rabbit reached an age of between fifty-two and sixty-six years, and at his death had governed Copan for twenty-eight years.

Three-Death

The structure of Three-Death's name phrase (Fig. 9-12) is analyzed in Table 9-8. The first two positions give his personal name, which is unique in the corpus of Copan texts.

Position I represents the number 13 (*ox lahun*). Position II should be rendered something like Smoke-Jaguar Sun-God, or just Smoke-Sun-God. Together, both give a structurally acceptable Maya name, with a numerical part followed by an animate object: Thirteen Smoke-Sun God. Position III is composed of subposition IIIa, read *ah*, followed by IIIb, read *chan* 'heavens'; *ah chan* is a common title for Copan rulers. Position IV contains the title God K, 'storm/rain god', which is also a very common title of Copan rulers, preliminarily read as *toh* or *tohil*.

BIRTH. CPN 52 may contain the record of Three-Death's birth, but this is not certain. The God K$_2$ title glyph refers to the person born; in addition to Three-Death, his predecessor, Eighteen-Rabbit, and his successors also used this title. It is impossible to reconstruct his birth date, because we lack a *k'atun*-age statement.

ACCESSION AND POSITION IN THE DYNASTIC SEQUENCE. The group of dates 23b/26/28 of CPN 158 (Table 9-2) has the characteristic pattern of accession dates appropriate to this monument, once the fragments are reassembled in their proper order.

The dates are identical: 9.15.6.16.5 6 Chicchan 3 Yaxk'in. They are identified as accession dates by the accession glyph, and the person who acceded is named Three-Death. The same date is repeated on CPN 26*bis*. The next glyph, however, has not yet been identified as an accession glyph. The concluding name is that of Three-Death. Date A of CPN 30 is stated as the accession of Yax K'uk' Mo'. If we choose the Long Count position, 9.15.6.16.17, for the Calendar Round date, it will fall just twelve days after Three-Death's accession. It seems possible, therefore, that Yax K'uk' Mo' is used here as a title for Three-Death, whose accession festivities could well have extended over a span of twelve days.

The inscription on CPN 26*bis* combines a 14-Hel glyph with the name phrase of Three-Death. On CPN 30, the fourteenth ruler is depicted sitting on T122.1093? Smoke-Sun-God, which is the second part of Three-Death's name. These two independent instances thus do not contradict each other.

REIGN. The text on CPN 158 apparently gives quite detailed information on Three-Death's reign, although most of it cannot be retrieved because of the stairway's poor state of preservation and current confused order. CPN 30 seems to provide some information on the first part of Three-Death's reign, if we accept the proposed Long Count positions for the dates connected with him under the guise of Yax K'uk' Mo'. A third possible monument related to Three-Death is CPN 7. He might even have commissioned this monument to commemorate his predecessor, Eighteen-Rabbit, and placed it appropriately among the Plaza group of that ruler's stelae. However, this remains speculative reasoning, based solely on the dedicatory date of that monument and its death-related iconography. The text does not contain the name of Three-Death, but speaks only of Eighteen-Rabbit.

LIFE SPAN AND DEATH. Three-Death's death date is not known. He should have died shortly before the accession of the next

TABLE 9-8. The Structure of Three-Death's Name Phrase

Position	I			(II)				III			IV		
Constituent signs	III	1046	23	122	563P 1010 Head	109 5	(178)	683b 181	561 746	23	122	1030	142 178
Decipherment	ox	la-hun	na		SMOKE SUN GOD	la		ah	chan	na	toh		la

FIGURE 9-12. Three-Death's name phrase on CPN 26*bis* (24–29). Drawing by Elisabeth Wagner.

ruler, Smoking-Squirrel, at 9.15.17.13.10. If this is correct, then Three-Death reached an age of approximately forty-seven years and ruled Copan for eleven years.

Smoking-Squirrel

Smoking-Squirrel's personal name occupies position I of the name phrase (Fig. 9-13; Table 9-9). Kelley (1976:240, Fig. 83) read T528 + 528 in a nominal context at Naranjo as *kuk* (from *ku* + *ku*). The reading *ku* for T528 had been proposed earlier by Yuri Knorozov (1967:91), following Diego de Landa's (1959:706) alphabet. In many Mayan languages, *kuk* or a cognate (e.g., *kuk* in Quiche, *chuch* in Chol, and *ku'uk* in Yucatec) means 'squirrel'. For this ruler, mentioned on Naranjo Stela 32, Kelley was able to reinforce his reading through a substitution pattern where T528 + 528 is substituted by T758. T758 has for some time been recognized as representing a rodent or a rabbit:

squirrel, gopher (*bah*), mouse (*ch'o*), and rabbit (*umul* or *t'ul*) all were proposed as the species represented. The squirrel identification is thus reinforced and has been widely accepted.

The two elements of this glyph that represent the squirrel are the basis for naming this Copan ruler. To account for the prefix T122, the recent literature names him more correctly as Smoking-Squirrel. This still leaves T17, an element also invariably present in his personal name but unrepresented in the reading.

The reading of the first sign in the second position is straightforward, *ah*. It forms a phrase with the following signs, which are read as *chan*. The whole compound can be read as *ah chan* 'heavenly lord'. Since this expression is also found in the name phrases of other Copan rulers, it must be a title rather than a personal name.

The glyph in the third position represents God K in two slightly varying forms. This also

143

TABLE 9-9. The Structure of Smoking-Squirrel's Name Phrase

Position	I				II				III			IV
Constituent signs	122(563a)	17	528	528	(126)	181 683	561 748 746	23	122	1030a 1030d	142	Copan Emblem
Decipherment	SMOKE	yax	ku	ku	ah	ah	chan	na		toh		

FIGURE 9-13. Smoking-Squirrel's name phrase on CPN 24 (A7). Drawing by Elisabeth Wagner.

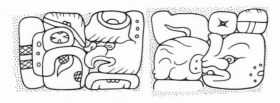

FIGURE 9-14. Rising-Sun's name phrase on CPN 37 (E1–F1). Drawing by Elisabeth Wagner.

is a title glyph, rather than a personal name, because it occurs quite regularly with all Late Classic Copan rulers. It might be read as *toh* or *tohil*.

The Emblem phrase is found in the fourth position. It consists of the Copan Emblem Glyph; sometimes, but rarely with this ruler, a *bakab* title glyph is added.

BIRTH AND ASCENDANCY. No text refers to the birth of Smoking-Squirrel. We should therefore try to calculate his birth date using the *k'atun*-age method (Riese 1980). The only two *k'atun*-age expressions associated with Smoking-Squirrel, both on CPN 158 (Steps 38:J, and 36:I), are not associated with any

date, and calculation of his birth date is not possible. A possible parentage statement on CPN 26*bis* refers to his father with an otherwise unknown name of a ruler of Copan. Thus, it remains unclear which ruler is meant.

ACCESSION AND POSITION IN THE DYNASTIC SEQUENCE. The date pair 11/11a on Steps 39 and 40 of CPN 158 contains a clear accession glyph associated with the date 9.15.17.13.10 11 Oc 13 Pop and the name phrase of Smoking-Squirrel. This paired statement corresponds to the accession pattern of the Hieroglyphic Stairway text, as discussed above. In the dynastic gallery of CPN 30, the fifteenth ruler of Copan sits on T122.?.17:528.528, which is the name glyph of Smoking-Squirrel (Fig. 9-1). Two Hel Counts are associated with Smoking-Squirrel's name on CPN 145 (Ap5–AP6) and CPN 141 (F'). Both agree in assigning him a Hel coefficient of 15, and they also agree with his position in the dynastic gallery on CPN 30. The complete agreement of evidence from three independent sources makes it certain that Smoking-Squirrel was considered the fifteenth official ruler of Copan. His accession date also conforms to this information, since it falls temporally between the fourteenth and sixteenth rulers' accessions.

DEATH AND BURIAL. No record of Smoking-Squirrel's death is preserved. We can only assume that he was dead before the next ruler, Rising-Sun, acceded to the throne on 9.16.12.5.17 6 Caban 10 Mol. His reign thus can be roughly calculated at fifteen years. It is possible that Smoking-Squirrel's tomb still lies undiscovered somewhere in Structure

144

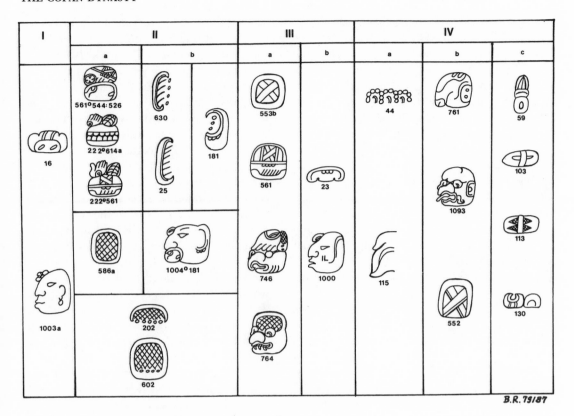

FIGURE 9-15. The structure of Rising-Sun's name phrase.

26, below the temple. This structure was investigated when the Hieroglyphic Stairway was restored during the 1940's and again during the 1980's; tunnels were dug into it to reveal its constructional sequence. However, the only tomb encountered during those excavations is much too early to be this ruler's.

Rising-Sun

Rising-Sun was the first Copan ruler discovered by modern investigations (Proskouriakoff 1960). He was first called Sun-at-Horizon and later New-Sun-at-Horizon; in Spanish his name has been rendered as Madrugada (Baudez 1983). In more recent publications, he is sometimes called Yax Pac. I call him Rising-Sun for reasons to be detailed below.

The structure of the name phrase is given in Figure 9-15. Position I is obligatory. It

contains two signs, T16 and T1003a, in a paradigmatic (substitutional) relation. It is well known from non-Copan texts that these are phonemically and semantically equivalent signs, to be read *yax*, meaning 'green, blue, fresh, new, strong' depending on the context.

Position II has a complicated structure with several subpositions. Subposition IIa contains two subgroups of paradigmatically related glyphs or signs. The first subgroup consists of glyphs which, although they vary somewhat, always contain a 'sky' sign (T561), a 'sun' sign (T544), and an 'earth' sign (T526), or some substitutes. Their placement in relation to one another in some cases is such that the sun seems to emerge or disappear between the sky and the earth (i.e., on the horizon). Because subposition IIa follows position I, this short clause must mean 'new

145

sun at horizon', specifying that sunrise is intended. This name clause has therefore been called Sun-at-Horizon, New-Sun-at-Horizon, or Rising-Sun. The second subgroup, of which T586 is the most common representative, is in a substitutional relation to the 'sun-at-horizon' glyph. It pictorially represents a net or netted bag. This picture also gives the clue to the reading: *paw* means 'net' in Yucatec Maya (Barrera Vásquez et al. 1980:635), to be discussed below.

Subposition IIb consists of two syntagmatic subgroups. T25, T630, and T1004°526 have a substitutional relation in subgroup 1, and T181 in subgroup 2. Graphically, this is not very evident, because T1004°526 and T181 are fused. T25 and T630 are simply graphic variants of each other. On the basis of ample evidence, they can be read as *ka* in Yucatec (*cha* in Chol). T1004°526 is a head with an infixed Caban sign in place of its mouth. If read phonemically, T526, the Caban sign, would result in *kab*, although it does not agree completely with the other two signs of this paradigmatic subgroup. The second syntagmatic subgroup here is T181, which is read *ah*.

We must now consider two signs, T202 and T602, which by themselves can stand in the second position without any further additions (or subpositions) as alternatives to the subpositions just discussed. Both contain a crosshatched central design and a row of dots on the lower fringe of the crosshatching. The crosshatching indicates the principal characteristic of T586 (*paw;* see above), and the row of dots indicates an incorporation of characteristic elements from T630, read *ka* (see above). Thus, these fused glyphs, T202 and T602, would be read as *pa(w)-ka,* according to the readings of the two constituent elements.

If all elements are taken together in their proper relationship, position II reads *pa(w)k* or *pa(w)ka(h).* Adding the established reading of position I to this, we get *yax pa(w)k* or *yax pa(w)kah.* This, indeed, as Floyd Lounsbury (personal communication) has shown, is very close to an expression for 'rising-sun' or 'dawn'. I therefore conclude that the personal

name of this ruler is Yaxpak or Yaxpakah, meaning 'Rising-Sun'; this can be rendered completely phonemically with syllabic signs, or in a mixed phonemic-iconic form.

Problems of morphological analysis remain to be resolved. If we consider the larger context of the following title glyph (see Fig. 9-15), the morphological analysis just discussed for position II is problematic. Essentially, there are three possibilities regarding the morphological placement of the *ah* element (T181). It can be considered the last syllable of the personal name, as suggested in the reading *yaxpak-ah,* or it can be considered the first part of the following title glyph, *ah-chan* (position III in Fig. 9-15). The second possibility is suggested by name phrases of other rulers, where we sometimes encounter the title *chan* with a prefixed *ah.* A third, but probably not very convincing, possibility in the specific context of Rising-Sun's name is to consider both the *ka* and the *ah* parts independent of either the personal name or the following *chan* title and to join them to form the title *kah.* This title has a precedent in other name phrases, where it is written either as *kah* or as the derivative *kahal* '(lord of) the town, city, territory'.

It would be premature to decide among these possibilities now. Likewise, it is premature to call this ruler by his real name, since its structure and exact spelling are still in doubt. Hence, there is a strong argument for conserving the traditional name Rising-Sun for the time being.

BIRTH. No direct statement of Rising-Sun's birth is preserved in the corpus of Copan texts. I therefore rely upon indirect evidence, using the *k'atun*-age method to calculate his birth date (Riese 1980:157–159). Basing my calculation on the three examples with securely fixed Long Count dates, I place his birth date between 9.15.12.6.3 and 9.16.0.0.0.

ASCENDANCY: HIS MOTHER, A LADY FROM PALENQUE. On CPN 55 (B6), a lady is identified by the Palenque Emblem Glyph at P2 as originating from that city, and she is linked

146

TABLE 9-10. The Structure of the Lady from Palenque's Name Phrase

Position	I	II				III	
Constituent signs	1000	110 16	533	102	515	1030	102
Decipherment	'lady'	'deceased'?				xok	

through a 'woman's child' relational glyph to Rising-Sun (Schele, Mathews, and Lounsbury 1982). This relationship strongly implies that she was married to a member of the Copan dynasty who probably was the father of Rising-Sun, but no parentage statement for Rising-Sun survives that could furnish positive evidence of this assumption. On CPN 34 she is stated to be the mother of another important male (?) person, Yahaw Chan Ah Baak (see discussion below).

Her name phrase (Table 9-10) is not easy to analyze because of the small sample available. In Position I the T1000 female classifier is encountered, which can be conveniently translated as 'lady'. Position II closely resembles the second and third part of the death statement first identified by Tatiana Proskouriakoff (1963; 1964) in Yaxchilan texts. Since the apparently decisive and constant first part is lacking, however, it is uncertain whether the same meaning applies here. If it is considered a death statement here, its integration into a name phrase is not surprising, since many Colonial examples in Highland Maya legal texts constantly use such an expression in connection with personal names. Position III is the head of the xok fish with a phonetic complement T102 to indicate the concluding consonant /k/. Xok is a known name for Classic Maya noblewomen, for which there is evidence at Yaxchilan.

Her own birth date can be roughly calculated from the dates in the life of her son, Rising-Sun, as falling into the interval from 9.13.10.0.0 to 9.14.10.0.0. No trace of her can be found in the inscriptions of Palenque, though. This is a result of the general lesser prominence given to females in genealogical accounts. On purely chronological grounds, she must have been of the same generation as Palenque rulers Chaacal III and Chac Zudz (= Chac Zutz' of Schele, Chapter 7 of this volume). She probably was an important member of the ruling lineage at Palenque; otherwise, she would not have been married to a member of the royal lineage of Copan, far to the east. Her importance is further, though indirectly, emphasized by the emergence of several Palenque-derived cultural and scientific patterns at Copan with the installation of her son there as royalty. Most of these patterns have been presented in an earlier publication (Riese 1988). One element pertaining to this pattern, which is not discussed in that publication, is connected with the greenstone mask with an inscription on the back (now housed in the British Museum in London). This mask was acquired in the middle of the nineteenth century in Comayagua, Honduras. As there are no known Maya ruins near that town, it is possible that a traveler or local inhabitant found the piece in the only Maya city of the region then known, Copan. The inscription on the back of this greenstone pendant mentions Pakal the Great from Palenque. Certainly, it was part of a hanging belt ornament worn by the elite, and it might have been inherited in the Palenque dynasty and passed from Pakal the Great to one of his descendants (Schele and Miller 1986:71, Pls. 21, 21a). As we have seen, the Lady from Palenque probably is a great-niece or granddaughter of Pakal. Thus, she could have kept this piece of jewelry as an heirloom when she married Rising-Sun of Copan. After her death, the mask might have been buried with her. If so, her burial could have been in one of the tombs excavated by Juan Galindo at the beginning of the nineteenth century in the East Court, which we have identified as the private residential and burial compound of her son, Rising-Sun. Although this is very speculative, the greenstone mask from Comayagua contains circumstantial evidence, which is easily interpreted in terms of this lady's biography.

Since both records possibly characterize her as deceased, her death must have occurred before the dedication of the earlier of the two monuments containing these records, that is, before 9.17.12.0.0, which is the dedicatory date of CPN 55. Since both limits of her life span are vaguely and hypothetically defined, the age she reached cannot be calculated at present.

RELATIONSHIP WITH SMOKING-SQUIRREL. Copan Valley Bench CV 43A records a relationship between Rising-Sun (G[right] –H?) and Smoking-Squirrel. The relational glyphs are to be sought in blocks I–K. The separation of Rising-Sun's name phrase from the relational clause is obscure, however. An heir-designation is represented in the iconography and possibly also mentioned in the text of CPN 26, which dates to the reign of his predecessor, Smoking-Squirrel.

RELATIONSHIP WITH YAX K'UK' MO'. Rising Sun is related to Yax K'uk' Mo' in the texts of CPN 30 and CPN 60. These texts are difficult to assess. If Yax K'uk' Mo' is a title used by different rulers, then this title could represent the ruler Three-Death on CPN 30, and Eighteen-Rabbit on CPN 60. If Yax K'uk' Mo' is considered the name of a specific person, it could be a mythical or real forebear, namely, an ancestor of the Rising-Sun lineage to which he pays homage.

ACCESSION AND POSITION IN THE DYNASTIC SEQUENCE. The accession of Rising-Sun at 9.16.12.5.17 6 Caban 10 Mol and its anniversaries are the most frequently given information in Copan texts. This reflects the facts that he commissioned the most monuments

and was the last active ruler of the city. We therefore know that Rising-Sun acceded to the lordship of Copan on the day 6 Caban 10 Mol, which corresponds to the Long Count position 9.16.12.5.17.

In three texts, Rising-Sun's name phrase contains a Hel-with-coefficient statement. In all three cases, the Hel coefficient is 16. On the west side of CPN 30, his accession date is written in abbreviated form as the Calendar Round date 6 Caban 10 Mol. This is embedded in the iconographic rendering of the Copan dynasty as discussed above. Conforming to this iconographic message and the Hel Count, Rising-Sun, seated on his name glyph T16.586.25:?, is pictured as the sixteenth and last ruler at the time this monument was carved.

DEATH AND BURIAL. No record of Rising-Sun's death or burial is known. This might be explained by two observations: in general, Copan lacks death statements of its rulers, and Rising-Sun was probably the last ruler at Copan before monumental inscriptions ceased to be recorded; perhaps no one remained to care about such a record. Nevertheless, architectural and iconographic research has advanced circumstantial evidence that Temple 18 is Rising-Sun's mortuary monument, and at least two of the sculptures associated with this temple, CPN 60 and CPN 31, might refer iconographically, and perhaps textually, to his death (Baudez 1983:2:493–494). His death date also has to be reconstructed from circumstantial evidence. The unique Long Count date inscribed on Temple 18 leads us to assume that his death occurred at about 9.18.5.0.0.

BUILDING ACTIVITIES. According to inscriptions associated with individual buildings and groups of buildings, two zones of general architectural activity stand out during Rising-Sun's reign. In the Main Group, the southern part of the acropolis around the East Court, and along the east and north sides of the West Court is such an activity zone. As Marshall Becker suggested (verbal communication to Claude Baudez), the East

Court group of buildings would have been the residential zone of Rising-Sun. Structures 21a, 22 (probably his official residence), and 18 and 19, which are connected with each other by the low platform Structure 17 and adjoining level areas, bear inscriptions that name him. Furthermore, there are several clearly identified residential structures, such as Structure 25 and late additions to the north side of Structure 16. Specialized buildings, a steam bath for example, also hint at the domestic nature of the buildings. Thus, the East Court ensemble would have contained all types of buildings necessary for the royal household and administration. Structure 11, dated somewhat earlier than the buildings surrounding the East Court, could have been the first building remodeled by Rising-Sun immediately after his accession and on later occasions. This would have been especially appropriate, since Rising-Sun's predecessor had an heir-designating monument (CPN 26) erected at the bottom of the stairway leading to Temple 11. If my assumption that 9.17.0.0.0 is the dedicatory date of that temple is correct, it would have taken seven years to complete, assuming that construction began immediately after accession of the new king.

The Western Court poses a problem. Except for Structure 12 and Temple 16, other buildings grouped around the Western Court are not associated with Rising-Sun. Could it be that he had not finished his building program here, but had only stated it with the remodeling of Structure 16 and by placing CPN 30 in front of its main stairway when death cut his efforts short?

The second major zone of architectural activity during Rising-Sun's reign lies to the east and northeast of the Main Group and is connected to it by a broad *sacbe*. Today, this group is called Las Sepulturas. It constitutes the second most important architectural group in the Copan Valley after the Main Group, judging from the size, masonry, and sculptural finish of its buildings. Four distinct Plaza Groups with hieroglyphic monuments name

Rising-Sun: the Grillo-Gasolinera Group, with the sculpted bench CPN 999; the CV 36 Group, from which, according to a hypothesis of William L. Fash (personal communication), CPN 101 might originate; the Structure 82 Group; and finally the CV 43 Group, with its hieroglyphic bench. These secondary groups of high rank would have been residences of persons associated with the ruler, or even related to him by kinship.

REMAINING PROBLEMS. A major problem with Rising-Sun's biography is the number of persons apparently mentioned during his reign, some of whom are associated with accession glyphs; thus, it is not clear whether his reign is to be considered a one-person rule or a system that allowed others to participate in the royal prestige. It is also possible that he was not the last ruler, but was succeeded by others, who connected their own accession reports with Rising-Sun.

CPN 34 mentions someone (Table 9-11) who acceded to the kingship at 9.17.9.2.12 3 Eb 0 Pop (Date F, at B3), and this accession is later celebrated with a 13-*haab* anniversary at 9.18.2.5.17 3 Caban 0 Pop, with his name repeated at P4. The remainder of this text refers to Rising-Sun, and also to this ruler's half-brother, Yahaw Chan Ah Baak. However, it is intriguing to compare the name phrase of the CPN 34 tertiary person with that of Rising-Sun. I have the strong impression that they are the same, but slightly varied through substitutions of equivalent signs. If this is correct, Rising-Sun acceded to some sort of supplementary royal office on the date mentioned here. On the whole, this reference to a third person in the text of CPN 34 remains problematic.

Yahaw Chan Ah Baak

Yahaw Chan Ah Baak (Fig. 9-16) was first reported and named by Schele and Grube (1987). The structure of his name phrase is analyzed in Table 9-12.

On CPN 34, Yahaw Chan Ah Baak is stated to be the son of the Lady of Palenque, who is

TABLE 9-11. The Structure of the Name Phrase of the Third Person on CPN 34

Constituent signs	16	672	142	178 683	126	Head	561	23
Decipherment	*yax*	RULER		*ah*	*ya*	?	*chan*	*na*

TABLE 9-12. The Structure of Yahaw Chan Ah Baak's Name Phrase

Position	I				II		III	
Constituent signs	282	126	683b	130	561c	23	12	1040
			168		561f 561c			
			128var					
Decipherment	?	*ya*	*ah*	*wa*	*chan*	*na*	*ah*	*baak*
			yahaw		*chan*			*chöm*

FIGURE 9-16. Yahaw Chan Ah Baak's name phrase on CPN 34 (I4–I5). Drawing by Elisabeth Wagner.

also the mother of Rising-Sun. His father is an otherwise undocumented person. The parentage statement of Yahaw Chan Ah Baak on CPN 34 gives his father's name as T1000:23 + 58or59.1:1070 + 60:1046. This makes it plausible that he was a half-brother of Rising-Sun, both born from one mother but from different fathers; the father of Yahaw Chan Ah Baak probably was the second husband of the Lady of Palenque, since Yahaw Chan Ah Baak seems to be considered younger than Rising-Sun, according to the dates associated with him. The monuments on which Yahaw Chan Ah Baak is mentioned date from 9.17.12.5.17 (CPN 33), 9.18.5.0.0 (CPN 34), and 9.18.10.0.0 (CPN 13). The last one seems to record his death. This corresponds to the second half of the reign of his elder half-brother, Rising-Sun.

Although Yahaw Chan Ah Baak was not a ruler of Copan, he apparently dedicated two monuments of his own, CPN 34 and CPN 33. These were found in the present village of Copan Ruinas, but when they were first reported, any possible association with ancient Maya buildings had been obliterated by modern construction work and the displacement of sculptures. Still, it is highly probable that these monuments were associated with a building complex at that site, since they are much too bulky to have been dragged to the village from far away.

SUMMARY OF THE COPAN DYNASTY

Table 9-13 correlates dynastic positions, names, and accession dates of all officially

TABLE 9-13. The Dynastic Sequence of Copan

Hel Number	Name	Accession or Time of Rule	
		Maya Date	Julian Date (A.D.)
1	Decorated-Ahaw or K'uk' Mo'	≈8.6.0.0.0	17 Dec 159
2	Tok'		
3	Ruler III		
4	Ruler IV		
5	Ruler V		
6	Ruler VI?		
7	Jaguar-Sun-God	≈9.4.10.0.0	22 Aug 524
8	Head-on-Earth	Before 9.6.10.0.0	25 Jan 564
9	?		
10	Cleft-Moon Leaf-Jaguar	9.5.19.3.0	22 May 553
11	Smoking-Heavens	9.7.5.0.8	15 Nov 578
12	Smoke-Jaguar Imix-Monster	9.9.14.17.5	3 Feb 628
——	Yax K'uk' Mo'	9.13.10.0.0	20 Jan 702
13	Eighteen-Rabbit	9.13.18.17.9	23 Nov 710
14	Three-Death	9.15.6.16.5	5 Jun 738
15	Smoking-Squirrel	9.15.17.13.10	12 Feb 749
16	Rising-Sun	9.16.12.5.17	26 Jun 763

recognized Copan rulers as of the date when CPN 30 was erected. A question mark after the Hel number indicates that the position in the dynastic sequence is insecure. A question mark in place of a name indicates that only the name glyph on CPN 30 has been identified so far, and a definitive name has not been assigned to that ruler. In cases in which accession dates are only approximate, the symbol ≈ or the word "before" precedes the date. Julian dates are calculated with the GMT correlation constant, 584,283.

The sequence presents some problems. In the section of rulers 7–10, one ruler remains to be identified, and the already-known rulers float among these numbers. In the section of Rulers 11–16, which seems complete, an interregnum from about 9.12.19.0.0 to 9.13.18.0.0 immediately precedes the accession of ruler 13. No officially recognized ruler is known for this period, but possibly a regent, Yax K'uk' Mo', was in charge. Table

9-13 does not reflect the situation during and after the reign of the sixteenth ruler either; others may have shared the rule with Ruler 16, and there may have been successors (e.g., Tok').

This fairly complete record of the Copan dynasty and the associated dates of the rulers enables us to extrapolate the date of its official founding, if we use approximate mean durations of reigns. According to my calculation, Copan's dynasty was founded in about 8.16.0.0.0, or 8.6.0.0.0 if Decorated-Ahaw is considered the founder and if the dates associated with him are considered historically correct. For other cities with similarly complete dynastic sequences, for example, Tikal and Yaxchilan, founding dates of local dynasties also cluster in the mid-to-late Baktun 8. It is possible that the concept of royalty with publicly displayed monuments was introduced into the Maya Lowlands from outside.

Architectural Activities

Each ruler seems to have chosen one of two architectural groups in which to concentrate his building program: either the Main Group or the present village of Copan Ruinas, formerly called Group 9. We do not yet know if the zone chosen by the ruler also contains his residential area and his tomb or burial. Until recently, Copan has been disappointingly poor in royal tombs in buildings, and archaeologists have not yet been very successful in locating residences of rulers and high-status persons or the places where their ritual, political, and economic activities took place. Exceptions are the discovery of the Sepulturas CV 36 group and the tentative identifications of the tombs of Smoke-Jaguar Imix-Monster, Rising-Sun, and the Lady of Palenque, which have been presented in this study.

Lacking at Copan is the clear pattern of monument-erection evident in the stelae rows in front of specific buildings that correlate with individual rulers at Piedras Negras (Proskouriakoff 1960) and Machaquila (Riese 1984a; 1988). Although the production of stelae and altars was more prolific at Copan than at many other Maya cities, they seem to be almost randomly distributed over the major activity zones. Only Eighteen-Rabbit followed a pattern when he erected his stelae in the Great Plaza; this pattern is repeated by his contemporary, Two-Legged-Sky, at Quirigua. Equally unrevealing has been the search for biography-related chronological sequences of iconographic themes depicted on stelae and other monuments.

Political and Social Events and Changes

The first political change or action that we can infer from the inscriptional record occurs during the reign of Smoke-Jaguar Imix-Monster. During this reign, the name of one Yax K'uk' Mo' appears conspicuously on some monuments. After Smoke-Jaguar Imix-Monster's death, a Yax K'uk' Mo' was apparently installed as ruler and held this position for eighteen years, but he was not included in

the official dynastic gallery on CPN 30 nor in the Hel Count of successive rulers. The most conspicuous monuments in Copan devoted to warfare are CPN 158 (the Hieroglyphic Stairway) and Temple 18. These show rulers in warrior costumes and prostrate captives, but no written information on warfare accompanies them, as is common at many other Maya cities. The only major hieroglyphic report of war that is related to Copan comes from neighboring Quirigua, where the defeat and capture of Copan ruler Eighteen-Rabbit is reported, and it is repeated on the Hieroglyphic Stairway at Copan.

Before his defeat, Eighteen-Rabbit had established a record of general political achievements in the text of CPN 1, which is comparable to only a few texts at Seibal and Tikal. The only other Copan ruler to boast of outside political ties and accomplishments is Rising-Sun. He had himself mentioned in the larger southeastern region, which he apparently dominated. Rising-Sun is also the only Copan ruler who we know had kinship ties with the outside world: his mother was a Lady from Palenque.

An important social change occurred at the end of Rising-Sun's reign: I would call it a general democratization, since it seems that other important persons, notably his half-brother Yahaw Chan Ah Baak and the lineage of calendar priests in the Sepulturas suburb (Webster 1989), were allowed to erect their own monumental palaces and inscriptions, although they were requested to mention the ruling king.

Intellectual History

The development and introduction of intellectual achievements at Copan during the Classic era—like the Long Count, certain additions to it, and their possible link with specific rulers—is documented in recent publications (Gaida 1990; Riese 1988) and will only be briefly summarized here. It appears that Smoke-Jaguar Imix-Monster (or his calendar priests) experimented with lunar astronomy. For half a century after his reign, little was added to the intellectual life of the city, and the few innovations cannot be linked to specific rulers. Only the last ruler, Rising-Sun, started experimenting again with the calendar. During his reign, the massive production of sculpture, hieroglyphic inscriptions, and buildings might mean that the number of people participating in the intellectual and artistic life of Copan increased and that leaders were eager to borrow innovations from prestigious foreign locales.

The Demise of Copan

A challenging question remains unanswered, since the comprehensive view of Copan's Late Classic history has not yet been related to broader issues of Maya cultural and social history: How are we to explain the demise of Classic-period culture at Copan? This demise seems to have overcome the Copan polity quite suddenly, after a peak in cultural activity and only a few decades of decline. It is marked by the successive cessation of dynastic reports, hieroglyphic texts in general, masonry architecture, and local polychrome ceramic production (Copador wares), with a concomitant decline in population.

ACKNOWLEDGMENTS

This article benefited greatly from cooperation with Claude F. Baudez on all aspects of Maya iconography, architecture, and religion, since our joint fieldwork in Copan began in 1977. Victoria R. Bricker has encouraged me in writing this article, and her indirect contribution through repeated commentaries is acknowledged. Help in translation into English was offered by Cynthia Kristan-Graham, and most drawings were faithfully and skillfully executed by artists Anke Blanck and Elisabeth Wagner.

10. The Middle American Calendar Round

MUNRO S. EDMONSON

THE INTENT OF this chapter is to give a summary account of the count of the solar year by the peoples of Middle America. It will deal with three principal aspects of their calendrics: (1) how their solar calendar relates to our Gregorian one, (2) how it was written, and (3) how it developed. Detailed documentation of these points has already been published (Caso 1967; Edmonson 1988a) and is accordingly omitted here, as it would expand the present summary to book length. Nonsolar calendars, such as the Olmec-Maya Long Count, and calendars generated during the Colonial period are likewise largely omitted.

Nearly sixty linguistic groups eventually came to share the solar cycle that has come to be called the Calendar Round (Nahuatl *xiuhmolpilli*, Maya *hunab*). This is a time count that combines cycles of $13 \times 20 = 260$ days (Nahuatl *tonalpohualli*, Maya *tzolkin*) and of $18 \times 20 + 5 = 365$ days (Nahuatl *xihuitl*, Maya *haab*). The 260-day cycle, or day count, was used to name both the days and the 365-day years, and the name days of the year were generally conceived as "year bearers," deities who bore the burden of time. All the numerals of the cycle of thirteen (Spanish *trecena*) and (in any given calendar) four of the numeral names of the cycle of twenty (Spanish *veintena*) could be used to name the year, in a permutative count that repeated itself after $13 \times 4 = 52$ years of 365 days each. It is this 52-year cycle that is called the Calendar Round, and it was central to the religious and social organization, as well as to the solar astronomy of Middle America.

The years of the Calendar Round were named either for the initial day (as in Yucatan) or for what was considered to be the final day, that is, the 360th (as in Tenochtitlan). In either case, the name day was considered to be the year bearer. The name of the first day recurs as the name of the 261st day, and the name of the 360th day is anticipated on the 100th day of the year. To specify a day within the year, therefore, it was sometimes necessary to specify its location within the $18 \times 20 + 5 = 365$-day count. This was usually done by numbering or naming the 18 "months," as well as the final "month" of 5 days. Zapotec, for example, did both. Often the 20 days of these months were also enumerated, either from 0 to 19, as in Zapotec, or from 1 to 20, as

154

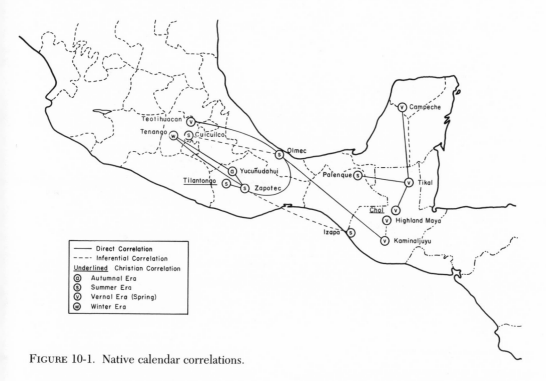

FIGURE 10-1. Native calendar correlations.

in Nahuatl.

Although the numerology of all this can get complicated, it should in principle be a simple matter to correlate a date in the Middle American Calendar Round with a date in the Julian or Gregorian calendar. In practice, it has not proved to be so. Many Middle American dates are fragmentary or difficult to read, and many European correlations are obscured by errors in the counting of leap years. Despite these difficulties, a single correlation is sufficient to place the two systems with respect to each other. The capture of Cuauhtemoc on 1 Serpent 3 Uo Tikal (13 August 1521 Julian) is such a correlation (Sahagún 1970–1982:12: 122; Cortés 1963:189).

The oldest of the Middle American calendars cannot be directly compared with European time. They can, however, be related to one another because of the frequent occurrence of correlational inscriptions, citing the date in two or more calendars. Most commonly, these are year bearer dates. They pro-

duce two networks of intercorrelations, focusing on the Zapotec and Tikal calendars, and illustrated in Figure 10-1. As luck would have it, the Zapotec and Tikal calendars can in turn be correlated with other calendars that can be directly related to the European ones. Thus, for example, the calendar of Teotihuacan is correlated with that of the Olmec, which is correlated with Zapotec, which is correlated with Tilantongo Mixtec, which is correlated with Julian. The Palenque calendar is correlated with that of Tikal, which survived among the Colonial Chol and is directly correlated with Gregorian. Thus the new year's dates (and year bearers) of even the oldest Middle American calendars can be fixed in European chronology.

Most of the remaining Preconquest calendars can be directly correlated with the Christian calendars. Many of them are intercorrelated by native inscriptions as well, thus confirming their placement. There are perhaps three degrees of certainty to the assign-

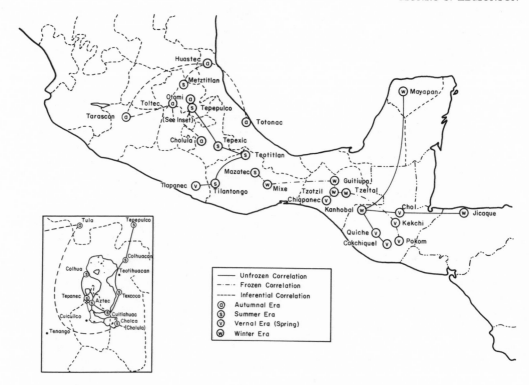

FIGURE 10-2. Christian calendar correlations.

ment of new year's dates in these calendars. The most satisfactory case is a contemporary and readable date in the native and European systems. These are the dates listed as "unfrozen" in Figure 10-2. In most cases, they are multiply attested.

But the confusion introduced by the European leap year also resulted in "frozen" correlations. It is not clear whether this was originally a native or a Spanish aberration, but the effect was to freeze the European calendar to the native one (or vice versa) at a particular date and to cease counting leap-year days thereafter. In most cases, this appears to have occurred directly after 29 February 1548 Julian. (The Mixe calendar correlation may have been frozen by 1531, and the Mazatec correlation as late as 1616.) As Figure 10-2 indicates, frozen correlations are the only data we have for the placement of the calen-

dars of Mazatec, Mixe, Guitiupa, Chiapanec, Tzotzil, Tzeltal, Kekchi, and Pokom. A number of other groups also used the frozen 1548 correlation, but can be independently directly correlated in unfrozen time. Perhaps the most consequential case is the famous one-day error in Diego de Landa's documentation of the calendar of Mayapan (Landa 1966:71).

The most problematic correlational difficulties are presented by the Cholula, Toltec, Tarascan, Huastec, Totonac, and Metztitlan calendars. I have described their placement (in Fig. 10-2) as "inferential." The inference rests on a combination of calendrical and geographical considerations, but in all cases we simply need more data. That there were Classic (or, in the case of Metztitlan, Postclassic) calendars in these areas is beyond question, but clinching calendrical correlations are simply lacking.

The evidence for the Classic-period calendars in question is almost entirely epigraphic. Central and northern Anahuac used no less than eight writing systems: those of Totonac, Huastec, Tarascan, Toltec, Cholula, Xochicalco, Yucuñudahui, and Teotihuacan. Although there is some degree of correspondence in their glyphs for the twenty days of the *veintena*, each system is distinguished by at least one unique glyph. They may have had a common numeral canon, involving a bar for the number 5, though that is not always attested. While we cannot assume automatically that a different writing system implies a different calendar (Xochicalco's script differs notably from the Ñuiñe script of Yucuñudahui, but they shared the same calendar), there would seem to be some plausibility to the idea.

A degree of corroboration is provided by a series of Postclassic calendars that appear to bear a regular transformational relationship to the problematic members of this group. In each case, the new year of the Postclassic calendar is one hundred days earlier than that of the Classic one (Table 10-1).

Although there may have been some relationship among ethnic, linguistic, calendrical, and writing systems, it was certainly not a one-to-one correspondence. A single calendar was written in several writing systems (Olmec), and a single script served several calendars (Maya); a single ethnic group used several calendars (Nahua) or more than one writing system (Zapotec); and a single writing system could be used by different ethnic groups (Tilantongo). Furthermore, the manner in which these various systems developed is clearly different. In what follows, only the manner of writing Calendar Round dates is considered.

The writing systems of ancient Middle America are markedly regional. As Figure 10-3 indicates, the data suggest the relatively autonomous development of four regions: (1) West, (2) Central, (3) South, and (4) East. Of course, there were contacts and areas of

TABLE 10-1. Classic-Postclassic Calendrical Correspondences

Classic	Postclassic
Yucuñudahui	Chalca
Cholula	Tepexic
Toltec	Colhuacan
Tarascan	Tepanec
Huastec	Cuitlahuac
Totonac	Teotitlan

overlap between regions, particularly between the Olmec, on the one hand, and Zapotec, Teotihuacan, and Maya, on the other. And the Late Postclassic expansion of the Nahuas may have spread awareness of their Tilantongo script to all four regions.

The West Mexican region is the least well documented, and the least securely defined geographically. It has generally been considered a frontier area, and its only known writing system was Tarascan. This appears to have been in use from Middle or perhaps Early Classic times, and probably recorded dates only in the Classic Tarascan calendar. By the time of the Conquest, this calendar had been replaced by the Tepanec one, but we do not know how Tepanec dates were written in Michoacan.

The Central region is more complex. It is probably best defined by the Classic Teotihuacan writing system, though that fact is very far from being adequately documented. There are, nonetheless, reasons to believe that the Teotihuacan writing system was known from Tampico to Veracruz and throughout the modern state of Guerrero, as well as in the intervening highland areas. It was eventually replaced successively by the Yucuñudahui (Classic) and Tilantongo (Postclassic) scripts and, more locally, by the Late Classic scripts of Totonac, Huastec, Tula, Cholula, and Xochicalco. The approximate areas involved are indicated in Figure 10-3. The area comprising Puebla, Tlaxcala, Morelos, the State of Mexico, and the Federal District also used

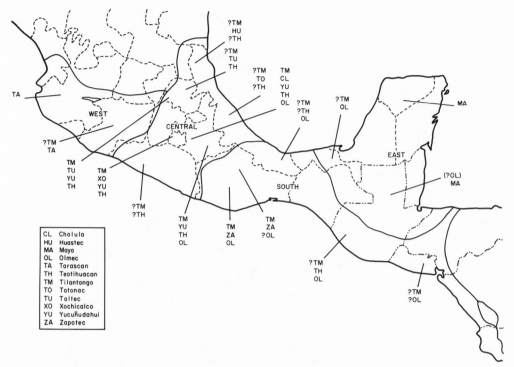

FIGURE 10-3. Calendar script distributions. In each column, the earliest script is at the bottom and the latest at the top.

Olmec script in Preclassic and Classic times.

The region of the South was primarily Olmec and Zapotec territory as far as writing is concerned, and all of the earliest inscriptions and calendrical dates come from this area and in these scripts. There is also direct evidence of the Teotihuacan writing system in Chiapas and Guatemala in the Preclassic period, and there is good reason to suppose that the entire area may have been exposed to the Tilantongo-Nahua script as far south as Costa Rica in the Postclassic, though direct evidence is lacking. Northern Oaxaca is an area of overlapping Olmec and Zapotec influence.

The region of the East wrote in Maya, though the predominantly Maya area of eastern Chiapas and the Guatemalan Peten appears to have been exposed to the Olmec script as well during the Classic period.

The glyphs used for writing the names of the twenty days of the *veintena* are illustrated, where known, in Figure 10-4, in thir-

teen Middle American systems of calendrical writing. Only the Tilantongo and Maya systems can be considered complete and secure; a number of the others can only be described as fragmentary. Although a number of the glyphs have a strong pictographic component, their use as day signs is primarily ideographic: taken together, they constitute a vigesimal number system. The English day names are translations of the Nahuatl names. Some of the same signs were sometimes used logographically, as in Nahuatl personal and place names, or syllabically, as in Maya texts, but not in calendrical contests.

The manner of writing Calendar Round dates was subject to some variation. Minimally, it required one glyph naming the year and marked as such with a year sign, accompanied by a numerical coefficient. Such an inscription can be read as referring to the first day of the first month (e.g., in Maya) or the last day of the eighteenth month (e.g., in

158

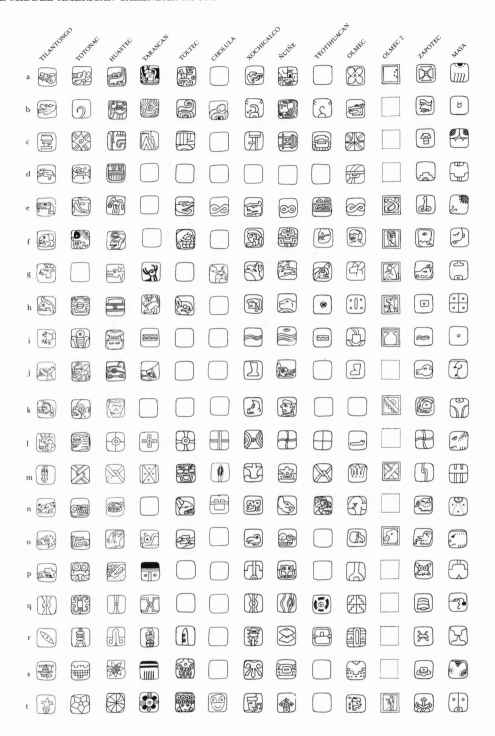

FIGURE 10-4. The day names in thirteen Middle American scripts.

Nahuatl), and is thus a unique date within the fifty-two-year cycle. To specify any other day of the year requires a second coefficient and glyph, identified as a day name (usually by omission of the year sign), and unless that day falls only once in the given year, it must be placed in one of the named (or numbered) nineteen months. The number of the day within the month may also be specified, though that is redundant.

The Mayan calendar of Tikal is the best established and most convenient reference point. Its nineteen month names are unequivocal and their order is fixed (which is not true even of Aztec). Hence, the simplest way of relating all the calendars to one another is to list the dates of their New Year's days in the Tikal calendar. Arbitrarily, I shall use the reference year 1549–1550, when the Tikal year began on 6 Wind 0 Pop, 14 July 1549 Julian. (This date corresponds to a correlation constant of 584,283; it is 11.16.9.15.2 in the Mayan Long Count.)

Table 10-2 gives all the information needed for translating a date in any one of these calendars into any other, within the framework of the Tikal calendar. Certain additional complications, having to do with the handling of numbers, are involved in accurately reading and interpreting the original inscriptions. Not only did the various scripts have different ways of marking the year; they also had different ways of writing numerals. In Zapotec, for example, both 1 and 5 were marked by the depiction of a finger: if the fingernail is indicated, it means 1; if not, it means 5. In the remaining Preclassic and Classic writing systems, the numerals from 1 to 4 were written as dots; 5 and multiples of 5 were written with horizontal (or sometimes vertical) bars. In all of the Postclassic writing systems, numerals were indicated by dots alone.

There were variations in the placement of the numerals as well. Zapotec, Yucuñudahui, and Xochicalco placed the numerical coefficient below the day sign to which it referred and read the signs from right to left and from top to bottom. In the remaining Preclassic

and Classic systems, the coefficients were placed vertically to the left of the day sign or horizontally above it. The order of reading was left to right or top to bottom.

A final complication is that the calendars of Teotihuacan and the Tlapanec (and they alone) counted the day count from 2 to 14 instead of from 1 to 13. Thus, the Tlapanec new year 5 Deer in Figure 10-2 would have been written 6 Deer in Tlapanec, and the Teotihuacan New Year's date of 1 Wind would have been 2 Wind in a Teotihuacan inscription.

The numerological relationships among the differing calendars provide internal evidence that they were part of a single historical system, which was designed from its inception to enable its users to place themselves in a larger cycle of time by comparing their new year's dates with actual observations of the quarters of the solar year: the solstices and equinoxes.

There is reason to believe that the very earliest calendars made an erroneous calculation of the length of the solar cycle, but with the calendar of Kaminaljuyu they landed on the correct calculation: that it took exactly 29 Calendar Rounds of 52 years each for the 365-day calendar to fall one full year behind the sun. In other words, $29 \times 52 = 1,508$ (years of 365 days each) $= 1,507$ (years of 365.2422 days each). The latter calculation is the modern estimate of the length of the tropical year, but the priests of Kaminaljuyu knew that millennia before Europe did: their calendar was presumably inaugurated at the spring equinox of 433 B.C.

The Kaminaljuyu calendar and its derivatives were keyed to the spring equinox. Earlier calendars had been tied to the summer solstice, and families of later calendars chose to link themselves to the winter solstice or the autumnal equinox. I am not able to document how the experts kept track of which of the four cycles they were related to, but it would have been a simple matter to make that datum unforgettable through ritual symbolism we have not yet decoded, and I would suppose that was how it was done.

The European attitude toward the discrep-

TABLE 10-2. The New Year's Days of Middle America in 1549–1550

Calendar	New Year	Other Users
Tikal*	6 Wind 0 Pop	(Chol*, Kekchi*)
Palenque	7 House 1 Pop	(Tarascan*)
Mayapan*	8 Iguana 2 Pop	(Campeche)
Toltec*	1 House 1 Uo	
Cholula*	8 House 1 Zip	
Teotihuacan*	1 Wind 0 Zotz'	
Yucuñudahui*	2 House 1 Zotz'	
	(Tzec)	(No calendar)
Highland Maya*	7 Deer 5 Xul	(Calendar D)
Mixe*	8 Rabbit 6 Xul	
Colhua	9 Water 7 Xul	
Olmec	13 Death 4 Yaxkin	
Kaminaljuyu*	1 Deer 5 Yaxkin	
Jicaque*	2 Rabbit 6 Yaxkin	
Metztitlan	3 Water 7 Yaxkin	
Cuicuilco	7 Death 4 Mol	
Izapa	8 Deer 5 Mol	
Zapotec	9 Rabbit 6 Mol	(Chatino)
Tilantongo	10 Water 7 Mol	(Chocho, Tlaxcalan)
Tzotzil*	3 Rabbit 6 Ch'en	(Chinantec)
Texcoco	4 Water 7 Ch'en	
Tzeltal*	10 Rabbit 6 Yax	
Aztec	11 Water 7 Yax	(Mazatec)
Lachixola	4 Rabbit 6 Zac	
Otomi	5 Water 7 Zac	(Tepepulco)
Cakchiquel*	10 Deer 5 Ceh	
Guitiupa*	11 Rabbit 6 Ceh	
Teotitlan	12 Water 7 Ceh	(Pipil)
Istacostoc*	5 Rabbit 6 Mac	(Colonial)
Cuitlahuac	6 Water 7 Mac	
Mitontic*	12 Rabbit 6 Kankin	(Colonial)
Tepanec	13 Water 7 Kankin	(Matlatzinca)
Tlapanec*	5 Deer 5 Muan	
Cancuc*	6 Rabbit 6 Muan	(Colonial)
Colhuacan	7 Water 7 Muan	
Chiapanec*	12 Deer 5 Pax	
Tepexic	13 Rabbit 7 Pax	(Huexotzinco)
Quiche*	6 Deer 5 Kayab	(Aguacatec*, Ixil*, Mam*, Pokom*)
Kanhobal*	7 Rabbit 6 Kayab	(Chuh*, Jacaltec*)
Chalca	8 Water 7 Kayab	(Tenango*)
Huastec*	1 Rabbit 6 Cumku	
	(Uayeb)	(No calendar)

*In those calendars marked with an asterisk, the new year's date given is also the year bearer; in all other cases, the year bearer falls on the 360th day of the year. Note that all dates are cited in the *Tikal* Calendar Round, in which the count of days of the month begins with zero (see Edmonson 1988a: 7).

ancy between a 365-day year and the true solar year was to introduce (add) occasional
leap-year days to bring the calendar abreast
of the apparent movement of the sun. The
Middle Americans took the opposite approach: their aim was predictive. They were
concerned with knowing in advance when
the 1,507-year solar cycle was destined to
end. They therefore took advantage of occasional religious and political pretexts to erase
the 1,508th year by moving their new year's
dates *backward* in 20-day increments (i.e., in
a direction opposite to the European leap-
year corrections). Eventually, they would
have to erase 18 months of 20 days each plus
the 5 final days of the 1,508th year. The moti-
vation to introduce such a correction was almost certainly politico-religious, but in every
case it seems to have been governed by a
commonly shared astronomical awareness: it
was timed correctly to the solar cycle.

To introduce any change in the calendar
was an act of political and religious schism. It
was accomplished in one of three ways: (1) by
moving the date of the new year back twenty
days; (2) by moving the date of the new year
forward one day; or (3) by a more complicated maneuver that included moving the
date of the new year back five days. The first
of these eliminates one of the eighteen months
of the astronomically erroneous 1,508th year
mentioned earlier. The third eliminated the
nineteenth (five-day) month. (This was done
independently only by the Teotihuacan and
Tikal calendars.) In the corrected Kaminaljuyu calendar and its derivatives, the one-day
advance was used to change the reference
date of the solar cycle from a solstice to the
preceding equinox or from an equinox to the
preceding solstice. On the evidence, none of
these changes were ever made until the arrival of the correct astronomical date for
making them.

The application of these transformational
principles enables us not only to reconstruct
the evolution and differentiation of the
Middle American calendar, but also to calculate the absolute (astronomical) dates of its bi-

TABLE 10-3. The Longest-Lived Calendars

Calendar	Duration (years)
Olmec	2,100
Zapotec	2,000
Tikal	1,600
Quiche	1,600
Tarascan	1,300
Huastec	1,200
Totonac	1,200
Toltec	1,200
Chiapanec	1,200
Teotihuacan	1,100
Otomi	1,100
Aztec	1,100
Texcoco	1,100

furcations. This calendrical genealogy is illustrated in Figure 10-5. In general terms, the
figure documents the operation of cultural
drift: occasional and seemingly random "mu-
tations" have resulted in a progressive differentiation of the system.

On closer inspection, there are a number
of instances in which particular calendrical
changes appear to have been influenced by
other cultural processes as well. Some calendars have manifested a marked resistance to
change, whereas others have been subjected
to important diffusional and acculturational
pressures.

At least thirteen of the calendars can be
shown to have endured without change for
more than a millennium. They are listed in
Table 10-3. Many of these (and perhaps a
number of others) might well have continued
longer, had it not been for the Spanish Conquest. Only the Quiche calendar is still intact
today. The prevalence of this kind of longev-
ity would seem to suggest that calendrical
change was not primarily intrasystemic or lineal, but rather a way of symbolizing ethnic
difference.

In the first phase of its development, the
Middle American calendar may be docu-
mentable at Cuicuilco as a Summer Era calendar with a new year at 4 Mol (Tikal). It

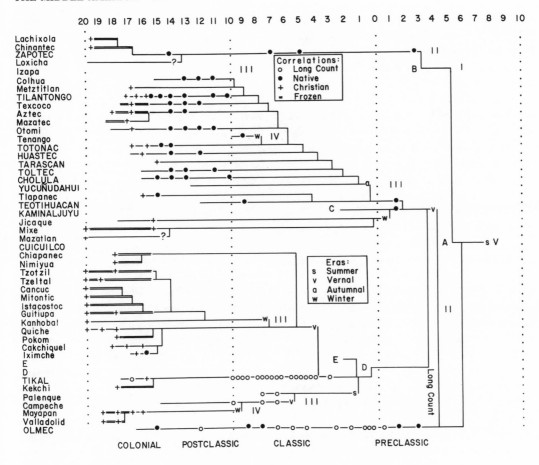

FIGURE 10-5. Calendrical genealogy (year bearers in Roman numerals).

counted the days of the months from 0 to 19 and placed its year bearer on the 360th day of the year. It was presumably inaugurated at the summer solstice of 739 B.C. The ethnic or linguistic identity of Cuicuilco is unknown, but it is not unreasonable to guess that it was non-Zoquean. Thus, when the calendar was transmitted to the Olmec, it may have crossed a cultural boundary. The Olmec signaled the difference by setting their new year back twenty days in 656 B.C.

The further diffusion of the calendar to Izapa from Cuicuilco in 520 B.C. may also have involved ethnic difference, but again we have no way of knowing. It was not mediated by the Olmec; so the route of contact may have been through Oaxaca. The distance, however, makes a cultural contrast highly likely. The effect was the establishment of a new Summer Era calendar by the advancement of the Cuicuilco new year by one day. (That the count of the era was not changed meant the perpetuation of the erroneous calculation of the cycle, mentioned above.) The Izapans may have been distinct from the Zapotecs as well as from the people of Cuicuilco. In any case, two centuries later the Zapotecs established their own Summer Era calendar by a further one-day advance in the date of new year (305 B.C.).

In the meantime, the Olmec calendar had spread from Puebla and Veracruz to Chiapas and Guatemala, and in 433 B.C. it produced its own progeny: the calendar of Kaminaljuyu. It advanced the Olmec new year by one day, established a new Spring Era, and moved the year bearers to the first day of the year. This was a momentous technical achievement, as has been described, but it may have been motivated also by the fact that the people of Kaminaljuyu were non-Zoquean—Xinca perhaps?

The immediate northwestern neighbors of the site of Kaminaljuyu were almost certainly the Highland Maya, and they may have been responsible for the otherwise hypothetical Calendar D of 350 B.C., generated by subtracting twenty days from the Kaminaljuyu new year.

Also present in Kaminaljuyu, at least by a century or so later, were the people of Teotihuacan, whose ethnic identity is also obscure and whose calendar is an ingenious transformation of that of Kaminaljuyu, inaugurated in 165 B.C. It moved the Kaminaljuyu new year from 5 Yaxkin to 0 Zotz'. It is documented in Guatemala and Chiapas and in several parts of Central Mexico, but the geographical connection between the two areas has not been traced. The evolution of the writing systems suggests to me that the language of Teotihuacan may have been Mixtec (Edmonson 1988b), though I do not think this conclusion is yet secure.

By this time, the Zoquean languages were probably distributed from Veracruz through Chiapas to southern Guatemala. They may have been in direct contact with Lenca or Jicaque as well as Kaminaljuyu. In any case, the Jicaque calendar was generated in 57 B.C. as a Winter Era calendar by advancing the Kaminaljuyu new year by one day, and the Mixe calendar was generated in A.D. 26 by subtracting twenty days from that. It is possible that each of these transformations crossed an ethnic/linguistic boundary (e.g., from Xinca [Kaminaljuyu] to Lenca [Jicaque] to Mixe). We would still appear to be missing one transformation (from Lenca to Jicaque), but there are many other instances in which the calen-

dar has crossed a cultural boundary *without* changing.

Whatever the linguistic identification of Teotihuacan may prove to be, its calendar is closely linked to the Mixtec calendar of Yucuñudahui, an Autumnal Era calendar generated in A.D. 42 by a one-day advance from the Teotihuacan new year. (The Mixtec abandoned the 2 to 14 enumeration of the day count at the same time.) The Yucuñudahui calendar was known and used at Teotihuacan. If its separation from the calendar of that site were ethnically motivated, that would imply that Teotihuacan may have spoken a language other than Mixtec.

In A.D. 85 the Highland Maya passed the calendar to the Lowland Maya, originating the calendar of Tikal. Like the transformation that initiated the calendar of Teotihuacan, this one was complex, but both involved a "Uayeb subtraction": both were motivated by deletion of the nineteenth month (of five days) from the supernumerary, 1,508th year of the solar cycle. This moved the Calendar D (Highland Maya) new year from 5 Xul to 0 Pop.

By A.D. 177 the Tikal calendar was probably generally shared by the Yucatecan and Cholan Maya of the Lowlands. But the transformation involved in the Palenque calendar of that year may imply some outside pressure as well. Palenque was close to the Olmec (Zoquean) frontier. Although its aberrant calendrical usage never became the standard even at Palenque itself, it followed Olmec usage in adopting the Summer Era and the terminal naming of the year (for its 360th day). This may have been a combination of Cholan (Chontal and northern Chol) nationalism and Olmec influence, but even so it remained a secondary calendar.

After the Preclassic—indeed, from 350 B.C. on—the genealogy of the Middle American calendars divides at the Isthmus of Tehuantepec, and subsequent developments east and west of that frontier appear to be largely independent. For clarity, I shall deal first with the east.

The Highland Maya of Chiapas and Guatemala switched to the Quiche calendar in A.D. 395 by moving the date of the new year back forty days from that of Tikal. They also distanced themselves from the Lowlanders by abandoning the 0 to 19 count of the days of the month. Of all of the Highland peoples, only the Kekchi, and perhaps the Chorti, remained on Tikal time. At this point, all of the Mayan peoples shared Spring Era calendars except for the occasional use of the Palenque calendar in the Usumacinta valley.

The Chiapanecs had a common frontier with the Chiapas Maya, and in A.D. 478 borrowed their calendar, distancing themselves at the same time by moving the date of the new year back twenty days, but retaining the other features of the Quiche calendar.

Western Yucatan and Campeche inaugurated the Campeche calendar in A.D. 568. Like the Palenque calendar from which it was seemingly derived, it was a secondary and occasional usage. Since it seems to have involved terminal naming of the year, it can be seen as a Zoquean-influenced change, but such an influence was probably secondhand—via the Chontal and northern Chol. The Campeche calendar advanced the Palenque new year by one day, making it a Spring Era calendar, like those of the other Maya peoples.

The calendars of the Cuchumatanes and Highland Chiapas separated from the Quiche calendar of Guatemala in A.D. 768 by advancing the Quiche new year by one day to create the new Winter Era calendar of Kanhobal. Substantial ethnic and linguistic differences separated the two areas, but they were both internally diverse as well, and it is not clear why the calendrical rift should have occurred along the Mam-Kanhobal border. The fact that the change was to a Winter Era could have been Mixe influence, implying perhaps that the change was initiated in Chiapas, rather than in Guatemala.

The Mayapan calendar of A.D. 937 was apparently derived from the Campeche calendar by a one-day advance in the date of the new year (producing a new Winter Era), and a simultaneous return to initial counting, placing the year bearers on the first day of the year. It appears not to have been formally initiated, however, until A.D. 1539, two years before the founding of Spanish Merida. By that time the calendar was a bone of contention between the Xiu and the Itza, but whether there was an ethnic dimension to its genesis is not clear. The growing Nahua influence on the western frontier may have been involved.

It was not until A.D. 1182 that the Tzeltalans (Tzeltal and Tzotzil) divorced themselves from the Kanhobal calendar with the calendar of Guitiupa. More than inter-Mayan ethnic differentiation may have been involved, as the Guitiupa new year sets that of Kanhobal a full one hundred days back. The choice of this date may have been influenced by the Teotitlan new year (one day later), since there may have been a substantial Nahuatl presence on the northern Chiapas frontier by the twelfth century, and their calendar was that of Teotitlan.

The occupation of coastal Chiapas by Pipils may have had something bearing on the genesis of the Tzeltal calendar in A.D. 1348, moving the Guitiupa new year back forty days so that it fell on the day before the Aztec new year. We have no independent proof that the Pipils of Chiapas were on the Aztec calendar, but the dates fit fairly well. The Tzotzils moved the new year date back an additional twenty days to produce their own calendar in A.D. 1431.

A final Mayan calendrical schism on the eve of the Spanish Conquest produced the Cakchiquel calendar, probably in A.D. 1480. The Cakchiquels had come under heavy influence from the Guatemalan Pipils, who were on the Teotitlan calendar, which may explain why they moved the Quiche new year back one hundred days, to land just two days before the Teotitlan new year. The date of the change, however, was clearly motivated by Quiche-Cakchiquel political rivalry rather than by calendrical considerations.

Ethnic relations to the west of the Isthmus

of Tehuantepec were considerably more complex than those to the east. There was greater linguistic diversity and there were more volatile population movements. The Classic period was marked by the diversification of the calendars of Teotihuacan and the Yucuñudahui Mixtec.

The Teotihuacan calendar may have attained some degree of currency throughout the Central region (see Fig. 10-3), particularly in the Early Classic. It was gradually replaced in much of the region by the calendar of Yucuñudahui and its derivatives and disappeared in the Late Classic, leaving only one direct descendant: the Tlapanec calendar of A.D. 415. This was derived by setting back the Teotihuacan new year seven months (140 days). It remained a Spring Era calendar and continued to count the day count from 2 to 14.

The remaining Classic period calendars were derived from that of Yucuñudahui. The Cholula calendar of A.D. 125 is problematic and ethnically unidentified. It seems most likely to have represented an Otomanguean-speaking group.

The Toltec calendar is equally problematic because its new year cannot be placed with certainty. Although I have hypothesized its inauguration in A.D. 208, a more plausible guess is that its new year was one hundred days earlier and its founding four hundred years later (A.D. 622). This would make it a direct ancestor of the Aztec calendar and identify it with Nahuatl speakers.

The remaining Classic calendars are more satisfactory. Each is generated by moving the new year back twenty days from the calendar before, and each involves passing the calendar to a new ethnic group: Tarascan (A.D. 291), Huastec (A.D. 373), and Totonac (A.D. 456). All of these calendars maintain the Autumn Era of Yucuñudahui, count the month days from 0 to 19, and name the years for the first day.

These calendars also imply population movements. Direct contact between Tarascan and Huastec is a surprise, but seems to be indicated for the fourth century, perhaps

in the area of Guanajuato. Similarities in certain day names and day glyphs appear to reflect an equally surprising direct contact between Tarascan and Totonac. This is underscored by the genesis of the Tenango calendar of A.D. 772, which advanced the Totonac new year one day to establish a Winter Era calendar, the only one in Central Mexico. At that date, therefore, there may have been Totonacs in the western State of Mexico, as well as in Puebla and Veracruz. The fact that the Tenango calendar moved to the Winter Era also suggests the possibility of Mixe influence.

Additional Classic-period calendars are possible, but remain undocumented: Proto-Otomi in A.D. 539 (Totonac new year minus twenty days), Proto-Aztec (Toltec?) in A.D. 622 (Proto-Otomi new year minus twenty days), Proto-Texcoco in A.D. 705 (Proto-Aztec new year minus twenty days), Proto-Tilantongo in A.D. 788 (Proto-Texcoco new year minus twenty days), Proto-Metztitlan in A.D. 870 (Proto-Tilantongo new year minus twenty days), and Proto-Colhua in A.D. 953 (Proto-Metztitlan new year minus twenty days). Each of these may have involved contrastive ethnic affiliations, albeit perhaps only minimally in the case of Aztec and Texcoco.

The Tilantongo Mixtec calendar of A.D. 988 marks the watershed between the Classic and the Postclassic in Central Mexico. It reflects a one-day advance from the Zapotec new year and the simultaneous change to counting month days from 1 to 20. It retains the Zapotec Summer Era and the terminal placement of the year bearers, and it eventually generated no less than twelve Postclassic calendars, all of them Nahuatl, differing only in their initial months, but otherwise structurally identical.

The ethnic implications of the Postclassic Nahuatl calendars are sometimes problematic; the Colhua (Nahuatl?), Cuitlahuac (Huastec?), Colhuacan (Nahuatl?), and Chalca (Mixtec?) calendars are particularly so. The remaining eight are at least geographically clear: Metztitlan (Northern Otomi), Tlaxcalan

(Nahuatl), Texcoco (Nahuatl), Aztec (Nahuatl), Tepepulco (Otomi), Teotitlan (Totonac), Tepanec (Tarascan), and Tepexic (Mixtec).

The genealogical construal of Middle American calendrical history demonstrates lineal continuities, but it also appears to show that the transmission of calendrical ideas from one ethnic group to another was an important motivator for calendrical change. Almost all of the structural changes seem to appear in this context. At the same time, there are numerous cases in which a single calendar is shared by a number of linguistically and ethnically differentiated peoples: the calendar has frequently crossed ethnic boundaries without changing. Not all ethnic differences become confrontational, but in historical Middle America, those that did were likely to be symbolized in calendrical differences. Despite the all-but-universal acceptance of technical and astronomical constraints, the history of the calendar is a history of ethnically oriented religious and political relations as well.

BIBLIOGRAPHY

ACUÑA, RENÉ
1984 (ed.) *Relaciones geográficas del siglo XVI*, vols. 2–3: *Antequera*. Instituto de Investigaciones Antropológicas, Serie Antropología 58. Mexico City: Universidad Nacional Autónoma de México.

ADAMS, RICHARD E. W.
1978 Routes of Communication in Mesoamerica: The Northern Guatemalan Highlands and the Peten. In *Mesoamerican Communication Routes and Cultural Contacts*, edited by Thomas A. Lee, Jr., and Carlos Navarrete. Papers of the New World Archaeological Foundation, no. 40:27–35. Provo, Utah.

ALVARADO, FRANCISCO DE
1962 *Vocabulario en lengua mixteca*. Edited by Wigberto Jiménez Moreno. Mexico City: Instituto Nacional Indigenista and Instituto Nacional de Antropología e Historia. (Facsimile copy of 1593 document.)

ANALES
Cuauhtitlan
1938 *Die Geschichte der Königreiche von Colhuacan und Mexico*. Translated by Walter Lehmann. Quellenwerke zur alten Geschichte Amerikas, no. 1. Stuttgart and Berlin: Kohlhammer. (Reprinted, 1974.)

Tlatelolco
1939 Unos annales históricos de la nación mexicana. Edited by Ernst Mengin. *Baessler-Archiv* 23:69–168.

ANDERS, FERDINAND, AND MAARTEN JANSEN
1988 *Schrift und Buch im alten Mexiko*. Graz: Akademische- Druck u. Verlagsanstalt.

ATTANASI, JOHN J.
1973 Lak T'an: A Grammar of the Chol (Mayan) Word. Ph.D. dissertation, Department of Linguistics, University of Chicago.

AUBIN, JOSEPH MARIUS ALEXIS
1885 *Mémoires sur la peinture didactique et l'écriture figurative des anciens mexicains*. Mission scientifique au Mexique et dans l'Amérique Centrale: Recherches historiques et archéologiques, part 1: Histoire. Paris: Imprimerie Nationale.

AULIE, H. WILBUR, AND EVELYN W. DE AULIE
1978 *Diccionario ch'ol-español, español-ch'ol*. Serie de Vocabularios y Diccionarios Indígenas Mariano Silva y Aceves, no. 21. Mexico City: Instituto Lingüístico de Verano.

BARLOW, ROBERT H.
1946 Materiales para una cronología del imperio de los mexica. *Revista Mexicana de Estudios Antropológicos* 8:207–215.

169

1961 El palimsesto de Veinte Mazorcas. *Revista Mexicana de Estudios Antropológicos* 17:99–110.

BARRERA VÁSQUEZ, ALFREDO, JUAN RAMÓN BASTARRACHEA MANZANO, WILLIAM BRITO SANSORES, REFUGIO VERMONT SALAS, DAVID DZUL GÓNGORA, AND DOMINGO DZUL POOT
1980 *Diccionario Maya Cordemex: Maya-Español, Español-Maya*. Merida: Ediciones Cordemex.

BATRES, LEOPOLDO
1902 *Exploraciones de Monte Albán*. Mexico City: Casa Editorial Gante.

BAUDEZ, CLAUDE F.
1983 (ed.) *Introducción a la arqueología de Copán, Honduras*. 3 vols. Tegucigalpa: Proyecto Arqueológico Copán and Secretaría de Estado en el Despacho de Cultura y Turismo.

BAUDEZ, CLAUDE F., AND PETER MATHEWS
1979 Capture and Sacrifice at Palenque. In *Tercera Mesa Redonda de Palenque*, edited by Merle Greene Robertson and Donnan Call Jeffers, pp. 31–40. Palenque, Chiapas: Pre-Columbian Art Research Center.

BAUDEZ, CLAUDE F., AND BERTHOLD RIESE
1990 Sculpture of Copan. Microfilm Collection of Manuscripts on Cultural Anthropology, no. 381, series 73. Chicago: University of Chicago Library.

BERLIN, HEINRICH
1958 El glifo "emblema" en las inscripciones mayas. *Journal de la Société des Américanistes* [n.s.] 47:111–119.
1959 Glifos nominales en el sarcófago de Palenque. *Humanidades* 2(10):1–8.
1960 Más casos del glifo lunar en números de distancia. *Antropología e Historia de Guatemala* 12(2):25–27.
1963 The Palenque Triad. *Journal de la Société des Américanistes* [n.s.] 52:91–99.
1968 The Tablet of the 96 Glyphs at Palenque, Chiapas, Mexico. In *Archaeological Studies in Middle America*, pp. 135–150. Middle American Research Institute, Tulane University, pub. 26. New Orleans.
1975 El texto del sarcófago, y su relación con otros textos palencanos. Unpublished.
1977 *Signos y significados en las inscripciones mayas*. Guatemala City: Instituto Nacional del Patrimonio Cultural de Guatemala.

BERLIN, HEINRICH, AND ROBERT H. BARLOW
1948 *Anales de Tlatelolco*. Fuentes para la Historia de México 2. Mexico City: Porrúa, Antigua Librería Robredo.

BERNAL, IGNACIO, AND ANDY SEUFFERT
1973 *Esculturas asociadas del Valle de Oaxaca*. Corpus Antiquitatum Americanensium 6. Mexico City: Instituto Nacional de Antropología e Historia.
1979 *The Ballplayers of Dainzú*. Translated by Carolyn B. Czitrom. Graz: Akademische Druck- u. Verlagsanstalt.

BEYER, HERMANN
1937 *Studies on the Inscriptions of Chichen Itza*. Carnegie Institution of Washington, pub. 483, contribution 21. Washington, D.C.

BIERHORST, JOHN
1985 *A Nahuatl-English Dictionary and Concordance to the Cantares Mexicanos: With an Analytic Transcription and Grammatical Notes*. Stanford: Stanford University Press.

BLOM, FRANZ, AND OLIVER LA FARGE
1926 *Tribes and Temples*, vol. 1. New Orleans: Tulane University.

BOONE, ELIZABETH HILL
1983 *Codex Magliabechiano and the Lost Prototype of the Magliabechiano Group*. Berkeley and Los Angeles: University of California Press.

BOOS, FRANK H.
1966 *The Ceramic Sculptures of Ancient Oaxaca*. London: Thomas Yoseloff; South Brunswick, N.J.: A. S. Barnes.

BRICKER, VICTORIA R.
1985a Noun Incorporation in the Dresden Codex. *Anthropological Linguistics* 27(4):413–423.
1985b The Use of Logosyllabic Principles of Writing in *The Book of Chilam Balam of Chumayel*. *International Journal of American Linguistics* 51(4):351–353.
1986 *A Grammar of Mayan Hieroglyphs*. Middle American Research Institute, Tulane University, pub. 56. New Orleans.
1987 Abbreviation Conventions in the Maya Inscriptions and the Books of Chilam Balam. *Anthropological Linguistics* 29(4):425–438.
1989 The Last Gasp of Maya Hieroglyphic Writing in the Books of Chilam Balam of Chumayel and Chan Kan. In *Word and*

Image in Maya Culture: Explorations in Language, Writing, and Representation, edited by William F. Hanks and Don S. Rice, pp. 39–50. Salt Lake City: University of Utah Press.

BRICKER, VICTORIA R., AND HARVEY M. BRICKER

1988 The Seasonal Table in the Dresden Codex and Related Almanacs. *Archaeoastronomy* 12:S1–S62. (Supplement to *Journal for the History of Astronomy* 19.)

BRUSH, JOHN E., AND HOWARD E. BRACEY

1955 Rural Service Centers in Southwestern Wisconsin and Southern England. *Geographical Review* 45:559–569.

BURGOA, FRANCISCO DE

1934 *Geográfica descripción*. 2 vols. Publicaciones del Archivo General de la Nación, nos. 25–26. Mexico City: Talleres Gráficos de la Nación. (Reproduction of 1674 ed.)

BURLAND, C. A.

1960 The Map as a Vehicle of Mexican History. *Imago Mundi* 15:11–18.

BYLAND, BRUCE E., AND JOHN M. D. POHL

1987 The Marriage of 12 Wind and 3 Flint at White Hill. *Thesis* 2(1):10–17.

CALNEK, EDWARD E.

1982 Patterns of Empire Formation in the Valley of Mexico, Late Postclassic Period, 1200–1521. In *The Inca and Aztec States, 1400–1800: Anthropology and History*, edited by George A. Collier, Renato I. Rosaldo, and John D. Wirth, pp. 43–62. New York: Academic Press.

CARLSON, JOHN B.

1977 Copán Altar Q: The Maya Astronomical Congress of A.D. 763? In *Native American Astronomy*, edited by Anthony F. Aveni, pp. 100–109. Austin: University of Texas Press.

CARRASCO, PEDRO

1984 Royal Marriages in Ancient Mexico. In *Explorations in Ethnohistory: Indians of Central Mexico in the Sixteenth Century*, edited by H. R. Harvey and Hanns J. Prem, pp. 41–81. Albuquerque: University of New Mexico Press.

CASO, ALFONSO

1928 *Las estelas zapotecas*. Monografías del Museo Nacional de Arqueología, Historia, y Etnografía. Mexico City: Talleres Gráficos de la Nación.

1946 Calendario y escritura de las antiguas culturas de Monte Albán. In *Obras completas de Miguel Othón Mendizábal* 1:113–143. (Reprinted in 1947 as a separate monograph with new pagination. Mexico City: Cooperativa Talleres Gráficas de la Nación.)

1949 El mapa de Teozacoalco. *Cuadernos Americanos* 8:145–181.

1957 Lienzo de Yolotepec. *Memoria de El Colegio Nacional* 3(4):41–55.

1960 *Interpretación del Códice Bodley 2858*. Mexico City: Sociedad Mexicana de Antropología.

1961 Los lienzos mixtecos de Ihuitlan y Antonio de León. In *Homenaje a Pablo Martínez del Río*, pp. 237–274. Mexico City.

1964 *Interpretación del Códice Selden 3135 (A. 2)*. Mexico City: Sociedad Mexicana de Antropología.

1965a Sculpture and Mural Painting of Oaxaca. In *Handbook of Middle American Indians*, vol. 3, edited by Robert Wauchope and Gordon R. Willey, pp. 849–870. Austin: University of Texas Press.

1965b Zapotec Writing and Calendar. In *Handbook of Middle American Indians*, vol. 3, edited by Robert Wauchope and Gordon R. Willey, pp. 931–947. Austin: University of Texas Press.

1965c Mixtec Writing and Calendar. In *Handbook of Middle American Indians*, vol. 3, edited by Robert Wauchope and Gordon R. Willey, pp. 948–961. Austin: University of Texas Press.

1966 The Lords of Yanhuitlan. In *Ancient Oaxaca*, edited by John Paddock, pp. 313–335. Stanford: Stanford University Press.

1967 *Los calendarios prehispánicos*. Instituto de Investigaciones Históricas, Serie Cultura Náhuatl, monograph 6. Mexico City: Universidad Nacional Autónoma de México.

1977 *Reyes y reinos de la Mixteca [I]*. Mexico City: Fondo de Cultura Económica.

1979 *Reyes y reinos de la Mixteca II: Diccionario biográfico de los señores mixtecos*. Mexico City: Fondo de Cultura Económica.

CASO, ALFONSO, AND IGNACIO BERNAL

1952 *Urnas de Oaxaca*. Memorias del Instituto Nacional de Antropología e Historia 2. Mexico City.

171

CHADWICK, ROBERT
1971 Native Pre-Aztec History of Central Mexico. In *Handbook of Middle American Indians*, vol. 11, edited by Robert Wauchope, Gordon F. Ekholm, and Ignacio Bernal, pp. 474–504. Austin: University of Texas Press.

CHIMALPAHIN, FRANCISCO DE SAN ANTÓN
1965 *Relaciones originales de Chalco-Amaquemecan.* Translated by Silvia Rendón. Biblioteca Americana, Serie de Literatura Indígena. Mexico City: Fondo de Cultura Económica.

CLOSS, MICHAEL P.
1985 The Dynastic History of Naranjo: The Middle Period. In *Fifth Palenque Round Table, 1983*, edited by Merle Greene Robertson and Virginia M. Fields, pp. 65–77. San Francisco: Pre-Columbian Art Research Institute.

CODICES
Azoyú 1
Original classified with no. 35–108 in the Biblioteca Nacional de Antropología e Historia, Mexico City.
Azoyú 2
Original classified with no. 35–109 in the Biblioteca Nacional de Antropología e Historia, Mexico City.
Becker, *see* Colombino-Becker
Bodley 2858
1960 *Interpretación del Códice Bodley 2858*, by Alfonso Caso. Mexico City: Sociedad Mexicana de Antropología.
Borbonicus
1974 *Codex Borbonicus, Bibliothèque de l'Assemblée Nationale, Paris (Y120).* Commentaries by Karl A. Nowotny and Jacqueline de Durand-Forest. Graz: Akademische Druck- u. Verlagsanstalt.
Boturini
1964 In *Antigüedades de México basadas en la recopilación de Lord Kingsborough*, edited by José Corona Núñez, 2:7–29. Mexico City: Secretaría de Hacienda y Crédito Público.
Chimalpopoca
1945 *Códice Chimalpopoca: Anales de Cuauhtitlán y Leyenda de los soles.* Translated by Primo Feliciano Velázquez. Instituto de Historia, Universidad Nacional Autónoma de México, pub. no. 1. Mexico City: Imprenta Universitaria.

Colombino-Becker
1961 *Codices Becker I/II.* Commentary by Karl A. Nowotny. Codices Selecti 4. Graz: Akademische Druck- u. Verlagsanstalt.
1966 *Interpretación del Códice Colombino*, by Alfonso Caso. Glosses by Mary Elizabeth Smith. Mexico City: Sociedad Mexicana de Antropología. (Facsimile copy.)
Cruz
1981 *Codex en Cruz.* Edited by Charles E. Dibble. 2 vols. Salt Lake City: University of Utah Press.
Egerton 2895
1965 *Codex E 2895.* Introduction by C. A. Burland. Codices Selecti 7. Graz: Akademische Druck- u. Verlagsanstalt.
Ixtlilxochitl
1976 *Codex Ixtlilxochitl: Bibliothèque Nationale, Paris (MS. mex. 65–71).* Commentary by Jacqueline de Durand-Forest. Graz: Akademische Druck- u. Verlagsanstalt.
Kingsborough
1912 *Códice Kingsborough: Memorial de los indios de Tepetlaoztoc al monarca español contra los encomenderos del pueblo*, edited by Francisco del Paso y Troncoso. Madrid: Hauser y Menet.
Magliabechiano
1983 *Codex Magliabechiano and the Lost Prototype of the Magliabechiano Group*, by Elizabeth Hill Boone. Berkeley and Los Angeles: University of California Press.
Mendoza
1925 *Colección de Mendoza; o, Códice Mendocino*, edited by Jesús Galindo y Villa. Mexico City: Museo Nacional.
1964 In *Antigüedades de México basadas en la recopilación de Lord Kingsborough*, edited by José Corona Núñez, 1:1–149. Mexico City: Secretaría de Hacienda y Crédito Público.
Nuttall
1987 *Codex Zouche-Nuttall.* Foreword by Ferdinand Anders; introduction by Nancy P. Troike. Codices Selecti 84. Graz: Akademische Druck- u. Verlagsanstalt.

Osuna
1976   *Pintura del gobernador, alcaldes y regi-
        dores de México*, vol. 2: *Estudio y trans-
        cripción por Vicenta Cortes Alonso.*
        Madrid: Ministerio de Educación y Ci-
        encia, Dirección General de Archivos y
        Bibliotecas.

Selden 3135 (A.2)
1964   *Interpretación del Códice Selden 3135
        (A.2)*, by Alfonso Caso. Mexico City: So-
        ciedad Mexicana de Antropología.

Sierra
1982   *Códice Sierra: Traducción al español de
        su texto náhuatl y explicación de sus pin-
        turas jeroglíficas por el doctor Nicolás
        León.* Mexico City: Museo Nacional de
        Arqueología, Historia e Etnografía.

Telleriano Remensis
1964   In *Antigüedades de México basadas en la
        recopilación de Lord Kingsborough*, ed-
        ited by José Corona Núñez, 1:151–337.
        Mexico City: Secretaría de Hacienda y
        Crédito Público.

Tudela
1980   *Códice Tudela.* 2 vols. Prologue by Don-
        ald Robertson; epilogue by Wigberto
        Jiménez Moreno; illustrations by Ferdi-
        nand Anders and S. Jeffrey K. Wilker-
        son. Madrid: Ediciones Cultura His-
        pánica del Instituto de Cooperación
        Iberoamericana.

Vaticano Latino 3738
1964   In *Antigüedades de México basadas en
        la recopilación de Lord Kingsborough*,
        edited by José Corona Núñez, 3:7–343.
        Mexico City: Secretaría de Hacienda y
        Crédito Público.

Codex Vaticanus 3738
1979   *Codex Vaticanus 3738.* Graz: Akade-
        mische Druck- und Verlagsanstalt.

Vindobonensis Mexicanus 1
1974   *Codex Vindobonensis Mexicanus 1.* In-
        troduction by Otto Adelhofer. Codices
        Selecti 5. Graz: Akademische Druck- u.
        Verlagsanstalt.

Xolotl
1980   *Códice Xolotl*, edited by Charles E.
        Dibble. 2d ed. 2 vols. Instituto de Inves-
        tigaciones Históricas, Serie Amoxtli 1.
        Mexico City: Universidad Nacional Au-
        tónoma de México.

COE, MICHAEL D.
1973   *The Maya Scribe and His World.* New
        York: Grolier Club.

COGGINS, CLEMENCY C.
1975   Painting and Drawing Styles at Tikal: An
        Historical and Iconographic Reconstruc-
        tion. Ph.D. dissertation, Department of
        Fine Arts, Harvard University. Ann Ar-
        bor: University Microfilms (76-03783).

CORDAN, WOLFGANG
1963   *Introducción a los glifos mayas, sistema
        de Mérida.* Merida: Universidad de
        Yucatán.

CÓRDOVA, JUAN DE
1886   *Arte en lengua zapoteca*, edited by
        Nicolás León. Morelia: Imprenta del
        Gobierno.
1942   *Vocabulario castellano-zapoteco.* Intro-
        duction by Wigberto Jiménez Moreno.
        Instituto National de Antropología e His-
        toria, Biblioteca Lingüística Mexicana 1.
        Mexico City. (Facsimile of 1578 original.)

CORTÉS, HERNÁN
1963   *Cartas y documentos.* Mexico City:
        Porrúa.

CRUZ, VICTOR DE LA
1983   *Genealogía de los governantes de Zaa-
        chila.* Oaxaca: Unidad Regional Oa-
        xaca, Dirección General de Culturas
        Populares.

DAHLGREN DE JORDÁN, BARBRO
1979   *La Mixteca: Su cultura e historia prehis-
        pánicas.* Oaxaca: Ediciones del Gobierno
        Constitucional del Estado de Oaxaca.

DAKIN, KAREN
1983   Consideraciones lingüísticas de los nom-
        bres de lugar del Códice Azoyú 1. In *Pri-
        mer Coloquio de Documentos Pictográ-
        ficos de Tradición Náhuatl.* Mexico City:
        Instituto de Investigaciones Históricas,
        Universidad Nacional Autónoma de
        México. In press.
1986   El náhuatl del Códice Azoyú 1 y el
        Lienzo de Tlapa. In *Primer Coloquio de
        Arqueología y Etnohistoria del Estado
        de Guerrero*, pp. 311–317. Mexico City:
        Instituto Nacional de Antropología e
        Historia and Gobierno del Estado de
        Guerrero.

DAVIES, NIGEL
1973   *The Aztecs: A History.* London: Mac-
        millan.

173

DAVOUST, MICHEL
1976 *Etude épigraphique 1: Les chefs mayas de Copan, Palenque, et un ancien glyphe emblème.* Angers.
1978 *Etude épigraphique 3: Les glyphes nominaux individuels et titres des chefs mayas.* Angers.

DE ARA, DOMINGO
1986 *Vocabulario del lengua tzeldal según el orden de Copanabastla,* edited by Mario Humberto Ruz. Instituto de Investigaciones Filológicas, Centro de Estudios Mayas, Fuentes para el Estudio de Cultura Maya 4. Mexico City: Universidad Nacional Autónoma de México.

DELGADO, ALONSO
1904 *Relación de los obispados de Tlaxcala, Michoacan, Oaxaca, y otros lugares en el siglo XVI.* Documentos Históricos de Méjico 2. Mexico City: Luis García Pimentel.

DEMAREST, ARTHUR A.
1986 *The Archaeology of Santa Leticia and the Rise of Maya Civilization.* Middle American Research Institute, Tulane University, pub. 52. New Orleans.
1989 Ideology in Ancient Maya Cultural Evolution: The Dynamics of Galactic Polities. MS on file, Department of Anthropology, Vanderbilt University, Nashville.

DIBBLE, CHARLES E.
1960 Spanish Influence of [on] the Aztec Writing System. In *Homenaje a Rafael García Granados,* pp. 171–177. Mexico City: Instituto Nacional de Antropología e Historia.
1971 Writing in Central Mexico. In *Handbook of Middle American Indians,* vol. 10, edited by Robert Wauchope, Gordon F. Ekholm, and Ignacio Bernal, pp. 322–332. Austin: University of Texas Press.

DURBIN, MARSHALL E.
1969 An Interpretation of Bishop Diego de Landa's Maya Alphabet. In *Philological and Documentary Studies,* vol. 2. Middle American Research Institute, Tulane University, pub. 12:169–179. New Orleans. (Issued as bound volume in 1977.)

EDMONSON, MUNRO S.
1988a (ed.) *The Book of the Year: Middle American Calendrical Systems.* Salt Lake City: University of Utah Press.
1988b Some Implications of Middle American Writing Systems. Paper presented at the 46th International Congress of Americanists, Amsterdam.

FERNÁNDEZ, MIGUEL ANGEL
1954 Drawings of Glyphs of Structure XVIII, Palenque, with notes by Heinrich Berlin. *Carnegie Institution of Washington, Notes on Middle American Archaeology and Ethnology,* no. 119, 5:39–44. Cambridge, Mass.

FONDS MEXICAIN 20
Ms. in Bibliothèque Nationale, Paris.

FOX, JAMES A., AND JOHN S. JUSTESON
1980 Mayan Hieroglyphs as Linguistic Evidence. In *Third Palenque Round Table, 1978, Part 2,* edited by Merle Greene Robertson, pp. 204–216. Austin: University of Texas Press.
1984 Polyvalence in Mayan Hieroglyphic Writing. In *Phoneticism in Mayan Hieroglyphic Writing,* edited by John S. Justeson and Lyle Campbell. Institute for Mesoamerican Studies, State University of New York at Albany, pub. no. 9:17–76.

FREIDEL, DAVID A., AND LINDA SCHELE
1989 Tlaloc-Venus Warfare and the Triumph of the Confederacy at Chichen Itza. Paper presented at the 54th Annual Meeting of the Society for American Archaeology, Atlanta.

FURST, JILL LESLIE
1978 *Codex Vindobonensis Mexicanus I: A Commentary.* Institute for Mesoamerican Studies, State University of New York, pub. no. 4. Albany.

GAIDA, MARIA
1990 Die kulturelle und politisch-ökonomische Stellung Copans im Maya-Gebiet in der klassischen Zeit (300–900 n. Chr.). *Beiträge zur allgemeinen und Vergleichenden Archäologie.* Bonn.

GALARZA, JOAQUÍN
1966 Glyphes et attributs chrétiens dans les manuscrits pictographiques mexicains du XVIe siècle: Le Codex Mexicanus 23–24. *Journal de la Société des Américanistes* [n.s.] 55:7–41.
1967 Prénoms et noms de lieux exprimés par les glyphes et des attributs chrétiens dans les manuscrits pictographiques mexicains. *Journal de la Société des Américanistes* [n.s.] 56:533–583.

1972 (ed.) *Lienzos de Chiepetlan.* Vol. 1 of *Etudes mesoamericaines,* general editor, Guy Stresser-Péan. Mexico City: Mission Archéologique et Ethnologique Française au Mexique.

1979 *Estudios de escritura indígena tradicional, azteca-náhuatl.* Mexico City: Archivo General de la Nación and Centro de Investigaciones Superiores del INAH.

GARCÍA, GREGORIO
1981 *Origen de los indios de el Nuevo Mundo.* Mexico City: Fondo de Cultura Económica. (Facsimile copy of 2d ed., 1729.)

GARCÍA MOLL, ROBERTO, DONALD W. PATTERSON BROWN, AND MARCUS C. WINTER
1986 (eds.) *Monumentos escultóricos de Monte Albán.* Materialien zur Allgemeinen und Vergleichenden Archaeologie, vol. 37. Munich: C. H. Beck.

GERHARD, PETER
1972 *A Guide to the Historical Geography of New Spain.* Cambridge Latin American Studies, no. 14. Cambridge: Cambridge University Press.

GIBSON, CHARLES
1967 *Los aztecas bajo el dominio español (1519–1810).* Mexico City: Siglo Veintiuno Editores.

GLASS, JOHN B.
1975 A Survey of Native Middle American Pictorial Manuscripts. In *Handbook of Middle American Indians,* vol. 14, edited by Robert Wauchope and Howard F. Cline, pp. 3–80. Austin: University of Texas Press.

GLASS, JOHN B., AND DONALD ROBERTSON
1975 A Census of Native Middle American Pictorial Manuscripts. In *Handbook of Middle American Indians,* vol. 14, edited by Robert Wauchope and Howard F. Cline, pp. 81–252. Austin: University of Texas Press.

GONZÁLEZ DE COSÍO, FRANCISCO
1952 *El libro de las tasaciones de pueblos de la Nueva España: Siglo XVI.* Mexico City: Archivo General de la Nación.

GORDON, GEORGE BYRON
1902 *The Hieroglyphic Stairway, Ruins of Copan: Report on Explorations by the Museum.* Memoirs of the Peabody Museum of American Archaeology and Ethnology, Harvard University, 1(6). Cambridge, Mass.

GRAHAM, IAN
1967 *Archaeological Explorations in El Peten, Guatemala.* Middle American Research Institute, Tulane University, pub. 33. New Orleans.

1979 *Corpus of Maya Hieroglyphic Inscriptions* 3(2): *Yaxchilan.* Cambridge, Mass.: Harvard University, Peabody Museum of Archaeology and Ethnology.

GRUBE, NIKOLAI
1988 Stadtgründer und "Erste Herrscher" in Hieroglyphentexten der Klassischen Mayakultur. *Archiv für Völkerkunde* 42:69–90.

GRUBE, NIKOLAI, AND DAVID STUART
1987 *Observations on T110 as the Syllable* ko. Research Reports on Ancient Maya Writing 8. Washington, D.C.: Center for Maya Research.

GUTIÉRREZ SOLANA, NELLY
1987 Avances en los estudios sobre los códices mixtecos (1973–84). *Anales del Instituto de Investigaciones Estéticas* 58:35–45.

HERRERA Y TORDESILLAS, ANTONIO DE
1947 *Historia general de los hechos de los castellanos en las islas y tierra firme del Mar Océano.* Madrid: Guaranía.

HOUSTON, STEPHEN D.
1984 An Example of Homophony in Maya Script. *American Antiquity* 49(4): 790–805.

1987 The Inscriptions and Monumental Art of Dos Pilas, Guatemala: A Study of Classic Maya History and Politics. Ph.D. dissertation, Department of Anthropology, Yale University. Ann Arbor: University Microfilms.

HOUSTON, STEPHEN D., AND KEVIN JOHNSTON
1987 Classic Maya Political Organization. Paper presented at the 86th annual meeting of the American Anthropological Association, Chicago.

HOUSTON, STEPHEN D., AND PETER MATHEWS
1985 *The Dynastic Sequence of Dos Pilas, Guatemala.* Pre-Columbian Art Research Institute, monograph 1. San Francisco.

HUERTA CARRILLO, ALEJANDRO
1988 Análisis de materiales del Códice Azoyú 1. In *Códice Azoyú 1: El reino de Tlachinollan.* Mexico City: Instituto Nacional de Antropología e Historia.

IXTLILXOCHITL, FERNANDO DE ALVA
1975 *Obras históricas*, vol. 1. Edited by Edmundo O'Gorman. 3d ed. Instituto de Investigaciones Históricas, Serie de Historiadores y Cronistas de Indias 4. Mexico City: Universidad Nacional Autónoma de México.
1977 *Obras históricas*, vol. 2. Edited by Edmundo O'Gorman. 3d ed. Instituto de Investigaciones Históricas, Serie de Historiadores y Cronistas de Indias. Mexico City: Universidad Nacional Autónoma de México.

JACOBS MÜLLER, FLORENCIA
1958 *El Códice de Cualac*. Mexico City: Instituto Nacional de Antropología e Historia, Dirección de Monumentos Prehispánicos.

JANSEN, MAARTEN E. R. G. N.
1982a *Huisi Tacu: Estudio interpretativo de un libro mixteco antiguo: Codex Vindobonensis Mexicanus I*. Amsterdam: Centrum voor Studie en Documentatie van Latijns Amerika.
1982b Viaje al otro mundo: La Tumba I de Zaachila. In *Coloquio internacional: Los Indígenas de México en la Epoca Precolombina y en la Actualidad*, edited by M. E. R. G. N. Jansen and Th. J. J. Leyenaar, pp. 87–118. Leiden: Rutgers B.V.
1988a The Art of Writing in Ancient Mexico: An Ethno-Iconological Perspective. *Visible Religion* 6:86–113.
1988b Dates, Deities, and Dynasties: Nondurational Time in Mixtec Historiography. In *Continuity and Identity in Native America: Essays in Honor of Bendikt Hartmann*, edited by Maarten Jansen, Peter van der Loo, and Roswitha Manning, pp. 156–192. Leiden: E. J. Brill.

JANSEN, MAARTEN E. R. G. N., AND MARGARITA GAXIOLA
1978 (eds.) *Primera Mesa Redonda de Estudios Mixtecos*. Oaxaca: Instituto Nacional de Antropología e Historia, Centro Regional de Oaxaca.

JANSEN, MAARTEN E. R. G. N., AND GABINA AURORA PÉREZ
1983 The Ancient Mexican Astronomical Apparatus: An Iconographical Criticism. *Archaeoastronomy* 6(1–4):89–95.

1986 Iyadzeha Anute: Valor literario de los códices mixtecos. In *Etnicidad y pluralismo cultural: La dinámica étnica en Oaxaca*, coordinated by Alicia M. Barabas and Miguel A. Bartolomé, pp. 173–211. Mexico City: Instituto Nacional de Antropología e Historia.

JIMÉNEZ MORENO, WIGBERTO, AND SALVADOR MATEOS HIGUERA
1940 *Códice de Yanhuitlan*. Mexico City: Instituto Nacional de Antropología e Historia.

JOHNSTON, KEVIN
1985 Maya Dynastic Territorial Expansion: Glyphic Evidence from Classic Centers of the Pasion River, Guatemala. In *Fifth Palenque Round Table, 1983*, edited by Merle Greene Robertson and Virginia M. Fields, pp. 49–56. San Francisco: Pre-Columbian Art Research Institute.

JONES, CHRISTOPHER
1977 Inauguration Dates of Three Late Classic Rulers of Tikal, Guatemala. *American Antiquity* 42:28–60.

JONES, CHRISTOPHER, AND LINTON SATTERTHWAITE
1982 *The Monuments and Inscriptions of Tikal: The Carved Monuments*. Tikal Report, no. 33; University Museum Monograph 44. Philadelphia: University Museum, University of Pennsylvania.

JUSTESON, JOHN S
1986 The Origin of Writing Systems: Preclassic Mesoamerica. *World Archaeology* 17:437–458.

JUSTESON, JOHN S., WILLIAM M. NORMAN, LYLE CAMPBELL, AND TERRENCE KAUFMAN
1985 *The Foreign Impact on Lowland Mayan Language and Script*. Middle American Research Institute, Tulane University, pub. 53. New Orleans.

JUSTESON, JOHN S., AND LAURENCE D. STEPHENS
1980 Syllable and Script: A Typological Study. Unpublished manuscript in the possession of the authors.

KARTTUNEN, FRANCES
1983 *An Analytical Dictionary of Nahuatl*. Austin: University of Texas Press.

KAUFMAN, TERRENCE S., AND WILLIAM M. NORMAN
1984 An Outline of Proto-Cholan Phonology,

Morphology and Vocabulary. In *Phoneticism in Mayan Hieroglyphic Writing*, edited by John S. Justeson and Lyle Campbell. Institute for Mesoamerican Studies, State University of New York at Albany, pub. no. 9:77–166.

KELLEY, DAVID H.

1962a Glyphic Evidence for a Dynastic Sequence at Quirigua, Guatemala. *American Antiquity* 27(3):323–335.

1962b A History of the Decipherment of Maya Script. *Anthropological Linguistics* 4(8): 1–48.

1965 The Birth of the Gods at Palenque. *Estudios de Cultura Maya* 5:93–134.

1968 Kakupacal and the Itzas. *Estudios de Cultura Maya* 7:255–268.

1976 *Deciphering the Maya Script*. Austin: University of Texas Press.

KIRCHHOFF, PAUL, LINA ODENA GÜEMES, AND LUIS REYES GARCÍA

1976 *Historia tolteca-chichimeca*. Mexico City: CISINAH and INAH-SEP.

KNOROZOV, YURI V.

1958a New Data on the Maya Written Language. *Proceedings of the Thirty-second International Congress of Americanists* (Copenhagen, 1956), pp. 467–475. Copenhagen: Munksgaard.

1958b The Problem of the Study of the Maya Hieroglyphic Writing. Translated by Sophie D. Coe. *American Antiquity* 23: 284–291.

1967 *Selected Chapters from the Writing of the Maya Indians*. Translated by Sophie Coe. Collaborating editor, Tatiana Proskouriakoff. Peabody Museum of Archaeology and Ethnology, Russian Translation Series, vol. 4. Cambridge, Mass.: Harvard University. (Chaps. 1, 6, 7, and 9 of *Pis'mennost indeitsev maiia*.)

KNOWLES, SUSAN M.

1984 A Descriptive Grammar of Chontal Maya (San Carlos Dialect). Ph.D. dissertation, Department of Anthropology, Tulane University. Ann Arbor: University Microfilms (84-20718).

KÖNIG, VIOLA

1979 *Inhaltliche Analyse und Interpretation von Codex Egerton*. Beiträge zur mittelamerikanischen Völkerkunde 15. Hamburg: Hamburgisches Museum für Völkerkunde; Munich: K. Renner.

1984 Der Lienzo Seler II und seine Stellung innerhalb der Coixtlahuaca Gruppe. *Baessler Archiv* (N.F.) 32(2):229–320.

KUBLER, GEORGE

1969 Studies in Classic Maya Iconography. *Memoirs of the Connecticut Academy of Arts and Science* 18. Hamden, Conn.: Archon Books.

1972 The Paired Attendants of the Temple Tablets at Palenque. In *Religión en Mesoamérica, XII Mesa Redonda*, edited by Jaime Litvak King and Noemi Castillo Tejero, pp. 317–328. Mexico City: Sociedad Mexicana de Antropología.

LANDA, DIEGO DE

1959 *Relación de las cosas de Yucatán*. Mexico City: Porrúa.

1966 *Relación de las cosas de Yucatán*. Mexico City: Porrúa.

LAUGHLIN, ROBERT M.

1988 *The Great Tzotzil Dictionary of Santo Domingo Zinacantán, with Grammatical Analysis and Historical Commentary*. 3 vols. Smithsonian Contributions to Anthropology, no. 31. Washington, D.C.

LIENZOS

Aztactepec y Citlaltepec
    No. 35–126 in the Biblioteca Nacional de Antropología e Historia, Mexico City.

Tlapa-Azoyú
    No. 35–110 in the Biblioteca Nacional de Antropología e Historia, Mexico City.

Totomixtlahuacan

1974 *Lienzo Totomixtlahuaca*. Introductory note by John B. Glass. Mexico City: Centro de Estudios de Historia de México and CONDUMEX.

LOUNSBURY, FLOYD G.

1973 On the Derivation and Reading of the "Ben-Ich" Prefix. In *Mesoamerican Writing Systems*, edited by Elizabeth P. Benson, pp. 99–143. Washington, D.C.: Dumbarton Oaks.

1974 Handouts for the Seminar on Maya Hieroglyphic Writing, Department of Anthropology, Yale University, for the academic year 1974–1975.

1975–1976 Handouts and notes from the 1975–1976 Seminar on Maya Hieroglyphic Writing and the Inscriptions of Palenque, Yale University.

1976 A Rationale for the Initial Date of the Temple of the Cross at Palenque. In *The*

Art, Iconography, and Dynastic History of Palenque, Part 3, edited by Merle Greene Robertson, pp. 211–224. Pebble Beach, Calif.: Robert Louis Stevenson School.

1980 Some Problems in the Interpretation of the Mythological Portion of the Hieroglyphic Text of the Temple of the Cross at Palenque. In *Third Palenque Round Table, 1978, Part 2*, edited by Merle Greene Robertson, pp. 99–115. Austin: University of Texas Press.

1982 Astronomical Knowledge and Its Uses at Bonampak, Mexico. In *Archaeoastronomy in the New World: American Primitive Astronomy*, edited by Anthony F. Aveni, pp. 143–168. Cambridge: Cambridge University Press.

1984 Glyphic Substitutions: Homophonic and Synonymic. In *Phoneticism in Mayan Hieroglyphic Writing*, edited by John S. Justeson and Lyle Campbell. Institute for Mesoamerican Studies, State University of New York at Albany, pub. no. 9:167–184.

1985 The Identities of the Mythological Figures in the Cross Group Inscriptions of Palenque. In *Fourth Palenque Round Table, 1980*, edited by Merle Greene Robertson and Elizabeth P. Benson, pp. 45–58. San Francisco: Pre-Columbian Art Research Institute.

MCGOWAN, CHARLOTTE, AND PATRICIA VAN NICE
1979 *The Identification and Interpretation of Name and Place Glyphs of the Xolotl Codex*. Katunob, no. 11. Greeley, Colo.

MACLEOD, BARBARA
1984 Cholan and Yucatecan Verb Morphology and Glyphic Verbal Affixes in the Inscriptions. In *Phoneticism in Mayan Hieroglyphic Writing*, edited by John S. Justeson and Lyle Campbell. Institute for Mesoamerican Studies, State University of New York at Albany, pub. no. 9: 233–262.

MARCUS, JOYCE
1976a *Emblem and State in the Classic Maya Lowlands: An Epigraphic Approach to Territorial Organization*. Washington, D.C.: Dumbarton Oaks.

1976b The Iconography of Militarism at Monte Alban and Neighboring Sites in the Valley of Oaxaca. In *Origins of Religious Art and Iconography in Preclassic Mesoamerica*, edited by H. B. Nicholson. UCLA Latin American Studies Series 31:123–139. Los Angeles.

1976c The Origins of Mesoamerican Writing. *Annual Review of Anthropology* 5:35–67.

1980 Zapotec Writing. *Scientific American* 242:50–64.

1983a The First Appearance of Zapotec Writing and Calendrics. In *The Cloud People: Divergent Evolution of the Zapotec and Mixtec Civilizations*, edited by Kent V. Flannery and Joyce Marcus, pp. 91–96. New York: Academic Press.

1983b Lowland Maya Archaeology at the Crossroads. *American Antiquity* 48:454–488.

1983c Teotihuacan Visitors on Monte Alban Monuments and Murals. In *The Cloud People: Divergent Evolution of the Zapotec and Mixtec Civilizations*, edited by Kent V. Flannery and Joyce Marcus, pp. 175–181. New York: Academic Press.

1984 Mesoamerican Territorial Boundaries: Reconstructions from Archaeology and Hieroglyphic Writing. *Archaeological Review from Cambridge* 3(2):48–62.

MARLETT, STEPHEN A.
1985 Some Aspects of Zapotecan Clausal Syntax. In *University of North Dakota Session*, edited by Desmond C. Derbyshire, *Work Papers of the Summer Institute of Linguistics* 29:83–155. Dallas: Summer Institute of Linguistics.

MARTÍNEZ GRACIDA, MANUEL
1986 *Los indios oaxaqueños y sus monumentos arqueológicos*. Oaxaca: Gobierno del Estado.

MATHEWS, PETER
1975 The Lintels of Structure 12, Yaxchilan, Chiapas. Paper presented at the Annual Conference of the Northeastern Anthropological Association, Wesleyan University.

1979a The Inscription on the Back of Stela B, Dos Pilas, Guatemala. MS on file, Department of Anthropology, Vanderbilt University, Nashville.

1979b Notes on the Inscriptions of "Site Q." MS on file, Department of Anthropology, Vanderbilt University, Nashville.

1983   Palenque's Mid-Life Crisis. Paper presented at the Quinta Mesa Redonda de Palenque (Palenque, Chiapas), June 1983.

MATHEWS, PETER, AND JOHN S. JUSTESON

1984   Patterns of Sign Substitution in Maya Hieroglyphic Writing: "The Affix Cluster." In *Phoneticism in Mayan Hieroglyphic Writing*, edited by John S. Justeson and Lyle Campbell. Institute for Mesoamerican Studies, State University of New York at Albany, pub. no. 9: 185–231.

MATHEWS, PETER, AND LINDA SCHELE

1974   Lords of Palenque—The Glyphic Evidence. In *Primera Mesa Redonda de Palenque, Part 1,* edited by Merle Greene Robertson, pp. 63–76. Pebble Beach, Calif.: Robert Louis Stevenson School.

MATHEWS, PETER, AND GORDON R. WILLEY

1986   Prehistoric Polities of the Pasión Region: Hieroglyphic Texts and Their Archaeological Settings. MS on file, Department of Anthropology, Vanderbilt University, Nashville.

MATRÍCULAS

Huexotzinco

1974   *Matrícula de Huexotzinco: Ms. mex. 387 der Bibliothèque Nacionale, Paris.* Edited by Hanns J. Prem. Graz: Akademische Druck- u. Verlagsanstalt.

Tributos

1980   *Matrícula de Tributos (Códice de Moctezuma): Museo Nacional de Antropología, México (Cod. 35-52).* Commentary by Frances F. Berdan and Jacqueline de Durand-Forest. Graz: Akademische Druck- u. Verlagsanstalt.

MAUDSLAY, ALFRED P.

1889–1902   *Biologia Centrali-Americana: Archaeology.* 4 vols. London: R. H. Porter and Dulau.

MILLER, ARTHUR G.

1973   *The Mural Painting of Teotihuacan.* Washington, D.C.: Dumbarton Oaks.

MORLEY, SYLVANUS GRISWOLD

1920   *The Inscriptions at Copan.* Carnegie Institution of Washington, pub. 219. Washington, D.C.

NICHOLSON, HENRY B.

1971   Major Sculpture in Pre-Hispanic Central Mexico. In *Handbook of Middle American Indians*, vol. 10, edited by Robert

Wauchope, Gordon F. Ekholm, and Ignacio Bernal, pp. 92–134. Austin: University of Texas Press.

1973   Phoneticism in the Late Pre-Hispanic Central Mexican Writing System. In *Mesoamerican Writing Systems,* edited by Elizabeth P. Benson, pp. 1–46. Washington, D.C.: Dumbarton Oaks.

NOWOTNY, KARL ANTON

1959   *Tlacuilolli: Die mexikanischen Bilderhandschriften.* Berlin: Gebrüder Mann.

1961   Die Hieroglyphen des Codex Mendoza: Der Bau einer mittelamerikanischen Wortbildschrift. *Mitteilungen aus dem Museum für Völkerkunde in Hamburg* 25:97–113.

NUTTALL, ZELIA

1903   *The Book of the Life of the Ancient Mexicans*, part 1: *Introduction and Facsimile.* Berkeley: University of California.

PADDOCK, JOHN

1983   *Lord 5 Flower's Family: Rulers of Zaachila and Cuilapan.* Vanderbilt University Publications in Anthropology, no. 29. Nashville.

PALACIOS, ENRIQUE JUAN

1935   Más gemas del arte maya en Palenque. *Anales del Museo Nacional de Arqueología, Historia y Etnografía,* época 5, 2:193–225.

PARMENTER, ROSS

1982   *Four Lienzos of the Coixtlahuaca Valley.* Studies in Pre-Columbian Art and Archaeology, no. 26. Washington, D.C.: Dumbarton Oaks.

PASO Y TRONCOSO, FRANCISCO DEL

1905   Relación de las minas de Zumpango. In *Papeles de Nueva España* 6:313–322. Madrid: Sucesores de Rivadeneyra.

PAUCIC, ALEJANDRO

1984   *Geografía histórica del Estado de Guerrero.* Mexico City: Editorial del H. Ayuntamiento de Acapulco, Estado de Guerrero.

PEÑAFIEL, ANTONIO

1978   *Nombres geográficos de México.* Introduction by César Macazaga Ordoño. Mexico City: Editorial Innovación.

1985   *Indumentaria antigua: Vestidos guerreros y civiles de los mexicanos.* Mexico City: Editorial Innovación.

179

PICKETT, VELMA
1971   Vocabulario zapoteco del Istmo: Caste-
        llano-zapoteco y zapoteco-castellano. 4th
        ed. Serie de Vocabularios Indígenas Ma-
        riano Silvo y Aceves, no. 3. Mexico City:
        Instituto Lingüístico de Verano.

PÍO PÉREZ, JUAN
1866–1877   Diccionario de la lengua maya.
            Merida: Imprenta Literaria de Juan F.
            Molina Solís.

PREM, HANNS J.
1970   Aztec Hieroglyphic Writing System—
        Possibilities and Limits. In Verhand-
        lungen des XXXVIII. Internationalen
        Amerikanistenkongresses   (Stuttgart-
        Munich 1968) 2:159–165. Munich:
        Klaus Renner.
1979   Aztec Writing Considered as a Paradigm
        for Mesoamerican Scripts. In Meso-
        américa: Homenaje al Doctor Paul Kirch-
        hoff, coordinated by Barbro Dahlgren,
        pp. 104–118. Mexico City: Instituto Na-
        cional de Antropología e Historia.

PROSKOURIAKOFF, TATIANA
1960   Historical Implications of a Pattern of
        Dates at Piedras Negras, Guatemala.
        American Antiquity 25:454–475.
1963   Historical Data in the Inscriptions of
        Yaxchilan, Part I. Estudios de Cultura
        Maya 3:149–167.
1964   Historical Data in the Inscriptions of
        Yaxchilan, Part II. Estudios de Cultura
        Maya 4:178–201.
1965   Sculpture and Major Arts of the Maya
        Lowlands. In Handbook of Middle
        American Indians, vol. 2, edited by
        Robert Wauchope and Gordon R. Willey,
        pp. 469–497. Austin: University of Texas
        Press.
1973   The Hand-grasping-fish and Associated
        Glyphs on Classic Maya Monuments. In
        Mesoamerican Writing Systems, edited
        by Elizabeth P. Benson, pp. 165–178.
        Washington, D.C.: Dumbarton Oaks.

PROSKOURIAKOFF, TATIANA, AND J. ERIC S.
THOMPSON
1947   Maya Calendar Round Dates such as 9
        Ahau 17 Mol. Carnegie Institution of
        Washington, Notes on Middle American
        Archaeology and Ethnology no. 79, 3:
        143–150. Cambridge, Mass.

RABIN, EMILY
1981   Chronology of the Mixtec Historical Co-
        dices: An Overview. Paper presented at
        the annual meeting of the American Soci-
        ety for Ethnohistory, Colorado Springs.
1982   Confluence in Zapotec and Mixtec Eth-
        nohistories: The 1560 Genealogy of Ma-
        cuilxochitl. Papers in Anthropology 23
        (2):359–368.

RANDS, BARBARA C., AND ROBERT L. RANDS
1961   Excavations in a Cemetery at Palenque.
        Estudios de Cultura Maya 1:87–106.

REECK, ROGER
1982   Sixteenth-Century Valley Zapotec: A
        Challenge for Linguistics and Ethnohis-
        tory. In Native American Ethnohistory,
        edited by Joseph W. Whitecotton and
        Judith Bradley Whitecotton. Papers in
        Anthropology, Department of Anthro-
        pology, 23(2):369–375. Norman: Uni-
        versity of Oklahoma.

REENTS, DORIE J., AND RONALD L. BISHOP
1985   History and Ritual Events on a Petexba-
        tun Classic Maya Polychrome Vessel. In
        Fifth Palenque Round Table, 1983, ed-
        ited by Merle Greene Robertson and
        Virginia M. Fields, pp. 57–63. San Fran-
        cisco: Pre-Columbian Art Research In-
        stitute.

RENSCH, CALVIN R.
1976   Comparative Otomanguean Phonology.
        Language Science Monographs, Indiana
        University Publications, vol. 14. Bloo-
        mington: Indiana University, Research
        Center for Language and Semiotic
        Studies.

REYES, ANTONIO DE LOS
1976   Arte en lengua mixteca. Vanderbilt Uni-
        versity Publications in Anthropology, no.
        14. Nashville.

REYES GARCÍA, LUIS
1977   Cuauhtinchan del siglo XII al XVI: For-
        mación y desarrollo histórico de un seño-
        río prehispánico. Wiesbaden: Steiner.

RIESE, BERTHOLD
1971   Grundlagen zur Entzifferung der Maya-
        hieroglyphen, Dargestellt an den In-
        schriften von Copan. Beiträge zur mit-
        telamerikanischen   Völkerkunde   11.
        Hamburg and Munich: Museum für
        Völkerkunde and Klaus Renner Verlag.
1975   Leitfaden zur Mayaschrift. 2 vols.
        Hamburg.

1980 Katun-Altersangaben in klassischen Maya-Inschriften. *Baessler Archiv* n.s. 28:155–180. Berlin.

1982 Kriegsberichte der klassischen Maya. *Baessler-Archiv* n.s. 30:255–321. Berlin.

1984a Dynastiegeschichtliche und kalendarische Beobachtungen an den Maya-Inschriften von Machaquilá, Petén, Guatemala. *Tribus* 33:149–154. (Additions and corrections in *Tribus*, [1988] 37:175–177.)

1984b Hel Hieroglyphs. In *Phoneticism in Mayan Hieroglyphic Writing*, edited by John S. Justeson and Lyle Campbell. Institute for Mesoamerican Studies, State University of New York at Albany, pub. no. 9:263–286. Albany.

1988 Epigraphy of the Southeast Zone in Relation to Other Parts of the Maya Realm. In *The Southeast Classic Maya Zone*, edited by Elizabeth Hill Boone and Gordon R. Willey, pp. 67–94. Washington, D.C.: Dumbarton Oaks.

RINGLE, WILLIAM M.

1985 Notes on Two Tablets of Unknown Provenance. In *Fifth Palenque Round Table, 1983*, edited by Merle Greene Robertson and Virginia M. Fields, pp. 151–158. San Francisco: Pre-Columbian Art Research Institute.

ROBELO, CECILIO A.

1962 Toponimía tarasco-hispano-nahua. In *Arte de la lengua tarasca*, by Diego Basalenque, pp. 165–193. Morelia: Editorial Erandi del Gobierno de Michoacán.

ROBERTSON, MERLE GREENE

1983 *The Sculpture of Palenque*, vol. 1: *The Temple of the Inscriptions*. Princeton: Princeton University Press.

RUZ LHUILLIER, ALBERTO

1956 Exploraciones arqueológicas en Palenque: 1954. *Anales del Instituto Nacional de Antropología e Historia* 10:117–184.

1973 *El Templo de las Inscripciones, Palenque*. Instituto Nacional de Antropología e Historia, Colección Científica, Arqueología 7. Mexico City.

1976 Nueva interpretación de la inscripción jeroglífica en el sarcófago del Templo de las Inscripciones. In *The Art, Iconography, and Dynastic History of Palenque, Part 3*, edited by Merle Greene Robertson, pp. 87–93. Pebble Beach, Calif.: Robert Louis Stevenson School.

1977 Gerontocracy at Palenque? In *Social Process in Maya Prehistory: Studies in Honour of Sir Eric Thompson*, edited by Norman Hammond, pp. 287–295. New York: Academic Press.

SAHAGÚN, BERNARDINO DE

1970–1982 *Florentine Codex*. Translated by Arthur J. Anderson and Charles E. Dibble. Salt Lake City: University of Utah Press.

SANDERS, WILLIAM T., AND DAVID WEBSTER

1988 The Mesoamerican Urban Tradition. *American Anthropologist* 90(3): 521–546.

SCHELE, LINDA

1974 Attribution of Architecture to Specific Rulers at Palenque. Paper presented at the 41st International Congress of Americanists, Mexico City.

1976 An Epigraphic and Iconographic Study of the Sarcophagus Sides at Palenque. Prepared for the Dumbarton Oaks Miniconferences on Palenque.

1978 A Preliminary Commentary on the Tablets of the Temple of Inscriptions at Palenque, Chiapas. Prepared for a publication of the miniconferences at Dumbarton Oaks.

1979a Genealogical Documentation on the Tri-Figure Panels at Palenque. *Tercera Mesa Redonda de Palenque*, edited by Merle Greene Robertson and Donnan Call Jeffers, pp. 41–70. Palenque, Chiapas: Pre-Columbian Art Research Center.

1979b Highland Rabbits and Lowland Lords. *Actes du XLIIe Congrès International des Américanistes* (Paris, 1976) 8:281–295. Paris: Société des Américanistes.

1981 Sacred Site and World-View at Palenque. In *Mesoamerican Sites and World-Views*, edited by Elizabeth P. Benson, pp. 87–117. Washington, D.C.: Dumbarton Oaks.

1982 *Maya Glyphs: The Verbs*. Austin: University of Texas Press.

1984 Human Sacrifice among the Classic Maya. In *Ritual Human Sacrifice in Mesoamerica*, edited by Elizabeth H. Boone, pp. 6–48. Washington, D.C.: Dumbarton Oaks.

1986a Architectural Development and Political History at Palenque. In *City States of the Maya: Art and Architecture*, edited by Elizabeth P. Benson, pp. 110–137. Denver: Rocky Mountain Institute for Pre-Columbian Studies.

1986b *The Founders of Lineages at Copan and Other Maya Sites.* Copan Note 8. Copan, Honduras: Copan Mosaics Project and Instituto Hondureño de Antropología e Historia.

1986c *Moon-Jaguar, the 10th Successor of the Lineage of Yax-K'uk'-Mo' of Copan.* Copan Note 15. Copan, Honduras: Copan Mosaics Project and Instituto Hondureño de Antropología e Historia.

1988 The Xibalba Shuffle: A Dance after Death. In *Maya Iconography*, edited by Elizabeth P. Benson and Gillett G. Griffin, pp. 294–317. Princeton: Princeton University Press.

1991 The Demotion of Chac-Zutz': Lineage Compounds and Subsidiary Lords at Palenque. In *Sixth Palenque Round Table, 1986*, edited by Merle Greene Robertson, pp. 6–11. Norman: University of Oklahoma Press.

SCHELE, LINDA, AND DAVID FREIDEL

1984 The Maya Message: Time, Text, and Image. Paper presented at the Conference on Art and Communication at the Israel Museum, Jerusalem.

1990 *A Forest of Kings: Royal Histories of the Ancient Maya.* New York: William Morrow.

SCHELE, LINDA, AND NIKOLAI GRUBE

1987 *The Brother of Yax-Pac.* Copan Note 20. Copan, Honduras: Copan Mosaics Project and Instituto Hondureño de Antropología e Historia.

SCHELE, LINDA, AND PETER MATHEWS

1979 *The Bodega of Palenque, Chiapas, Mexico.* Washington, D.C.: Dumbarton Oaks.

SCHELE, LINDA, PETER MATHEWS, AND FLOYD G. LOUNSBURY

1977 Parentage Expressions in Classic Maya Inscriptions. MS on file, Department of Anthropology, Vanderbilt University, Nashville.

1982 Parentage Expressions in Classic Maya Inscriptions. Revision of Schele, Mathews, and Lounsbury (1977).

1983 Parentage Expressions in Classic Maya Inscriptions. Revision of Schele, Mathews, and Lounsbury (1982).

SCHELE, LINDA, AND JEFFREY H. MILLER

1983 *The Mirror, the Rabbit, and the Bundle: "Accession" Expressions from the Classic Maya Inscriptions.* Studies in Pre-Columbian Art and Archaeology, no. 25. Washington, D.C.: Dumbarton Oaks.

SCHELE, LINDA, AND MARY ELLEN MILLER

1986 *The Blood of Kings: Dynasty and Ritual in Maya Art.* Fort Worth, Tex.: Kimbell Art Museum.

SCHELE, LINDA, AND DAVID STUART

1986 *Butz'-chaan, the 11th Successor of the Yax-K'uk'-Mo'.* Copan Note 14. Copan, Honduras: Copan Mosaics Project and Instituto Hondureño de Antropología e Historia.

SCHMIDT SCHOENBERG, PAUL, AND JAIME LITVAK

1986 Problemas y perspectivas de la arqueología en Guerrero. In *Primer Coloquio de Arqueología y Etnohistoria del Estado de Guerrero*, pp. 27–51. Mexico City: Instituto Nacional de Antropología e Historia and Gobierno del Estado de Guerrero.

SCHUMANN G., OTTO

1973 *La lengua chol de Tila (Chiapas).* Centro de Estudios Mayas, cuaderno 8. Mexico City: Universidad Nacional Autónoma de México.

SCOTT, JOHN F.

1978 *The Danzantes of Monte Alban.* 2 vols. Studies in Pre-Columbian Art and Archaeology, no. 19. Washington, D.C.: Dumbarton Oaks.

SELER, EDUARD

1961 Aus dem Berichte über die achtzehnte Tagung des Internationalen Amerikanistenkongresses in London. In *Gesammelte Abhandlungen* 5:152–167. Graz: Akademische Druck- u. Verlagsanstalt. (Reprint of 1915 ed.)

SIMPSON, JON ERIK

1976 The New York Relief Panel—and Some Associations with Reliefs at Palenque and Elsewhere, Part 1. In *The Art, Iconography, and Dynastic History of Palenque, Part 3*, edited by Merle Greene Robertson, pp. 95–105. Pebble Beach, Calif.: Robert Louis Stevenson School.

SMITH, A. LEDYARD
1982 *Excavations at Seibal, Department of Peten, Guatemala,* no. 1: *Major Architecture and Caches: Excavations at Seibal, Department of Peten, Guatemala.* Memoirs of the Peabody Museum of Archaeology and Ethnology 15. Cambridge, Mass.: Harvard University.

SMITH, MARY ELIZABETH
1973a *Picture Writing from Ancient Southern Mexico: Mixtec Place Signs and Maps.* Norman: University of Oklahoma Press.
1973b The Relationship between Mixtec Manuscript Painting and the Mixtec Language: A Study of Some Personal Names in Codices Muro and Sánchez Solís. In *Mesoamerican Writing Systems,* edited by Elizabeth P. Benson, pp. 47–98. Washington, D.C.: Dumbarton Oaks.
1979 Codex Becker II: A Manuscript from the Mixteca Baja? *Archiv für Völkerkunde* 33:29–43.
1983 Codex Selden: A Manuscript from the Valley of Nochixtlan? In *The Cloud People: Divergent Evolution of the Zapotec and Mixtec Civilizations,* edited by Kent V. Flannery and Joyce Marcus, pp. 248–255. New York: Academic Press.
1988 It Doesn't Amount to a Hill of Beans: The Frijol Motif in Mixtec Place Signs. In *Smoke and Mist: Mesoamerican Studies in Memory of Thelma D. Sullivan,* edited by J. Kathryn Josserand and Karen Dakin. BAR International Series 402(2):696–671. Oxford.

SOSA, JOHN R., AND DORIE J. REENTS
1980 Glyphic Evidence for Classic Maya Militarism. *Belizean Studies* 8(3):2–11.

SPINDEN, HERBERT J.
1924 *The Reduction of Mayan Dates.* Papers of the Peabody Museum of Archaeology and Ethnology, Harvard University 6(4). Cambridge, Mass.

SPORES, RONALD
1967 *The Mixtec Kings and Their People.* Norman: University of Oklahoma Press.
1974 Marital Alliance in the Political Integration of Mixtec Kingdoms. *American Anthropologist* 76:297–311.

STUART, DAVID
1984a Epigraphic Evidence of Political Organization in the Usumacinta Drainage. MS on file, Department of Anthropology, Vanderbilt University, Nashville.
1984b A Note on the "Hand-Scattering" Glyph. In *Phoneticism in Mayan Hieroglyphic Writing,* edited by John S. Justeson and Lyle Campbell. Institute for Mesoamerican Studies, State University of New York at Albany, pub. no. 9:307–310.
1984c A Reconsideration of Directional Count Glyphs. Paper presented at the 30th Annual Meeting of the American Anthropological Association, Denver.
1985 The "Count of Captives" Epithet in Classic Maya Writing. In *Fifth Palenque Round Table, 1983,* edited by Merle Greene Robertson and Virginia M. Fields, pp. 97–101. San Francisco: Pre-Columbian Art Research Institute.
1986 The "Lu-Bat" Glyph and Its Bearing on the Primary Standard Sequence. Paper presented at the First World Symposium on Maya Epigraphy, Guatemala City.
1987 Ten Phonetic Syllables. *Research Reports on Ancient Maya Writing* 14. Washington, D.C.: Center for Maya Research.
1989 Kinship Terms in Mayan Inscriptions. Paper prepared for The Language of Maya Hieroglyphs, a conference held at the University of California at Santa Barbara.

STUART, DAVID, AND STEPHEN D. HOUSTON
1989 Classic Maya Place Names. MS on file, Department of Anthropology, Vanderbilt University, Nashville.
n.d. *Classic Maya Place Names.* Research Reports on Ancient Maya Writing. Washington, D.C.: Center for Maya Research.

STUART, DAVID, AND LINDA SCHELE
1986 *Yax-K'uk-Mo', the Founder of the Lineage of Copan.* Copan Note 6. Copan, Honduras: Copan Mosaics Project and Instituto Hondureño de Antropología e Historia.

SUÁREZ, JORGE A.
1973 On Proto-Zapotec Phonology. *International Journal of American Linguistics* 39:236–249.

SWADESH, MORRIS
1947 The Phonetic Structure of Proto-Zapotec. *International Journal of American Linguistics* 13:220–230.

THOMPSON, J. ERIC S.
1950 *Maya Hieroglyphic Writing: An Intro-duction.* Carnegie Institution of Washington, pub. 589. Washington, D.C.
1960 *Maya Hieroglyphic Writing: An Intro-duction.* Norman: University of Oklahoma Press.
1962 *A Catalog of Maya Hieroglyphs.* Norman: University of Oklahoma Press.
1965 Maya Hieroglyphic Writing. In *Handbook of Middle American Indians*, vol. 3, edited by Robert Wauchope and Gordon R. Willey, pp. 632–658. Austin: University of Texas Press.
1970 *Maya History and Religion.* Norman: University of Oklahoma Press.
1972 *A Commentary on the Dresden Codex, a Maya Hieroglyphic Book.* Memoirs of the American Philosophical Society, vol. 93. Philadelphia.

TOURTELLOT, GAIR III, JEREMY A. SABLOFF, AND ROBERT SHARICK
1978 *Excavations at Seibal, Department of Peten, Guatemala*, no. 2: *A Reconnaissance of Cancuen.* Memoirs of the Peabody Museum of Archaeology and Ethnology 14. Cambridge, Mass.: Harvard University.

TOZZER, ALFRED M.
1941 (trans. and ed.) *Landa's Relación de las cosas de Yucatán.* Papers of the Peabody Museum of American Archaeology and Ethnology, Harvard University, vol. 18. Cambridge, Mass.

TROIKE, NANCY P.
1974 The Codex Colombino-Becker. Ph.D. dissertation, University of London.
1978 Fundamental Changes in the Interpretations of the Mixtec Codices. *American Antiquity* 43(4):553–568.
1982 The Interpretation of Postures and Gestures in the Mixtec Codices. In *The Art and Iconography of Late Post-Classic Central Mexico*, edited by Elizabeth H. Boone, pp. 175–206. Washington, D.C.: Dumbarton Oaks.

TSCHOHL, PETER
1964 *Kritische Untersuchungen zür spätindianischen Geschichte Südost Mexikos*, part 1: *Die aztekische Ausdehnung nach den aztekischen Quellen und die Probleme ihrer Bearbeitung.* Hamburg.

VEGA SOSA, CONSTANZA
In press *Códice Azoyú 1: El reino de Tlachinollan.* Mexico City: Fondo de Cultura Económica.

VENTRIS, MICHAEL, AND JOHN CHADWICK
1956 *Documents in Mycenaean Greek.* 1st ed. Cambridge: University Press.

VILLACORTA C., J. ANTONIO, AND CARLOS A. VILLACORTA
1976 *Códices mayas.* 2d ed. Guatemala City: Tipografía Nacional.

VON WINNING, HASSO
1987 *La iconografía de Teotihuacan: Los dioses y los signos.* 2 vols. Instituto de Investigaciones Estéticas, Estudios y Fuentes del Arte en México 47. Mexico City: Universidad Nacional Autónoma de México.

WAUCHOPE, ROBERT, AND GORDON R. WILLEY
1965 (eds.) *Archaeology of Southern Mesoamerica*, vol. 3 of *Handbook of Middle American Indians*. Austin: University of Texas Press.

WAUCHOPE, ROBERT, GORDON F. EKHOLM, AND IGNACIO BERNAL
1971 *Archaeology of Northern Mesoamerica*, vol. 10 of *Handbook of Middle American Indians*. Austin: University of Texas Press.

WEBSTER, DAVID
1989 (ed.) *The House of the Bacabs, Copan, Honduras.* Studies in Pre-Columbian Art and Archaeology, no. 29. Washington, D.C.: Dumbarton Oaks.

WHITECOTTON, JOSEPH W.
1983 The Genealogy of Macuilxochitl: A Sixteenth-Century Zapotec Pictorial from the Valley of Oaxaca. *Notas Mesoamericanas* 9:58–75.

WHITECOTTON, JUDITH BRADLEY
1982 Colonial Linguistic Writings as Ethnohistorical Sources: Spanish Friars and the Zapotec Language. In *Native American Ethnohistory*, edited by Joseph W. Whitecotton and Judith Bradley Whitecotton. Department of Anthropology, Papers in Anthropology 23(2):267–284. Norman: University of Oklahoma.

WHITTAKER, GORDON
1976 On the Decipherment of Early Monte Alban Hieroglyphics. Paper presented at the 41st Annual Meeting of the Society for American Archaeology, St. Louis. On

file at the Centro Regional del I.N.A.H., Oaxaca City.

1977 From Zapotec Hieroglyphics to the Mixtec Codices. Paper presented at the 42d Annual Meeting of the Society for American Archaeology, New Orleans. On file at the Centro Regional del I.N.A.H., Oaxaca City.

1980 The Hieroglyphics of Monte Alban. Ph.D. dissertation, Department of Anthropology, Yale University. Ann Arbor: University Microfilms (80-25319).

1981 *Los jeroglíficos preclásicos de Monte Albán*. Instituto Nacional de Antropología e Historia, Estudios de Antropología e Historia, no. 27. Oaxaca: Centro Regional de Oaxaca.

1982 The Tablets of Mound J at Monte Alban. In *Coloquio international: Los Indígenas de México en la Epoca Prehispánica y en la Actualidad*, edited by Maarten E. R. G. N. Jansen and Th. J. J. Leyenaar, pp. 50–86. Leiden: Rutgers B.V.

1983 The Structure of the Zapotec Calendar. In *Calendars in Mesoamerica and Peru: Native American Computations of Time*, edited by Anthony F. Aveni and Gordon Brotherston. BAR International Series 174:101–133. Proceedings: 44th International Congress of Americanists (Manchester, 1982), general editor Norman Hammond. Oxford.

1990 *Calendar and Script in Protohistorical China and Mesoamerica: A Comparative Study of Day Names and Their Signs*. Published version of 1984 Habilitationsschrift submitted to the University of Tübingen. Bonn: Holos Verlag.

In press *The Study of North Mesoamerican Place Signs*. Indiana 12. (MS, 1988.)

WILLIAMS, BARBARA J.

1980 Pictorial Representation of Soils in the Valley of Mexico: Evidence from the Codex Vergara. *Geoscience and Man* 21:51–62.

1984 Mexican Pictorial Cadastral Registers: An Analysis of the Códice de Santa María Asunción and the Codex Vergara. In *Explorations in Ethnohistory: Indians of Central Mexico in the Sixteenth Century*, edited by H. R. Harvey and Hanns J. Prem, pp. 103–125. Albuquerque: University of New Mexico Press.

ZAVALA, LAURO JOSÉ

1951 Informe personal: Exploraciones arqueológicas, segunda temporada, 1950. MS in possession of Linda Schele.

ZIMMERMANN, GÜNTER

1963 *Die Relationen Chimalpahin's zur Geschichte Mexico's*, vol. 1: *Die Zeit bis zur Conquista 1521*. Hamburg: Cram, de Gruyter.

INDEX

187